STREETWISE®
E-COMMERCE

Establish Your Online Business,
Expand Your Reach,
and Watch Your Profits Soar!

Aliza Risdahl

Adams Media
Avon, Massachusetts

Copyright © 2007 by F+W Publications, Inc.
A Streetwise® Publication. Streetwise® is a registered trademark of
F+W Publications.

Published by Adams Media, an F+W Publications Company
57 Littlefield Street
Avon, MA 02322
www.adamsmedia.com

ISBN-10: 1-59869-144-9
ISBN-13: 978-1-59869-144-3

Printed in the United States of America.

J I H G F E D C B A

**Library of Congress Cataloging-in-Publication Data
is available from the publisher.**

*This book is available at quantity discounts for bulk purchases.
For information, please call 1-800-289-0963.*

CONTENTS

Dedication

To my loving husband and kick-ass baby.
You are my world.

To my family.
Love always.

Acknowledgments

Even experts turn to other experts to get things right, so my many thanks go to smart people like my wonderful agent Jacky Sach of BookEnds; cyber-lawyer Peter S. Vogel of Gardere Wynne Sewell LLP; the savvy folks and companies I feature throughout this book; and the online community of Internet gurus, mavens, bloggers, and wonks who challenge and inspire me every day.

Introduction

When it comes to introducing Internet strategies and tactics into your current business activities, basic business principles make for sound decisions. You can't successfully use the Internet for your business until you've thought through who you are, whom you are trying to reach, and what you are trying to achieve in the marketplace. This book spells out processes step by step to help you better manage and implement your Internet projects.

When you are embarking on an online marketing campaign, it's important to learn how to think like an Internet marketer. If you are wondering about building an online community or starting a blog to help market your company, know the pros and cons of such an undertaking.

You also need to understand the legal issues behind getting your commercial message out there and doing business using Internet tools. Just because it is possible to do something online does not mean that you should.

When considering e-commerce strategies you don't want to make costly mistakes. If you plan to sell anything on the Internet, you'll want an e-commerce strategy that continues to grow and improve over time. This book explains the theories behind great online shopping experiences in order to help you build an online store or transactional site that best presents your products or services to potential customers or clients.

No matter what stage you've reached in integrating the Internet into your business, this book can guide you to make wise decisions backed up by proven strategies. Even if you already have a company Web site, you can use this book to assess if it is working for or against you and learn how to make it more effective. You can't afford to make bad business decisions, and the Internet offers just as many bad opportunities as good ones. This book is your map, starting you at the planning stage and leading you through the assessment stage to make sure you are on the road toward success.

You can't know everything there is to know about the Internet, but with this book you can know what is essential about using the Internet to establish your business online, expand your reach, and watch your profits soar!

What Is the Internet Good For, Really?

PART 1

What Is E-business?

Depending on whom you ask, you will probably get a variety of definitions of the phrase "e-business." In simplest terms, e-business is the process of doing business electronically or on the Internet. It is often used interchangeably with the term e-commerce, but it is more accurate to say that e-commerce means conducting transactions or other commerce-related activities electronically or on the Internet. E-commerce can be considered a subset of e-business.

E-Business Activities

When someone refers to "doing e-business," he or she is usually talking about conducting business activities through electronic means—most often over the Web or with Internet-based tools. More specifically, e-commerce refers to business transactions that use electronic tools to generate revenue or exchange currency in some way. With these basic definitions in mind, e-commerce activities can include the following online activities:

- ⮥ **Selling:** Sales transactions are completed with Internet-based tools.
- ⮥ **Shopping:** Customers purchase products online, often through a Web site.
- ⮥ **Payments:** Payment for services is made with Web-based tools such as Paypal.com.
- ⮥ **Banking:** Standard banking activities, such as money management and account transfers, are performed through a secure Web site.

E-business can involve everything from electronic purchasing to processing orders, from digital communications with vendors and other business partners to customer service activities conducted online. For the smaller company, e-business can mean using Internet tools and activities to help market something (a business, product, or service). It can also be a means for the business owner to interact with potential and current customers or clients, in some cases with the intent of selling a product or service.

E-Business Relationships

Depending on your company's target market, you will most likely gear your online efforts to one of two common e-business and transactional relationships: business to business, known as B2B, or business to consumer, known as B2C. Other business relationships include business to peer (B2P), a more closed, private transactional relationship with a select group of customers, and peer to peer (P2P), which includes transactions between individuals, such as auctions on eBay. Keep in mind that these transactional relationships don't necessarily mean that money has to change hands. Exchanging information and carrying out negotiations are also forms of transactions.

E-Business Tools

The Internet offers a variety of communication options, many of which can help you conduct business more effectively and efficiently. Each of these tools can be used to perform a business task, often more quickly than through traditional means. Some basic e-business tools and tactics include these:

- ⊃ **E-mail:** This instantaneous method of communication allows for correspondence with individuals and larger groups through mass e-mails, mailing lists, and e-newsletters.
- ⊃ **Web sites:** These may come in a variety of forms, including corporate Web sites, online catalogs, marketing sites, and blogs.
- ⊃ **Message boards:** Online user forums create and solidify online communities, also referred to as posting boards.
- ⊃ **Online ads:** Ads may be Web-based or delivered via e-mail and can contain graphics or consist of text only.
- ⊃ **Online catalogs:** This type of Web site uses a shopping cart to facilitate secure online purchases.

Technology is ever-changing, and the Internet and Web are no exception. New tools are constantly being developed. These include the emergence of wikis or online whiteboards, where multiple users can edit the same documents online; audio publishing commonly known as podcasting; and video publishing, or videocasting.

Not every new technology is relevant to every business, and newer technologies can be more expensive to implement than those that have been in use for years. **Part of making the right decisions about integrating e-business into your business is first understanding—at least on a cursory level—how the technologies work.** Don't get caught up in the jargon and buzz. You can make sound decisions based on clear understandings of both your business and the e-business tools available to you.

Birth of the Internet

You might be surprised to learn that the Internet was not created as a tool for doing business; it was actually intended for government and military communication. What, if anything, does this mean for you and your business?

Today it is clear that the Internet is a valuable business resource. Knowing a little bit about the origins and evolution of the Internet, however, can be helpful in understanding why the Internet and the Web don't always work the way you think they should.

How It All Began

In the 1960s, an agency called Defense Advanced Research Projects Agency (DARPA), part of the U.S. Department of Defense, wanted to develop a system of communications that could withstand any disaster—even a nuclear war. The system had to consist of loose, independent networks of computers with pathways for sending communications data in packets. The network pathways had to be easily rerouted in case part of the network went down. The diverse computers needed to be able to talk to each other for a seamless exchange of data.

The original name for this network was ARPANET. Computers making up the network were first called nodes and were later known as servers. Many of the early nodes were located at universities such as UC Santa Barbara and the University of Utah. MIT was also involved in conceptualizing the earliest stages of ARPANET.

Communicating with Others

E-mail was introduced to the system in the early 1970s. In the late 1970s, CompuServe became the first dialup service to offer connectivity, e-mail, and other online services to members of the public. Within a few years, Prodigy and a small upstart named America Online appeared on the scene alongside more homegrown bulletin board systems (BBSs) such as The WELL and EchoNYC. BBSs were typically started by hobbyists and not businesspeople and were often based on someone's home computer.

In 1980, CompuServe pioneered a tool facilitating online chat. Also in the 1980s, the military portion of ARPANET was separated from the public parts. At the time, the people accessing the network came primarily from universities. The National Science Foundation (NSF) got involved in the project, and the term Internet was coined and eventually used to represent the ever-expanding network. The Web was not invented until the early 1990s.

The Web and the Internet

While the World Wide Web is a part of the Internet, the Web is not the entire Internet. The Internet is the network within which the Web functions on Web servers. But there are also other types of servers on the Internet, and not all of them use Web sites or Web pages to access the data they house. E-mail servers and file transfer protocol (FTP) servers that manage the storing, uploading, and downloading of files also reside on the Internet. Over time, some Internet tools and functions have become Web-based, such as e-mail or tools used to access an FTP site. Still, "the Internet" is the correct way to refer to the entire network, while "the Web" refers specifically to the multimedia portion of the Internet.

E-Mail and the Web

E-mail has proven to be the mainstay of Internet communications, and its popularity supports the theory that the main reason people get online is to communicate directly with one another. Nothing else—not Web searching, Web site browsing, or uploading and downloading files—matches the popularity of e-mail. Even in countries or remote areas that lack faster broadband Internet connections, text-only e-mails can still be sent and received with relative ease.

Opening the Online Floodgates

Back in the early 1990s, commercial online services like CompuServe, Prodigy, and America Online began to reach out beyond hobbyists and target the mainstream public. These services were closed systems on protected servers where subscribers, especially new users unfamiliar with the Internet, could access e-mail, forums, live chat rooms, and databases of articles and information. While some of these services did offer limited access to the Internet at large and Internet resources such as Usenet newsgroups, the eventual goal of the online services was to keep people within their closed system to better capitalize on their undivided attention.

Around the same time, more experienced Internet users could be found on Usenet newsgroups, the Internet's original text version of message boards, and smaller online services. These people communicated globally and built online communities that crossed real-world borders. Having been online for a while, they enjoyed open access to the Internet and felt invested in the virtual spaces where they congregated with like-minded fellow users.

Eventually, commercial online services began to provide more access to the Internet at large, and the floodgates opened. On some services, access to Usenet newsgroups were still limited or in a few cases censored, but the influx of relatively new Internet users into the territory of more experienced users caused a ruckus in some online circles, with people complaining about the invasion of newbies (new Internet users) who didn't understand the proper etiquette of the virtual world.

The influx of large numbers of new users accessing the Internet and later the Web attracted the attention of companies large and small. Where there were people, there were potential customers. While initially companies did not know how to effectively reach Internet users for marketing and commercial purposes, they eventually started spending a lot of money to figure out a solution to the problem.

Where Have the Commercial Online Services Gone?

In the early 1990s, CompuServe (CIS), Prodigy, and America Online (AOL) were three of the largest bulletin board systems. While there were others, including GE's venture called GEnie and Apple's system called eWorld, these were the three big ones. Of the three, CompuServe was known as a service for techies, and Prodigy was positioned as a general consumer service. Eventually America Online surpassed them both to become the top service, reaching out to new computer and Internet users. Today, AOL owns CompuServe, which is now an internet service provider (ISP). Prodigy was acquired by SBC Communications and eventually phased out, and GEnie and eWorld went bust.

The Wild, Wild Web

During the time that newbies were first discovering life outside their subscription-based commercial online services, the Web was still a new and relatively unknown tool. Devised by Tim Berners-Lee, a programmer at CERN, the European Organization for Nuclear Research, hypertext markup language (HTML) was used on the World Wide Web as a way to link text documents together with cross-referencing hyperlinks. The actual codes that created these links and other specifications for the text—such as boldface, italics, and headers—were called HTML tags.

The Web's Purpose

Berners-Lee's initial impetus for developing HTML was to help researchers share and update information. Soon, Berners-Lee's specifications for Web browsers and setting up Web servers, which he published on his Web site, sparked other programmers to begin building sites of their own. Berners-Lee also founded the World Wide Web Consortium, also known as the W3C, to create and set standards to help maintain the quality of the Internet and the Web.

Early Web Sites

Web sites began simply as files on a Web server connected together with hyperlinks using HTML. At first those files consisted of text only, and Web pages were basic and bland with dull gray backgrounds. As more programmers began developing on the Web, the W3C expanded the number of HTML tags. Soon Web-page background colors could be changed. Then graphic files. such as illustrations and photographs and later animation, could be added to sites, which now also include sound and video. Today, a Web site can take the form of a blog or contain audio and digital video. Many Web sites are dynamic, with pages created "on the fly," meaning that each time a site visitor selects a link on a database-driven site, a page of content is constructed at that moment to deliver the most current information available in the site's database.

Big Business and the Internet

Big businesses were not very involved with the Internet in the early 1990s. Major corporations were reluctant to focus their attentions and resources on a medium that was text-only, hard to navigate, boring to look at, inflexible, and limited in scope. But with the creation of the Web within the Internet environment, companies began to take note. Once graphic files were introduced and other multimedia developments took Web pages far beyond the plain vanilla of a text-only Internet, companies began exploring this new medium in which information could be shared anywhere at any time.

The Start of E-Business

In the early days of the Web, once the general public gained access to it, people built sites that reflected a myriad of interests and served diverse purposes. But absent in the early incarnations of the Internet and Web were commercial ventures and advertising. With major corporations eyeing the Web as a potential new place for doing business, the idea of online advertising quickly took hold.

One of the earliest tools of e-business was the corporate Web site. To get people to their new sites, companies first turned to offline advertising and later to online advertising. Ads began appearing in the form of banners across the tops of Web sites, linking back to the advertisers' sites.

The more people who went online, the more attractive the Internet and Web became to businesses. Soon, the Internet and Web teemed with advertising. Even e-mail became fair game to companies that wanted to get their commercial messages across to the public.

Early adopters of the Internet and Web were offended by the commercialization of their private virtual spaces. Yet as the number of users on the Internet and Web continued to grow, people realized that without money from companies around the world, the Internet and Web could not support that growth.

Selling on the Web

Once companies developed a Web presence, the next step was to use their Web sites to make money. Facilitating online transactions became a priority, and soon programmers had come up with the first online shopping-cart system—a virtual experience that allowed customers to view products, save them to a cart, and then check out when they were ready to complete their purchase.

The orders from the Web were e-mailed to the business, and companies handled packaging and shipping in the same way they handled their catalog orders. An early challenge for businesses that were selling by mail order and were starting to sell online was how to make sure their inventory systems were integrated. Problems arose when online orders could not be fulfilled because items were sold out by mail order or vice versa.

Another early complication in online buying and selling was security. Hackers had a field day with the Web, and most people were hesitant to put their credit cards numbers into a form on a Web site. Gradually businesses became savvier about protecting their servers. Pioneering online sellers like Amazon.com not only helped to develop more secure shopping carts and servers but also communicated the message that their online stores were secure. It took time and money to communicate reassuring messages through advertising that overcame people's fears. Too often the media latched onto sensational stories of hacked servers and stolen credit cards.

As the Web Turns

So what does this history lesson about the Internet and Web mean to you as a business owner? The first thing to remember is that the Internet and the World Wide Web were not created for commercial pursuits or business purposes.

The Reality of E-Business

E-business was not an early goal of the Internet. That said, the Internet and Web have been modified and enhanced over time by programmers and companies to be more business-friendly. People have come to expect marketing, advertising, and selling online. Still, there are good ways to market, advertise, and sell online, and there are bad ways. **Understanding the origins of the Internet and Web can help you appreciate the spirit that built them.** Your goal should be to build a better Web site, engage others through effective—not offensive—e-mail campaigns, and to find ways to appropriately use the Internet and Web for commercial purposes without turning people off.

Who Is Online Anyway?

The growth of the Internet happened because more of the general public adopted it and began using it on a regular basis. According to research firm IDC, in 1995 there were 16 million Internet users. By October 2006, Internet World Stats (*www.internetworldstats.com*) placed the Internet population at over 1 billion.

According to Internet World Stats, 29.7 percent of all Internet users communicate online in English, followed by 13.4 percent in Chinese; 7.9 percent in Japanese; 7.5 percent in Spanish; and 5.4 percent in German.

Depending on where you look, the proportion of women to men on the Internet is similar to the world population breakdown. Women make up 51 percent of the overall Internet population. In some studies, however, women lag slightly behind men in how often they use the Internet.

The Pew Internet & American Life Project Tracking Survey, conducted from February 15 to April 6, 2006, breaks down some Internet demographics in the United States as follows:

Age	Percentage of each age group using the Internet
18–29	88%
30–49	84%
50–64	71%
65-plus	32%

Race/ethnicity	Percentage of each ethnic group using the Internet
White, Non-Hispanic	73%
Black, Non-Hispanic	61%
English-speaking Hispanic	76%

Community type	Percentage of Internet usage in each community
Urban	75%
Suburban	75%
Rural	63%

According to the Pew report, 91 percent of people with household incomes over $75,000 and an education level of college or higher are Internet users. Among home Internet users, 34 percent are still using dialup while 62 percent are getting access through a high-speed connection such as DSL or cable modem.

For the most part, online demographics reflect the world we live in. Understanding who is online and how they use the Internet can help you better target your audience.

What Really Works Online

Understanding some of the basic ways to do business on the Internet and Web can help you strategize your e-business efforts. Not everything you can do online is right for every business. Until you know your options, you won't be able to make an educated decision about what to use and what to avoid.

E-Business Activities

The benefit of using the Internet these days is that you can scale your activities to the size of your business, the size of your customer base, and your budget.

Some common e-business activities for small to mid-sized businesses include the following:

➲ Building and maintaining a basic Web site presence
➲ Conducting business with clients and vendors via e-mail and the Web
➲ Building and leveraging online communities
➲ Providing online customer service
➲ Selling products or services online
➲ Engaging in e-mail marketing campaigns

Success depends on how e-business activities are carried out, not necessarily how much money you spend to make them happen. What might be effective for one company might not be effective for another.

Effective E-Business

Success is in the eye of the beholder. One business may see success as getting people to visit its Web site and exposing them to its branding and marketing messages. Another business might measure success as the number of people who not only visit its Web site but also fill out a form to request more information. To another business, being able to provide better customer service around the clock with fewer personnel means success.

Business practices that work on the Internet and Web can be described as follows:

- Clear, succinct, and easy to understand
- Noninvasive and respectful of the privacy of others
- Repetitive without being annoying
- Focused more on building relationships than triggering one-time actions
- Integrated appropriately and thoughtfully into the online medium

The companies that take time to determine how best to use the Internet and the Web for e-business are the ones that experience greater success in achieving their business goals. E-business takes time to set realistic goals and to come up with viable strategies. Once implemented, e-business tactics require time to catch on. Going online is not a quick business fix.

 ▶▶ TEST DRIVE

Before you begin doing business online, particularly building a Web site, consider the following:

- How long have I been online, and what aspects of the Internet am I most familiar with?
- What changes have I seen on the Internet and Web since I first went online?
- How has the Internet affected my industry over the years?
- How are other companies in my industry using the Internet?
- Why do I want to use the Internet for my business?

Using the Internet with Care

The Internet offers individuals and businesses a variety of ways to communicate. You may be tempted to try to use them all before considering what impact each may have on other people. What you do on the Internet rarely happens in a vacuum. If you are sending e-mail, you are affecting the recipients. If you have a Web site online, even if you don't market it, people will eventually find it and will instantly get an impression about you or your company because of what they see and read.

Everything you do on the Internet can be found, traced, pointed to, and in some cases tampered with, so you should take care with anything you build or publish online. Even if you believe what you are doing online is private and protected, always act as if it is not. This will help minimize problems that could stem from inappropriate use of Internet communications tools.

Before you spend any effort integrating new Internet tools into your business tool kit, take the time to learn how to best use those tools. Knowing how to use Internet communications tools is only one aspect of learning how to properly do business online. Understanding how to craft your messages appropriately for various online formats and forums is key to getting the most out of the Internet for your business needs.

The Ubiquity of E-Mail

Nobody can deny that e-mail has become an integral way for people to communicate with one another. E-mail is the most popular Internet tool, bar none. As with any form of communication, e-mail has had its share of problems, from downed technology to faulty software, from e-mail "bombs," by which hackers bombard an e-mail account with continuous fake e-mails, to unsolicited commercial messages (also known as spam), from etiquette errors to gross misunderstandings. E-mail is not perfect, but it is arguably your most valuable Internet tool for business.

Through the years that e-mail usage has grown, people's feelings about it have evolved from curiosity to concerns about managing correspondence and protecting privacy. Part of the shift in perceptions and feelings about e-mail comes from the multitude of abuses perpetrated by unscrupulous marketers who send unsolicited e-mail ads indiscriminately. Bad marketers have given online marketing a bad name.

E-mail can be used in several ways for business:

- ➲ General business correspondence
- ➲ Customer service (feedback response)
- ➲ Customer retention through ongoing messaging
- ➲ Prospecting through e-mail marketing campaigns
- ➲ Document delivery with attached files
- ➲ Traffic driver leading recipients to your business site

E-mails can be crafted and distributed in a variety of ways to serve many business needs. Viewing e-mail as an essential business and marketing tool rather than simply a communications tool can help you see the opportunities e-mail presents for your business.

Why Is It Called Spam?

Nobody really seems to know exactly why unsolicited or junk e-mails are called spam. The term is not to be mistaken with the Hormel canned meat product called Spam (short for spiced ham). Some say that the Internet term refers to a skit by the British comedy troupe Monty Python's Flying Circus in which a waitress, while reading the menu to a customer, repeatedly says "spam." A group of Vikings dining at the restaurant bursts into song: "Spam, spam, spam, spam . . . lovely spam! Wonderful spam!" As the Internet gained popularity, the term spam was used for anything repeated ad nauseum, such as posts on message boards and unsolicited e-mails.

Pushing E-Mail

Most traditional marketing employs push tactics. You must send, or push, your message or advertisement out to many people in order to capture a few new customers or clients. Push media for marketing includes radio, television, and billboards. Some Internet marketing tactics, such as banner ads on Web sites, are push tactics.

Pull advertising—the act of drawing people to your Web site—uses other Internet marketing tactics, such as search engine optimization and listings in directories. E-mail is a push tactic, as you have to send e-mail to recipients in order for them to get your message.

With a push tactic like e-mail comes the need for greater sensitivity than with broadcasting a television or radio ad. People can choose to turn a television or radio on or off, so they control whether or not they receive your message. But not everyone can effectively and consistently block unsolicited e-mails from their e-mail inbox. Too often, Internet marketers disregard an individual's right to privacy or the right to choose what he or she receives via e-mail.

Interestingly, most people perceive their e-mail inboxes to be much more private and personal than their regular mailboxes. People are used to getting unsolicited mail in the form of direct-mail pieces—fliers, brochures, special offers that they never requested. They toss such material into the trash, often unread.

But unsolicited e-mail, commonly known as spam, often gets an emotional reaction. People will tell you that they hate getting unsolicited e-mails.

Building Relationships

Marketers like to say e-mail has several capabilities for building relationships with potential and existing customers. **E-mail is both a one-to-one and one-to-many broadcast medium.** You can e-mail someone directly— that is, you and one other person can communicate one-to-one. E-mail can also have a broader reach. You can e-mail many people at once—that is, one to many people.

Some people broadcast an e-mail message to many people by putting all the e-mail addresses for the recipients in the blind carbon copy or bcc field. A more effective way of implementing the one-to-many marketing technique is to use e-mail lists, also known as listservs, discussion lists, and group lists. E-mail lists are created using software or Web-based systems that store recipient e-mail addresses. Once you set one up, you send a single e-mail to the main e-mail address representing the entire list. The system broadcasts that message to all subscribers or list members. As a business owner, e-mail gives you the ability to build relationships with your customers or to cultivate relationships with potential customers, either by e-mailing individuals directly or sending a message out to many people at once.

How Not to Break the Law

The CAN-SPAM Act of 2003 (in full, the Controlling the Assault of Non-Solicited Pornography and Marketing Act) took effect at the beginning of 2004. It requires unsolicited commercial e-mails to be labeled as advertisements. Penalties can include up to twenty years in jail and fines exceeding $10,000 per offense. These e-mails must contain a way for the recipient to unsubscribe or opt out from the sender's e-mail list. The e-mails must also contain the sender's physical address, and they must not use deceptive subject lines and false headers. The federal law can pre-empt state laws, and most of the fifty states have their own detailed SPAM laws as well. Before embarking on an e-mail marketing campaign, you may want to consult with a lawyer familiar with Internet law in your area.

E-Mail Impressions

Picking the right e-mail software program, also known as an e-mail client, is critical to professional business communications. E-mail clients are downloaded onto your computer. The e-mail you send and receive is processed within the software program and can be saved on your hard drive. Most of these software programs allow you to customize how your e-mails appear to the recipient.

Some of the more commonly used e-mail clients include these:

- Outlook (Mac, Windows)
- Eudora (Mac, Windows)
- Mail (Mac)
- Mozilla Thunderbird (Windows, Mac, Linux)
- Pegasus Mail (Windows)

Can free e-mail programs convey the same kind of business professionalism as e-mail clients? If you send your e-mail campaign using Hotmail.com or Yahoo! e-mail, will the recipient think less of your company?

| Inside Track | The Spam Kings |

Over the last decade, several individuals have earned the notorious title of Spam King for their wanton abuse of e-mail for alleged marketing purposes. In 1998, Sanford Wallace, owner of Cyber Promotions, called a "junk e-mailing powerhouse" by CNET News, was charged $2 million to settle the final portion of a lawsuit brought against his company. The payment went to the ISP Earthlink, which got Wallace to agree to refrain from sending any further junk e-mail messages through its network. In 2005, Alan M. Ralsky, another "king of bulk e-mail" and "poster-boy for spam," as he was labeled by the *Detroit News*, had his $750,000 home raided by the FBI, a mansion built from the profits from his junk e-mail marketing business. In 2002, Ralsky paid a cash settlement of an undisclosed amount to end a lawsuit from Verizon Internet Services and agreed not to send spam through the company's networks. The FBI raid put Ralsky out of business, or so he claimed.

One Spam King who hoped to capitalize on the term Spam King by launching a clothing line under the moniker saw his venture dashed by a cease-and-desist letter from Hormel, the makers of Spam, the food product. In the end, spam does not pay.

The more you control the appearance and distribution of your marketing and business e-mails, the more effective they'll be. First impressions are important when it comes to e-mail, and the recipient often takes no more than a few seconds to determine whether or not she or he will open or read an e-mail from an unknown party. If the impression is a bad one, the recipient won't hesitate to hit the delete button.

The Ever-Changing Web

The Web consists of Web sites linked together in web-like fashion through the use of hyperlinks within special coding known as hypertext, or HTML. Behind the scenes, a Web site is really nothing more than a database of files on a Web server. The types and quality of the files you use to build your site and the way you assemble those files and present them to the viewer is what makes or breaks your site. Presenting information in not only an organized fashion but in a compelling and attractive manner is key to having an effective Web site for business.

Back in the Early Days

When Web sites first made their public debut in the early 1990s, the technology was so primitive that most Web sites looked alike. All sites had gunmetal grey backgrounds with black text. The font type was based on whatever the viewer's Web browser was set at and the size of the font could be very small, small, medium, large, or extra large.

Opt In Versus Opt Out

When someone knowingly and willingly subscribes to a list in order to receive e-mails from another party, he has chosen to opt in to the list. When an e-mail is sent to someone without that person's permission, and she has to deliberately unsubscribe from the sender's e-mail list to stop receiving the unwanted messages, she is being forced to opt out. Most reputable e-marketers agree that allowing recipients to opt in or actively choose to be added to an e-mail list is far more effective than forced opt-outs. Some e-marketers even implement a double opt-in procedure. The subscriber must enter her e-mail address to opt-in to an e-mail list and will receive a confirmation e-mail in which it is necessary to click a link to confirm the subscription.

Images could be embedded into a page, but they often appeared either above or below text, flush left or in the center of the Web page.

While the earliest Web sites may sound boring in their simplicity, there were some benefits of having limited choices in color, layout, and design, including the following:

1. **Pro:** There was less of a chance of cluttering up a page with too many bells and whistles.
2. **Con:** Most Web pages had too much text on a page and required more reading to get to the point.
3. **Con:** There was little differentiation between Web pages unless the Web developer was somewhat skilled with graphics.

4. Pro: If you did anything unusual or visually interesting with your site, you were likely to draw a large readership rather quickly.

5. Con: There were very few ways to follow up with the people you attracted to your site for business purposes.

As Web technology rapidly progressed and Web sites expanded beyond personal or creative platforms and academic or professional resumes, businesses began to invest money in the Web. With more money and business interests came even faster technological advances and more business-oriented Web features, including shopping carts.

Pull Them In and Make Them Act

While e-mail is a push technology, a Web site tries to pull people toward information that will trigger some kind of action. Actions someone might take through your Web site include the following:

- Subscribing to receive regular e-mails from you, often in the form of e-newsletters
- Filling out a form to request more information or to be contacted
- Purchasing a product or service
- Providing feedback
- Filling out a questionnaire or survey to provide valuable marketing data

As a business owner, you need to think of your Web site as a gateway to your company's information and an alternate access point to your products or services. A Web site should be more than informational; it should be action oriented. You must determine the key actions you want your site visitors to take.

Doing Business on the Web

Most businesspeople look at Web sites as great communications and marketing tools. Web sites can be much more than a basic or in-depth marketing brochure that simply provides information to the visitor. Some of the more common business uses for a Web site include the following:

➲ An online presence for marketing purposes
➲ A customer service tool to build and maintain customer relations
➲ A transactional tool to facilitate sales
➲ A community-builder to strengthen customer relations
➲ An alternate revenue generator

Not all Web sites that generate revenue do so through direct sales of products or services. Other ways a Web site can provide revenues to a business include these:

Affiliate programs   *Online advertising*
Sponsorships   *Content syndication*

Affiliate Programs

Affiliate programs are automated Web-based systems through which one company allows another company or individual to carry and sell its products on the other company's Web sites. If you have affiliates, they can be like an external sales force for your company. Amazon.com has a popular affiliate program and makes additional revenue by allowing anyone to feature products on their site that link back to Amazon's site to fulfill the orders.

The other side of an affiliate program is to become the affiliate. You can supplement your own product inventory or carry other companies' products on your site without ever needing your own inventory by becoming an affiliate of other companies that have affiliate programs.

Advertising

The overall concept of Web advertising is straightforward. An advertiser pays to advertise on your Web site. You guarantee their ad will be seen by a certain number of visitors to your site. If you plan to sell advertising on your Web site, you should have some or all of the following:

➲ A high volume of site traffic or a highly targeted audience
➲ A reliable, detailed, and verifiable Web traffic tracking system to measure page views

⮑ Carefully researched marketing data, such as demographics and psychographics, on your Web site visitors

⮑ An automated system for rotating the ads and for measuring ad views and ad click-throughs, or the number of times visitors actually click on an ad

⮑ A written agreement with the advertiser specifying the terms and length of the advertising contract

Web sponsorship is similar to Web advertising. The main difference is that rather than simply placing an ad graphic on your Web site, the advertiser sponsors an entire section of your site. You can either develop a specific content area and approach potential sponsors, or you can approach sponsors first with a concept and convince them to pay you up front to develop and implement the section on your site. In return, the sponsor gets extensive branding throughout the section that may include its company logo, a prominent statement saying it is the sponsor, and multiple links to its Web site.

Content Syndication for Profit

Content syndication means that not only do you produce content for your own site, you also distribute it to other sites for a fee. Many businesses do not have time and resources to develop extra content for their site, but they realize there is value in providing their customers with useful information. They may opt to pay other companies for the rights to republish content on their own sites. If you are the company they turn to for extra content, you can charge them a licensing fee. By doing so, you are syndicating your Web content.

Tools for Web Building

There are do-it-yourself tools for building your own company Web site. Still, most experts agree that rather than creating your own site, you are better off in the long run investing in a qualified, professional Web developer and designer.

If you are thinking of building your own business Web site, even as a test site before turning to a developer, some of your options include the following:

- ⮞ Free or low-fee Web-based publishing tools, such as Tripod.com or Homestead.com
- ⮞ Fee-based Web-based tools provided by ISPs such as Earthlink. net or AOL.com or by domain-registration companies such as Register.com or NetworkSolutions.com
- ⮞ Basic text-editing software, such as BBEdit
- ⮞ Web development software for beginners, such as Microsoft FrontPage
- ⮞ More advanced Web development software, such as Adobe's Dreamweaver or GoLive

A Web developer may use off-the-shelf development and design tools as well as custom programming. It is usually true that the more customized the site, the more costly it becomes. As a business owner, your time is money, so spending your time trying to figure out Web site development does not make good business sense.

While you may save money in the short term by building your own site, you will inevitably need help taking your site to a more professional level with more effective features for doing business online. Trying to do business with an inefficient site could end up costing you far more over the next few years than it would to do things right the first time.

The Evolution of Message Boards

A message board is any Internet-based environment that allows visitors to post a message, read other messages, and reply to messages. Also known as a bulletin board, forum, or a posting board, a message board also archives all of these messages in an organized format in one location. Message boards evolved from the Usenet newsgroups of the early Internet, where people congregated to discuss a specific topic; posted conversations, or threads, that were linked so any visitor could follow and contribute to the discussion. These boards took on a more organized and user-friendly form on commercial online services such as America Online.

Modern-Day Message Boards

Today, most message boards are Web-based. Web-based message boards now present messages using graphics and features such as folders and subfolders to organize discussions. They represent threads visually in a myriad of ways to make it clear who is responding to whom and where a conversation on a particular issue continues and ends.

Hosting message boards on your Web site or sponsoring a message board on someone else's site can be a great way to build your company brand. Message boards can build communities of like-minded people who in turn can help you increase customer loyalty, facilitating an ongoing dialogue between you and your current and potential customers. From an e-business standpoint, any time you can provide valuable resources on your Web site that keep visitors coming back, you are potentially doing something positive to help grow your business.

Building a Board

There are many ways to approach incorporating a message board system into your Web site. Most message or bulletin board systems require some degree of programming expertise beyond basic HTML. Despite the added expense, hiring a Web programmer may be the best way to go.

You can use free software, such as WWWBoard and phpBB, to build your board. Other software companies, like COMMbits, host boards on their Web site for a nominal monthly fee. These are customized to look like your site so most visitors will not even realize they're no longer on your Web site. Costs begin to increase as you move toward more custom-built solutions.

Free Web-based message boards that are hosted by a third party, such as Yahoo! Groups, are easy to set up and maintain, but they lack customization and branding. As a business, your logo and overall brand and design are an important part of your identity. Using generic message board solutions defeats part of the reason you'd want to set up and maintain an online forum in the first place—to build your brand.

What About Blogs?

A blog (short for Web log) is nothing more than a Web site that has a relatively accepted standard format. These are the basic elements of a blog:

- Time-stamped and dated posts presented in reverse chronological order
- Headers for each post
- Link to let visitors submit a comment on any post
- Automated archive of past posts
- List of most recent posts
- List of most recent comments
- Two- or three-column layout

The Blog Advantage

Building a blog can be easy, but maintaining it definitely is more of a challenge.

Because most people have come to expect blog content to be current and frequently updated, blogging can be extremely time consuming. Unless you are in the business of content creation, blogging can become burdensome and expensive.

If you are struggling to get your Web site off the ground, however, you can opt to put up a blog in lieu of a site. By taking advantage of the more advanced tools that have been developed for blogging, you can put a blog up more quickly and cheaply than you can a standard Web site.

The Right Tools for Your Business

The Internet offers businesses an array of tools for doing their work more quickly, effectively, and comprehensively. Not every business, however, needs to use all of the tools available in order to be successful. In fact, you are better off strategizing with your goals, market, and other business considerations in mind before putting time or money toward tools that you really shouldn't be using.

E-mail is, of course, a no-brainer for any business. For both internal and external communication, e-mail is by far the most efficient communication option next to the telephone. The benefit of e-mail over the telephone is that it provides an electronic paper trail of business discussions and transactions. Notes taken while on the phone will never be as accurate as e-mail records.

Companies most commonly build a Web site to establish their online presence for branding, marketing, and communications. Web sites with more advanced features can attract and retain customers, provide marketing data, and sell products or services.

Message boards and blogs are useful tools for business, but they may not be right for everybody. Both require resources that can potentially detract from business goals, thus making them costly in the long run even if they are free to set up.

As with any other business endeavor, setting solid goals is the first step to success and is crucial in determining what tools you'll need to get there. Technology decisions should always be made with plenty of consideration.

▶▶ TEST DRIVE

Before you embark on an entirely new Internet strategy, evaluate how you are currently using the Internet and determine where you need to extend more effort. Ask yourself these questions:

- ➲ How and when am I using e-mail for business?
- ➲ How action-oriented is my Web site?
- ➲ How much business does my Web site bring in?
- ➲ How am I strategically integrating message boards into my marketing program? If I'm not, should I?
- ➲ How does blogging fit into my business communications strategy? If I don't have a blog, should I consider setting one up?

What Is the Internet Really Good For, Anyway?

What Are Your Business Goals?

If you are exploring how to best use the Internet for business purposes, or you are looking into ways to better integrate the Internet into how you do business, there is some good news. Technology aside, any decisions you make regarding the Internet will be based on tried-and-true business logic.

E-business planning is like any other kind of business planning. You need to ask yourself a series of questions, take time to consider and research the answers, and document where you are today and where you want to be in both the short and long term.

Some possible immediate goals may include these:

➲ Announcing your new business
➲ Debuting a new product or service
➲ Driving customers to your physical business location
➲ Driving customers to your Web site or blog

Some longer-term goals might include these:

➲ Building your company's overall image or brand
➲ Changing your company's image or brand
➲ Increasing sales
➲ Strengthening customer relations

Once you determine your business goals, you have completed only the first step in Internet strategizing. An awareness of what you are trying to achieve will help clarify how you should use the Internet.

Who Is Your Audience?

Defining your company's goals is just the beginning of e-business planning. Next you must look outside your company to your existing and potential customers. In traditional marketing, this step is called "determining your market"—that is, targeting existing and potential customers.

Customers are categorized in two main ways: by means of demographics or psychographics. Demographics are quantitative data that express objective and verifiable facts about an individual. Psychographics are qualitative data that describe a person's more subjective personal attitudes or preferences.

Demographic Data

If you know the demographics of your existing customers, you can better target your likeliest new customers because they share similar traits that may have an effect on the products they buy and services they use. Common demographic breakdowns include the following:

- ➲ Gender
- ➲ Age
- ➲ Geographic location
- ➲ Education level
- ➲ Occupation
- ➲ Income level

Knowing customer demographics will guide you in marketing your product or service. If you provide a service for seniors, for example, you don't want your marketing campaign to target teenagers.

The Internet is a natural medium through which to reach a teen market. To reach the senior market, however, you need a more specialized strategy. If your market is purely local or regional, your Internet marketing target is much more specific than if you were trying to reach a statewide, nationwide, or global audience.

Determining Psychographics

Identifying customers by psychographics is not as straightforward as using demographics. To best determine psychographics, you may well need to interview or survey your customers to obtain more personal data about them. If you don't yet have customers, interview or survey people you think might be natural prospective customers. Conducting a formal or informal focus group is a common way to gather psychographic information about customers.

Psychographics include these types of information:

- Risk tolerance
- View of money
- Political views
- Cultural tastes
- Comfort with technology

Some psychographic details that may be especially useful for your e-business strategy are the following:

- Favorite Internet activities
- Feelings about credit card safety online
- Types of items commonly purchased online
- Likelihood of paying for a service via the Internet
- Tolerance for receiving promotions through e-mail

Psychographic information helps flesh out the bare-bones demographic data and paint a clearer picture of your market and your existing or potential customers.

Getting That Marketing Data

While major corporations pay thousands of dollars for custom marketing data, the Internet provides tools to conduct marketing research online, usually via electronic surveys or questionnaires. Such surveys can be integrated into even basic Web sites. This provides you with the means to find more out about your site visitors.

A good Web programmer can create an interactive survey form that asks readers to respond to carefully crafted questions with a finite set of answers. **The ideal survey form captures the responses in database form and allows you to generate reports that provide relevant breakdowns.** For example, you should be able to learn the gender breakdown of survey respondents as both a number and a percentage.

You may want to hire a marketing consultant to assist with developing effective survey questions that will get the information you need to grow your business. Keeping your survey or questionnaire short and simple is key in getting a response from potential participants.

An online survey can include several response formats, each of which encourages a different type of answer.

➲ **Check boxes:** When clicked, a checkmark appears in the selected square box.

➲ **Radio buttons:** When clicked, a dot appears in the selected round circle.

➲ **Pull-down menus:** The respondent selects the most relevant response from a list of defined choices.

➲ **List box:** The respondent is permitted to select multiple responses from a list of defined choices.

➲ **Text field:** Allows for a response to be typed into an open field.

Check boxes can be used to indicate single or multiple responses. Radio buttons, however, are best used for a single response. When a respondent clicks on one circle to select an answer, all other buttons will be blank. With a pull-down menu, respondents cannot see all the choices until they click on the menu, and they pull down the cursor to make a selection. Pull-down menus are nice space savers but should be used sparingly and only when you have a very long list.

List boxes allow users to scroll through a list of possible responses. They take up more space than other survey formats, but they also allow users to select as many responses as are applicable.

Text fields can be used when you want to allow the respondent to fill in a blank with a personal response that cannot be defined in a set of standard answers. Larger text fields allow a respondent to elaborate on an answer and provide a more detailed response. Analyzing the answers to open-ended questions can be problematic because responses must be weighed individually, rather than measured in percentage terms.

Surveys Made Easy

For a fast, easy, and inexpensive Web-based survey, you can turn to sites such as SurveyMonkey.com or Zoomerang.com. Both services provide a free basic subscription that allows you to create a ten-question survey and receive up to 100 responses. For a fee, you can store and analyze data for unlimited surveys with unlimited parameters. The fee-based services also offer features to better customize and brand your surveys. This type of service is helpful when you don't know HTML or want to spare your business the expense of a programmer or Web developer. As with any pre-packaged Web-based service, however, you may encounter limitations with the features offered and may later turn to a programmer for more customization and control.

Surveying your visitors is an important tactic to better identify your target market and their needs to better serve them both online and offline.

What Are Your Traditional Marketing Efforts?

The Internet can be a useful tool for your business marketing needs. Before you go online, however, you may want to first take inventory of your existing marketing strategy. Most traditional marketing tactics have an online equivalent.

Traditional Marketing Tactic
Press release
Brochure
Direct mail
Television ad
Radio ad
Press kit
Print ad
Business card

Internet Marketing Tactic

Electronic press release

Basic Web site

E-mail marketing campaign

Web video ad

Audio ad

Online press kit

Web ad

Signature file

The same principle applies to business tactics—for every traditional business tactic, there is an online version.

Online Versus Offline Approaches

In some cases, the Internet offers a new twist on an old tactic. Web ad targeting is a prime example. In traditional advertising, such as commercials produced for television and radio, ads cannot be specifically targeted to an audience; that is, all viewers see the same ad. On the Web, ads can be highly targeted, with a person's Web usage profile determining what version of an ad they see. This instant user analysis is generated through cookies or text messages saved to a file in the user's Web browser, which can be accessed by the Web server hosting the sites they visit.

Tracking Electronically

When you do business or market online, you can track the movement of visitors as they navigate through your Web site. Tracking can also be achieved using cookies. The Web server that hosts your site or online store places text messages on the cookie files within the browsers of people visiting your site to mark the actions taken while there.

Did they come to the home page and then leave without clicking on anything? Did they go directly from the home page to a product page? Did they put several items into their shopping cart without checking out? The answers to these and other questions about what customers do on your site can help you better serve them.

> ## Common Web Tracking Parameters
>
> Some of the best basic information you can obtain about visitors to your Web site includes what pages they viewed, the path they took through your site, the amount of time they spent on your site, and even what site referred them to yours. You can also track their country of origin and what kind of network they are using, such as an educational institution (.edu), organization (.org), network (.net), a government agency (.gov), or the military (.mil), among others. Even this general information can give you insight into who is visiting your site.

Integrating Online Tools for Marketing

The key to Internet marketing success is knowing how to translate your traditional marketing tactics into appropriate and effective online marketing tactics. Here are some factors you need to consider when you are moving from traditional to Internet marketing:

- ➲ **Be concise.** Most Internet-based marketing should be shorter and punchier than traditional marketing, so don't take your regular marketing piece and put it online unchanged.
- ➲ **Use small files.** File sizes determine download times, so try to create the smallest files possible for electronic marketing pieces.
- ➲ **Build trust.** People are more wary of advertising online, so find ways to build relationships via the Internet.
- ➲ **Provide customer security.** Security and privacy are valid concerns online, so establish policies for how you'll protect customer information.
- ➲ **Coordinate efforts.** Online marketing should complement offline marketing, so don't put anything online that is in conflict with what you are doing offline.

Some people unfortunately are intimidated by conducting marketing or doing business on the Internet because they think it means throwing out everything they have already learned about marketing and business.

The truth is that online marketing and e-business are simply enhanced versions of traditional marketing. Don't forget the fundamentals of sound business and good marketing when using the Internet. Common sense applies no matter what the medium.

Expanding into Selling Online

If you've never sold a product or service before and plan to start doing so by going straight to the Internet, you may have certain advantages over an established business.

Pros and Cons of Internet-First Businesses

There are many advantages to opening an online business first, including these:

- The old way of doing things, including old processes and technology, won't get in the way.
- You may not have to make a large investment in leasing space for your business, especially if your storefront is exclusively online.
- You can take advantage of Internet tools for communications, marketing, and sales.
- You can instantly have a global reach if that is what you want for your business.
- You aren't constantly trying to drive visitors to your site offline so they can take advantage of your product or service offerings.

But there are also some disadvantages to opening a business online without already having an established business:

- You don't have an established brand so will have to spend time and money building one.
- You don't have a customer base yet so will need to work on building a clientele from scratch.
- You may not have a lot of business experience.

➲ You haven't worked out the fundamental issues of providing services or selling, such as customer relations, return policies, and product fulfillment issues.

➲ You don't have the online and offline presence that can help reach more customers in various settings.

Even having an established business that sells products by traditional methods—storefront, catalog, and other offline means—doesn't eliminate all the challenges of setting up an online presence.

From Bricks to Clicks

The term bricks and mortar is often used to refer to a business with a real-world presence, such as an actual store or building. Clicks and mortar describes a bricks-and-mortar business that has gone online. Some immediate issues you may face when you become a clicks-and-mortar business include the following:

➲ Understanding how to create an online shopping experience that is complementary to what you do offline

➲ Integrating online sales systems with offline sales systems to properly track inventory

➲ Resolving fulfillment issues if you didn't start out as a mail-order or catalog business

➲ Strategizing how to best integrate online marketing and sales efforts with offline efforts

➲ Providing online customer service in addition to what you already do offline, including responding to e-mails in a timely manner

Selling your services online doesn't have to be complicated if you think through the process step by step and look for the best—not necessarily the cheapest—solutions for setting up your online presence. The more complex your business model, the more complex the issues you'll face. The more research you do beforehand and the more experience you have with the business, the easier the setup.

Things Amazon.com Does Well

While traditional companies looked for ways to do business on the Internet in the mid 1990s, other companies formed as Internet-based businesses. A pioneer of e-business is Amazon.com, founded in 1994 in the garage of e-entrepreneur Jeff Bezos. Although it took a decade for the company to turn a profit, Bezos did more than create just an online bookstore. He combined community with selling to allow everyday book lovers and shoppers to review books and to create product recommendation lists. Bezos and his Amazon team also developed features on the Amazon.com Web site that at the time were revolutionary and are now considered some of the best practices of selling online. Amazon.com helped to popularize the tabbed-navigation look—an easy-to-use navigation tool bar at the top of its Web pages that looks like the tabs on manila folders. The site jump-started the "E-mail a friend" feature for e-commerce, encouraging users to notify others about products they found on the site. After registering for free with Amazon.com, customers are greeted on the home page with both a short list of items they recently viewed plus recommendations of products based on their previous purchases. At the end of every purchase, customers have the option to "Share the Love" or make a similar purchase for people they know. Another helpful shopping feature is the "Buy now with 1-Click" feature that condenses the online shopping process from several steps to one. Amazon.com also offers a wish list feature so people can save and share items they would like to receive from others, as well as a specific wedding registry and baby registry. All of these features work together to not only create a rich online shopping experience but to encourage customers to market the site and help Amazon.com sell more products.

Benchmarks and Measurements

The Internet offers you the tools to target and track the visitors to your site, something that is a lot more challenging offline. Unless you literally follow customers through your store, for example, and keep a close eye on them to observe their buying habits, chances are you are not getting as detailed a picture of your customer offline as you are able to gain online.

Tracking Web Visitors

You can track the activities of visitors to your Web with special Web tracking software. Popular Web tracking software, also known as Web analytics software, includes Google Analytics and Web Trends. Because this tracking software needs to be installed on the Web server that hosts your Web site, you may need your ISP to install and administer it for you. Chances are if your ISP is in the business of Web hosting, it already has Web tracking in place and will offer you the service either for an additional fee or as part of your existing Web hosting fee. There are also free Web-based options for Web tracking, but they are much more limited in the features they offer.

Leveraging Electronic Information

With all this data available to you, you must find the best way to take advantage of this information. You can do this by establishing systems of measurement, usually by purchasing or utilizing the right Web tracking software to capture and analyze the information.

When you track any kind of data about your business, you can make the best use of it by determining benchmarks or measurements at intervals over time. For example, if you start out with 200 visitors to your site per month, that is a benchmark for the first few months. You can then set a goal to increase the number of visitors to your site by 10 percent each month over the next three months. Because 200 visitors is your original benchmark, your goals for visitors over the next three months would be 220, 242, and 268. When you have a benchmark, you can look at the numbers or data collected over time and have a basis for comparison.

►► TEST DRIVE

Are you asking yourself the right questions before proceeding with developing your e-business strategies?

- ➲ What are my big-picture business goals?
- ➲ Who is my customer or potential customer (my audience) and what are they doing online?
- ➲ What have I been doing offline to market my business to date?
- ➲ What sales processes are already in place that I'll need to integrate with my Internet presence?
- ➲ What customer service processes are in place, and how will I prepare for new issues arising from taking my business online?
- ➲ How do I measure my business success, and how will I measure my e-business success?

Basic Communications and Marketing Online

PART **2**

The Ins and Outs of Permission Marketing

E-mail is both a public and a private communications tool. People use e-mails to send messages to strangers, colleagues, friends, family, and everyone in between. On the one hand, people are eager to receive e-mail, but on the other hand, they most likely do not want to receive e-mail from people they don't know.

Over the years, unscrupulous Internet marketers have abused the privilege of e-mailing potential customers. Even today, these marketers take the following unethical shortcuts to getting hold of people by e-mail:

1. They obtain e-mail addresses by lifting them off Web pages, including message boards, to bolster their e-mail marketing lists.
2. They purchase e-mail lists from (or sell their lists to) others who use similar tactics to build their lists.
3. They send e-mails to unsuspecting people on these lists. These e-mails may include information on how to unsubscribe, but most do not.
4. They use the e-mail they receive from angry recipients of their marketing e-mails as a way of verifying that a "real person" is at the other end of the address.
5. They bombard people with unsolicited messages.

The first way to avoid these mistakes is to purchase e-mail lists only from companies that can prove their recipients opted to be on their lists. A second way to keep from making bad e-mail marketing errors is to operate your Internet marketing campaigns with permission marketing in mind.

Permission Marketing Defined

The basis of permission marketing is informed consent. Recipients give you permission to add their e-mail addresses to your marketing list and to send them e-mails. There are two kinds of permission a person can give to you:

Express permission: When customers select an option that says, "I give you permission to add me to your e-mail list and to send me e-mails each month," they are giving explicit permission for you to send them additional e-mails.

Implied permission: When customers subscribe to your e-newsletter, they are implying permission for you to send them that e-newsletter on a regular basis.

Most people will not tell you it is okay to send them unlimited e-mails. Usually, they are giving their permission for a defined number of e-mails at a specified frequency. They are also giving permission for particular types of e-mail messages or for very specific information to be sent to them. If customers subscribe to a monthly e-newsletter, for example, they have not given you permission to send them daily notices about sales or specials.

Getting to "Yes"

You don't have to bribe people to get them to sign up to receive your e-newsletter or e-mail messages. Instead, create real value that piques interest and motivates viewers to enter their e-mail address and hit the Submit button. Be clear about what you offer. People like to receive tips and advice they can act on immediately. They also like to receive lists of useful resources and links to other relevant sites.

Types of E-Mail Lists

An effective way to send e-mail to a large number of people is by using an e-mail list. There are three main types of e-mail lists that you can set up, manage, and maintain:

Unmoderated discussion: Subscribers post their messages to the list for all subscribers to read, and ongoing conversations take place.

Fully moderated discussion: Subscribers post their messages to the list, but a moderator screens messages before sending to all list subscribers.

Fully moderated announcement-only: Subscribers receive announcements generated by the list owner (you), and responses go only to the list owner.

For the purposes of e-mail marketing campaigns, the fully moderated announcement-only list setup works best. The more control you have over e-newsletters or business or marketing-related e-mail messages sent to your entire list, the better.

Getting Permission

Your Web site is the best place to ask people for permission to add them to your e-mail marketing list and to send them e-mails. The most effective place on your Web site to do this is prominently on the home page and also in a consistent place on every other page of the site. You cannot give visitors to your site too many opportunities to sign up and give you permission to contact them in the future.

There is nothing more valuable than a person who wants to receive messages from you in his private and personal e-mail box. By getting permission, you help your e-mail cut through the clutter of unsolicited and unwanted e-mails, making it one that may actually get opened and read by the recipient.

When you ask people for their permission, be specific about exactly what you plan to send them and how often. Some things you may send include the following:

- A monthly e-newsletter
- Weekly specials or discounts
- Daily tips or news items
- Quarterly reports
- Regular notices with useful information

By stating that you'll be sending regular notices, you give yourself some latitude as to the frequency with which you contact people on your e-mail list. You should interpret "regular" to mean periodic but not so frequent that the recipient will get annoyed. Take care that each e-mail you send at any time is valuable and worth receiving.

Honoring Permission

These days, permission isn't given lightly, but it may be given accidentally. In fact, it is pretty easy to trick someone into giving their permission. The most common way companies fool visitors into opting in or electing to subscribe to e-mail notices is by having them fill out a form on a Web site.

The Double Opt-In

Best practice for e-mail marketing goes beyond requiring someone to opt in to your e-mail list. To make sure your subscribers really want to be on your list, use the double opt-in technique, in which subscribers are presented with a second message to confirm their subscription. This second message is often e-mailed to the subscriber address, who must then link to a Web site where the subscription is verified. Double opt-in reduces confusion about subscribing and better guarantees that subscribers want to receive your e-mails.

There are three ways to program checkboxes or radio buttons in a Web-based form. The first way is to leave them blank so that visitors make their own selections. The second way is to select "No" as the default response. If visitors are really interested in subscribing, they must change this selection to "Yes."

The tricky third way is to program "Yes" as the default answer. Now the visitor must notice he is being subscribed to something. Chances are he won't, and when he finishes filling out the form, he has also subscribed unwittingly to your list. This method is not recommended.

If you trick someone into joining your list or abuse the privilege of the permission you have been granted, you'll risk losing subscribers. Treat the list you build as a precious commodity. A list of people who have opted in and given you express permission is one of the most valuable marketing tools any company can possess.

Building Your E-Mail List

There are many ways to ask for permission to add a new subscriber to your list. No matter what method you use, you should always be clear about what subscribers will get once they submit their e-mail address. Some methods for acquiring more addresses for your list include the following:

- Put a subscription field on your home page.
- Include the option to subscribe in all Web-based forms on your site.
- Ask when you are corresponding via e-mail with customers.
- When you receive a business card, ask if you can add that person to your e-mail list.
- If you have customers fill out forms or surveys on paper, add a question asking for permission to add them to your list.

Whether it's in your store, at your office, or on your site, with every contact you make you should get permission to add that person to your e-mail list.

Private and Secure

The two major concerns of most people using the Internet are privacy and security. This is especially important to remember when you ask for people to provide you with their personal information, including their names, mailing addresses, e-mail addresses, and credit card information.

One way to build user confidence is to post prominent privacy and security policies. A privacy policy usually includes a statement describing why you are asking for certain information and what you plan to do with it and assuring visitors that you will not sell or abuse what they provide to you. A security policy states your Web site is secure and that the visitor's credit card is safe. It details the type of software and secure certificate you are using as well as other technical details that explain how you carry out secure measures.

Some of the most common topics you may want to address in either your privacy or security policy include the following:

- ➲ Definition of the type of customer information you are collecting
- ➲ Explanation of how that personal information will be used
- ➲ Details of how you will keep their credit card information secure
- ➲ Explanation of how you use technology such as cookies and why
- ➲ Statement that you will not reveal, give away, or sell personal information

While some businesses do sell their lists and customer data, best practices in Internet marketing keep customer information safe and secure and do not distribute it to third parties in any way. By not selling your customers' e-mail addresses, you preserve their trust. While keeping that information private, you can still get permission from your customers to send them e-mail marketing messages on the behalf of third parties. This is a less onerous way of leveraging your list while providing both privacy and value to your list members.

Tried and True

Two e-mail-list management solutions that have been around since the early days are Majordomo and Listserv. Majordomo is still free and is distributed through Great Circle Associations (*www.greatcircle.com*). Although e-mail lists are sometimes called listserves, Listserv is a brand name for list software that has been around since 1986 and that is now owned and licensed through L-Soft (www.lsoft.com).

Good E-Mail Marketing

Given that the climate for using e-mail for advertising purposes has changed, take special care when developing an e-mail marketing campaign. To make e-mail marketing work, you need to do the following:

- ⊃ Get permission from the recipient to send them e-mails.
- ⊃ Remind them in your e-mails that they subscribed to your list.
- ⊃ Make it easy for them to unsubscribe from the list.
- ⊃ Keep a consistent schedule for sending e-mails.
- ⊃ Keep your e-mails short, with the most important information in the first few sentences.
- ⊃ Use less text and more links to lead readers to your Web site for more information.
- ⊃ Unsubscribe users the moment they ask to be removed from your list.

Your goal for effective Internet marketing is to have willing subscribers who are fully aware that they subscribed to your list and who are clear on what you will send them and how often. If they don't want to be on your list, there is no value having them there, so make sure you have systems in place to facilitate immediate removal when requested.

Managing That Growing E-Mail List

Managing your e-mail list takes on a greater importance as the list grows. While a smaller list may seem quite manageable, there will come a time when your favorite e-mail program will no longer be powerful enough to manage and monitor your e-mail marketing campaigns.

Doing It In-House

Most business owners start off using their standard e-mail program to send out e-newsletters or other e-mail announcements. With this method, the e-mail program's address book stores e-mail addresses. When sending a mass e-mailing, the addresses are then captured in the bcc so nobody can see all the addresses on the list.

When your list consists of dozens of subscribers, such an e-mail program seems to work. But this method is not scalable—that is, there is no easy way to handle growth. To be valuable to your e-business efforts, your e-mail list must be able to handle hundreds or thousands of addresses.

A regular e-mail program is not usually equipped to manage such a large list. The program may be able to store the addresses, but there is far more involved with list management.

There are software programs that can help a business affordably manage e-mail lists. Some can be loaded onto your computer (client side); others must be installed on a Web server (server side). The processes of installation, setup, implementation, and administration all involve a learning curve.

Free E-Mail Lists

You can set up an e-mail announcement-only list through Web-based services such as Yahoo! Groups. Keep in mind, though, that when you get something for free, there is usually a catch. Most free services place advertising on your list that you cannot remove unless you upgrade to a premium paid version. In some cases, you can select the category or theme, such as travel or business, for the ads that are automatically placed on your e-mail messages. The better business practice is to invest in an e-mail list package that is not driven by advertising and that lets you decide whether or not you want ads on your e-mail messages.

Beyond E-Mail Management

There is much more to managing an e-mail list for marketing purposes than just storing e-mail addresses. In order to effectively conduct e-mail marketing campaigns, you must do the following:

1. Store large numbers of e-mail addresses.
2. Easily manage e-mail bounces, update addresses, and subscribe or unsubscribe list members.
3. Provide an easy, automated way for members to subscribe and unsubscribe themselves from your list.
4. Trace e-mail activity, such as the number of recipients who delete your e-mail unopened or who open the e-mail.
5. Track the number of people who click through to your Web site from links within your e-mail.
6. Track actions taken through your Web site, such as clicking through to purchase an item or to fill out a survey.

7. Provide user-friendly Web-based administrative tools and archives of previous announcements or discussions.

Software available for managing your e-mail marketing includes Constant Contact and IntelliContact. Instead of simply selecting the cheapest option, you should seek the package that gives you the greatest control over your data and the most detailed analysis features.

Text Versus HTML E-Mails

Personal preference affects many things about technology. The differences between a Windows-based PC and a Mac, for instance, can affect your business in a variety of ways, all the way from ease of use to the type of software available to you. The Web browser you choose can also affect your Web-browsing experience.

No Attachments Please

Unless you have express permission from your recipients to send e-mails with attachments, do not attach files to your marketing e-mails. The only exception to this rule is when sending an HTML e-mail—the graphics can show up as attachments, which also makes for a good reason to keep the graphic file sizes small. You may be tempted to send a Word document or a spreadsheet, but unless you know what software your recipients are using, how fast their Internet connections are, and that you are both protected by virus detection software, sending attached files could potentially wreak havoc on an e-mail system and computer.

When it comes to e-mails, particularly e-mails sent as marketing messages, some people like to receive formatted HTML e-mails with graphics that look like a Web page. There are also those who prefer to receive text-only e-mails that have no graphics and no formatting.

As a business owner, there are several things to keep in mind as you decide between these options:

1. Your personal preference for HTML or text e-mails does not necessarily dictate what your customers and potential customers prefer.

2. Not everyone is able to view HTML e-mails, depending on the e-mail program in use.

3. Text e-mails load quickly and can be seen by anyone, even those with a basic e-mail program and slow Internet connection.

4. Text e-mails may be less compelling than a well-formatted HTML e-mail.

5. If you are using the right e-mail marketing management software, you can allow recipients to choose the type of e-mails they receive.

Giving your list subscribers the choice of their preferred format is the best way to ensure them access to the e-mails you send. As in all aspects of business, including e-business, the customer always comes first.

Designing HTML E-Mails

Given that most commonly used e-mail marketing management systems allow you to send both types of e-mail, the challenge is in designing an effective HTML message. Just as you want a designer with Web design experience to create your business Web site, chances are that you want a pro to design your own HTML e-mails. Some Web developers have experience designing HTML e-mails.

Much of the e-mail marketing management software out there offers design templates. However, these programs may not be flexible enough to create a layout and design consistent with your Web site and overall company brand.

Whether you do it yourself with templates or your well-honed design skills or you hire someone, you'll want to keep the following in mind when it comes to developing HTML e-mails:

⮕ Use graphics judiciously to keep the size of the e-mail manageable.

⮕ Use smaller graphics that have been properly compressed for the Web.

⊃ Design the e-mail keeping your Web site design in mind.

⊃ Use your company logo or related graphics so recipients recognize your e-mail.

⊃ Choose a layout that isn't too busy or large for the size of a standard e-mail.

⊃ Use graphics to draw attention to important information, not to detract from it.

⊃ Use less text by including the opening of an article then linking to the rest of it on your Web site.

Crafting the Perfect E-Mail

There is an art to writing an effective e-mail, whether it's for personal correspondence or for business and marketing. Long e-mails can be hard to read. While acceptable when communicating with friends, they are less desirable when courting and serving customers.

To help ensure your marketing e-mails create a positive and lasting impression, use these tips:

1. When you register your domain name (as described in Chapter 7), you may be given the option to also set up e-mail accounts using your own customized e-mail address with your company's domain name (i.e. *yourname@yourcompany.com*). Otherwise, your internet service provider or Web developer can help you to set it up so you are sending your marketing e-mail with a branded e-mail address.

2. Craft a clear, concise subject line for your e-mail that attracts attention without being annoying.

3. Keep the content of the e-mail short and to the point.

4. Make sure your opening statement encapsulates the message you are trying to get across.

5. Use links strategically within the e-mail message to lead the recipient to your business Web site.

From the Guru of Permission Marketing   Inside Track

Entrepreneur and marketer Seth Godin (*www.sethgodin.com*) is credited with coining the term "permission marketing" for his book of the same name. In the early 1990s, Godin started an Internet company called Yoyodyne Entertainment that put permission marketing into action, proving it could be good for business. A few years later Yahoo! purchased his company for millions of dollars. Godin's premise is that permission marketing is the antidote to traditional marketing, which he calls "interruption marketing." Says Godin, "Marketers must make us pay attention for the ads to work. If they don't interrupt our train of thought by planting some sort of seed in our conscious or subconscious, the ads fail." According to Godin, permission marketing "encourages consumers to participate in a long-term, interactive marketing campaign in which they are rewarded in some way for paying attention to increasingly relevant messages."

He points to Amazon.com, which spends time and money building its customer base, which in turn has become a "permission asset." Says Godin, "Amazon has overt permission to track which books you buy and which books you browse. They have explicit permission to send you promotional e-mail messages." Amazon can send an e-mail to millions of people to promote products with links back to the company's site to make purchases. All those people have given the company permission to send them the e-mail. Using permission, Amazon can fundamentally reconfigure the entire book industry, disintermediating and combining every step of the chain until there are only two: the writer and Amazon." That is the power of permission.

The Smart Subject

Before your recipients choose to read your e-mail, they usually do two things: check the e-mail address or sender's name to see if it's familiar, and decide whether the subject line is relevant. **Coming up with a subject line for your marketing e-mails that compels the recipient to open the e-messages is an important step to ensuring their overall effectiveness.**

What makes a good e-mail subject line varies depending on your audience. The best e-mail subjects are short—usually no more than six to eight words—and convey the content of the e-mail as a whole. Here are some good and bad e-mail subject lines to give you an idea of what works well and what doesn't.

Bad Subject	Good Subject
Best Discounts Ever on All Of Our Inventory!!	Discounts & Special Offers *YourCompany Name*
Buy Now and Save, Save, Save!!	This Month's Specials from *YourCompany Name*
Great Information You Can Really Use!	Exclusive E-Newsletter for *YourCompany Name* Customers—September Issue
Don't Miss Out!!!	Special Event from *YourCompanyName* This Week—Details Enclosed

It may be tempting to use gimmicks and a lot of exclamation points to attract attention. But if you follow the best practices for building relationships with your customers and potential customers by getting their permission to e-mail them, you don't need tricks to get them to pay attention to your messages. You save your recipients time and headaches by identifying yourself in the e-mail subject and clearly and succinctly presenting what you are sending them.

The longer your e-mail subject, the more likely it is that the last few words will be cut off in the recipient's inbox viewing window. If you don't put the most important key words at the start of the subject, the recipient may not understand the message you are trying to convey.

Tight Text

The main subject of your message should always be at the top of the e-mail and should be stated in a short opening paragraph consisting of one to three sentences. If you cannot get the main points of your message across in a small number of words, spend more time honing your message.

When someone is reading an e-mail, she is usually scanning it for key information. She often starts by reading the first few sentences. If you haven't made your point in those first few lines, you may lose the reader.

All text after the opening paragraph should be background information, links to your Web site, or other details not critical to the main message.

The type of e-mail you send can dictate the way you craft your opening paragraph. In a monthly e-newsletter, the opening paragraph can greet the reader and summarize the highlights of the information contained within the text of the newsletter. If you are sending a periodic announcement of sales or discounts, the opening paragraph should explain any parameters of the discounts, such as the discount amounts, the dates they are valid, and what the recipient must do to receive the discounts.

Use links often in a marketing e-mail. Links reduce the amount of text you need to get a point across by allowing you to write brief teasers with links to lead the reader to your site, where he can get more complete and detailed information. For an e-newsletter, write the headline for an article and include only the first few sentences of that article in the e-mail with a statement such as "Read More . . ." that links to your Web site. Suddenly, what might be a 500-word e-mail shrinks down to 200 words, with links making it easier to read and understand.

E-Mail Etiquette

Several rules apply to e-mails you are composing for business and marketing purposes. Never use all capital letters for the text of your e-mail; not only are all caps very difficult to read, in Internet-speak, they mean you are shouting or are angry. Don't use emoticons or the smiley text symbols that people often use in personal e-mails, such as : -) for a smile and ; -) for a wink. The rare exception may be if you are writing for a younger audience that expects to see these symbols in the correspondence they read.

Do's and Don'ts of E-Mail Marketing

It may seem like there are many rules to crafting effective business or marketing e-mail. Here are ten basic rules to follow:

- ➲ Don't send spam.
- ➲ Do ask permission.

- Don't force your users to opt out.
- Do keep it short.
- Don't send attachments.
- Do use links.
- Don't sell your list.
- Do post a privacy policy.
- Don't break trust.
- Do build a relationship.

Your goal is to engage the recipients of your e-mails, not invade their inboxes. You want to attract, not intrude. Your marketing e-mail should be a gateway to your Web site and a motivator to your customer or potential customer.

▶▶ TEST DRIVE

Take a look at the e-mails you are currently sending for e-marketing purposes, such as marketing campaigns or even general e-business communications. Ask yourself these questions:

- How clear and concise are the subjects of my e-mails?
- How quickly do I get to the point in the text?
- How long are my e-mails, and how can I shorten them?
- How efficient is the method or software I'm using to send out e-mails?

Compelling Signature Files

There are many complex and technologically sophisticated ways to use the Internet to build your business. There is, however, one simple and often overlooked way of marketing what you do: using a signature (or "sig") file at the bottom of each e-mail you send and every post you publish on message boards or on blogs.

A sig file is a small text file saved within your e-mail program. Its contents are automatically added to the end of your e-mails. Most e-mail programs have this feature. Some allow you to create more than one sig file so you can choose the most appropriate one. A signature for an e-mail going to a client may differ from a signature for e-mail correspondence with a vendor.

What's in a Signature?

From an e-business standpoint, some of the most common information in a sig file includes the following:

- Your full name and title
- Your company name
- Contact information
- The Web address (URL) of your site
- A one-line company description or slogan

When it comes to signature files, the more compact and concise, the better. Here are some examples of signature files:

Jane S. Doe, President
ABC Company
Ph: 212-555-1212
www.abccompanysite.com

Trust us to get the job done!
Bob L. Smith, CPA
Serving customers by the numbers...
www.bobsmithcpa.com

Because life is more than business…

John L. Doe
Business Coach
www.johnthecoach.com
e-mail: coach@johnthecoach.com

Getting Creative with Sig Files

Most sig files are separated from the body of the e-mail with a line. Some people use continuous asterisks, dashes, or a combination of symbols. Here are some examples of separators:

```
----------------------------------------------------------------------

* * * * * * * * * * * * * * * * * * * * * * * * * * * * * * * * * * * * * * * *

*_*_*_*_*_*_*_*_*_*_*_*_*_*_*_*_*_*_*_*_*_*_*_*_*_*

===============================================

++++++++++++++++++++++++++++++++++++++++++++++++

<*)))<--- <*)))<---<*)))<---<*)))<---<*)))<---<*)))<---<*)))<-

@))>--->--- @))>--->---@))>--->---@))>--->---@))>--->---
```

Some people make a design or form an image with the symbols, something referred to as ASCII art. ASCII is a standard code represented by letters, numerals, punctuation marks, and control signals—what you'd find on a standard computer keyboard.

But don't get carried away. The simpler and cleaner the signature, the more effective it is in conveying your message.

Some message boards allow you to create your own sig file to appear at the bottom of each post. If not, you may want to create a text file with your signature and save it to your hard drive to copy and paste on your messages, both in e-mails and on boards.

Guerrilla Posting

Placing your marketing message in your signature file at the bottom of your post on a message board is a subtle way of promoting who you are and what you do. Because most message boards forbid commercial posts, signature files become an unobtrusive way of getting people to visit your Web site.

There are appropriate ways to post to message boards to convey a marketing message. There is a fine line, however, between a message that is valuable and relevant to the board and one that is deceptive. A deceptive message, for example, might be one in which you or someone you hire pretends to be someone else. There are honest ways of combining valuable information to the community on a board with an appropriate marketing message.

Honesty Is the Best Policy

When posting messages on boards for your business, there are some rules to keep in mind so you don't offend the online community. Remember to follow these steps:

1. Read existing threads first to see what topics are being discussed.
2. Respond directly to a post only if you have something relevant and valuable to contribute.
3. Immediately disclose who you are in your post and why you are providing the information.
4. Be succinct in conveying the information.
5. Tone down the marketing speak, and be conversational instead.
6. Let your sig file do the talking.

If you have something to contribute to the conversation related to services or products your offer or because of your expertise, it is appropriate to share this information with any relevant online community. The way you craft your post, however, can be the difference between your message being welcome and being banned.

Using Blogs and Bloggers

While message boards have been around since the early days of the Internet, and Web sites were created over fifteen years ago, the standard blog format was developed about 1998 and became popular in 2000. Blogs combine the best of Web sites and message boards.

Blogs are content-driven Web sites that usually have a built-in feature allowing readers to post comments pertaining to the content. Whereas message boards allow for threads or conversations to be grouped or linked and have more sophisticated organizational features, the comments section of a blog is basic in format but effective for communication. Commenting on a blog can be instantaneous unless the blog owner or blogger moderates the comments section.

Avoiding Flame Wars

In the early days of the Internet, when people in online communities verbally attacked one another, the ensuing text-based battle was called a "flame war." Today, most online communities police themselves to get inflammatory messages removed before a flame war can start. If you come into an established online community, however, and post something on their message board that is blatantly commercial, you may experience a backlash including some personal written attacks. Most likely your post will also be removed. Bad behavior in an online community is bad for business.

When it comes to e-business, you can utilize blogs and blogging to do the following:

- ⮑ Monitor what is being said about your company on blogs.
- ⮑ Check what your competition is doing with blogs.
- ⮑ Start your own blog.
- ⮑ Post comments on other blogs.
- ⮑ Enlist bloggers to blog about your company.

For further discussion of blogs and their value as business tools, see Chapter 21.

Posting Comments on Blogs

Many of the same rules of posting to message boards apply when it comes to posting comments on blogs. The most important things to keep in mind are these:

- Be open about your identity and affiliations.
- Post only comments that are relevant to the discussion at hand.
- Refrain from posting commercial messages.
- Use a link to a relevant Web site, yours if it fits.
- Put your URL after your name if it isn't relevant to link to your site within the comment.

Because of the frequent updating of blogs, comments on a particular topic are mostly accessed while a post is current. The minute a new blog post is published, conversation and community often move along to the next topic. The shelf life of your comment, therefore, can be as short as a few hours or as long as a week or so. While comments may be archived indefinitely, the most attention a comment will get happens within the first forty-eight to seventy-two hours of commenting on a current blog post.

Bringing Bloggers on Board

Not all blogs allow comments. Some blogs do not include a comments section because managing a comments area can be a legal liability and a time-consuming process. A blog without a comments area should be approached in a different manner for use as an effective online communications tool.

If you have found blogs that reach an audience with the potential for becoming customers, you can approach the blogger—usually through an e-mail address on the blogger's home page or About Me page—and make a proposal to the blogger outlining how you might work together. Most savvy bloggers will want to be compensated for promoting your company, product, or service on their blog. Some bloggers may also allow you to advertise on their blog.

Considering "Catablogs"

While it is still an open question whether blogs can actually sell products, that doesn't stop people from experimenting with e-commerce-enabled blogs, also known as catablogs. The term catablogs also refers to catalogs that use RSS feeds to distribute notifications for sales, special promotions, and other product news. Looking at e-commerce-enabled blogs, in 2005, self-taught artist John T. Unger experimented with a blog format to sell his artwork online at *http://john tunger.typepad.com/artbuzz*. His work included one-of-a-kind mosaic fish and scrap-yard abstracts made with recycled and reused materials. In his first year using catablogs, Unger generated $10,000 in revenues. Year two yielded nearly $25,000. Unger says he makes a third of his overall revenues from about six catablogs, the rest from art gallery and art show sales. If the online numbers continue to grow, he anticipates leaving the gallery system behind at some point. Unger originally went online with his artwork in the late 1990s. Says Unger, "In all the years my portfolio existed as a regular Web site, I got one commission. The site was always current, well designed, and actually got quite a bit of traffic—as many as 20,000 visits per month, but it never sold work." Unger says his blogs are easier to maintain and generate not only sales but also global media attention. He eventually converted his traditional Web site into a blog. In his spare time, Unger, who worked for a while as a Web designer, is collaborating with blog companies to help develop new features that will better facilitate selling through blogs.

Online Press Releases

As with any online communications, online press releases or e-releases should not be exactly like your offline press releases. There are similarities and also some major differences. Both can contain some or all of the following features:

- Contact information at the top
- Headline
- Subhead (optional)
- Body text
- Contact info repeated at bottom of page

➲ Links

➲ Embedded images (optional)

➲ Attached documents (optional but not recommended)

One of the main differences between traditional and e-releases is that the body text can be longer on paper. While a printed release sometimes can be two or three pages long—although one page is preferable—an e-release would only be about one-half to three-fourths of a single page if printed out. Electronically, the release should be only three to four short paragraphs of about three sentences each.

In print, links can be included in the text as a reference, but electronically, those links can be used to click through to a site. In print, additional documentation can be attached to the back of the release. Electronically, files can be attached to the e-release that is distributed via e-mail. Attaching files without permission, however, is a surefire way to turn off an unsuspecting recipient as computer viruses are usually transmitted through attachments. In both versions, graphics and photographs can be embedded. But with the electronic version, take into consideration the sizes of the image files.

Pitch Versus Press Release

Many reporters prefer a short pitch to a release. The release can be used as background or additional information, but a pitch is easier to read in an e-mail than an entire release.

A pitch is a short, conversational e-mail that gets straight to the point of the message you are trying to convey. If you are pitching a reporter via e-mail, you should include the following:

➲ Who you are

➲ Why you are pitching the recipient

➲ What you are pitching

➲ Why it is important or interesting for their audience to know

➲ Why you are the person they should speak with about the topic

➲ Additional information or resources you can provide

A pitch should grab their attention first by the e-mail's subject then by the first few sentences of the e-mail.

The Ideal Release

To help make your releases more effective, be clear you are sending a release or a pitch by beginning your subject line with RELEASE or PITCH, followed by a brief, catchy headline.

Be careful copying and pasting text from Word or another text file. Although you may not see a problem in your own e-mail program, copied-and-pasted text often arrives garbled on the other end. Send the release to yourself first, as well as to one of two other people who are using different types of computers and e-mail programs to see how the finished release looks. First impressions count, and that includes how easy a release is to read electronically and how relevant and concisely the information is presented.

Content Syndication

Syndicating your Web site or blog content means that you offer the content through a variety of distribution methods either for free or for a fee. **Free content syndication is a way to get your name or your company name out there for reputation and brand-building purposes.** Charging a licensing fee is a way to get paid for the content you provide to others for their Web sites and blogs.

Using RSS Feeds

RSS—for really simple syndication—is a text file format tagged in XML markup language that allows Web content to be easily distributed. Most blog publishing tools produce an XML version of blog posts. Blog visitors can subscribe to the RSS feed, and each time the blog is updated they receive a summary in their e-mail box. Once you have your RSS feed up and running, register it at feed aggregators such as Feedburner.com and Feedster.com. With an RSS feed, others can syndicate your content on their sites or blogs, helping to build your brand through your content.

There are several easy ways to syndicate content, though some are more time consuming than others. They include the following:

License-free content: This method allows people to copy content from your site or blog as long as they properly credit you and your company with a link back to your site.

Content for purchase: You create a shopping cart where people can purchase content from you. Before they can access it, they must first pay a licensing fee.

RSS feed: When publishing a site or blog using blog-publishing tools, an RSS feed is usually a built-in feature, and RSS feeds are usually distributed for free.

Syndication deal: Prolific writers might enlist a syndication company to distribute content. Most business owners don't produce enough content to strike up this kind of deal.

If content is your business, it makes sense to spend time and resources not only on producing more of it but also marketing the fact that you have it for syndication or sale. Content development can be a revenue stream for some businesses, but don't change your business model if it doesn't make financial sense.

Offering license-free content is most often a tactic used by companies that have useful and usable content but that are not in the content-development business. License-free content can be harder to control and track, but it is also the least resource-intensive method of content syndication.

Content developers should invest in protecting and profiting from their content through written licensing agreements and licensing fees. Here are five important clauses to include in a licensing agreement or contract:

1. **Scope of license:** Defines how the other party is allowed to use your content—for example, where they can publish it.
2. **Duration of license:** Defines how long the licensing agreement lasts, such as one year, three years, five years, or more.

3. Terms of use: Defines any restrictions or rules about the way in which the licensee uses your content.

4. Breach of contract: Allows you to cancel the contract at any time if the licensee does not adhere to the terms.

5. Ownership: Clearly states your ownership and rights without limitations to the content.

Get a lawyer to help you with licensing fee contracts and legal issues.

Beyond Text

On the Internet, there are several ways to present content. While text is the most popular format and the easiest to access and download, audio and video content is increasingly becoming popular. Audio files are often called podcasts, audio casts, or Internet radio. Common file formats include .WAV and MP3. For video, the common file format is .MOV. Audio and video files can be protected by copyright. In audio, the copyright notice is included at the end of the broadcast. In video, the copyright notice can appear on the screen at the end as well. For both, the copyright notice can also appear on the Web page containing the link to the audio or video files.

Copyrighting Content

Laws protect the content you develop, whether it is text, graphics, photographs, or any other medium. Original work that you produce can be copyrighted. **In the United States, your own work is automatically copyrighted when you produce and publish it.** By putting a copyright notice on your work, you can exert that copyright. At the bottom of every Web page you produce, place one of the following statements or another appropriate variation:

➲ ©2007 Your Name/Company. All Rights Reserved
➲ ©2007–2008 Company Name. All Rights Reserved
➲ ©2007 Your Name. All Rights Reserved

A lawyer can help you determine what is copyrightable and how to best protect your work, particularly with the complexities of publishing on the Internet.

You can also trademark your company name or product or service names. If you have a unique name, you can protect it by doing the following:

1. Do an Internet search to see if the name is being used in similar ways by anyone else.
2. Pay for a trademark search through Thomson Compumark to check the databases of the U.S. Patent and Trademark Office for similar names.
3. Hire a lawyer to search and obtain the trademark for the name or names you are seeking to protect.
4. Include a trademark or servicemark symbol within the design of your logo or after the name you are trying to protect.
5. After you obtain a completed copyright registration from the U.S. Patent and Trademark Office, include the registered trademark symbol.

A trademark is used to protect a trade name, such as your company name or the original name of your product or service. A small TM after the name means that you are exerting trademark rights and are filing for a registered trademark. If you have a service business or want to protect the name of a service you provide, you would use a small SM after the name. See the following examples:

➲ The John Doe Company™
➲ The Great Service℠
➲ Coolest Product®

The last symbol shown above is the finalized registered trademark sign that states the name has been officially registered with the U.S. Patent and Trademark Office. You should not use this symbol until you have the proper registration paperwork from the government.

First Appearance Rule

The "first appearance" rule means that if you use a trademark or servicemark after your company name or a product or service name in a body of text, you only have to use the TM or SM symbol where the name first appears on the page. Subsequent mentions do not need the symbol as long as it is prominent and visible in the first mention. When it comes to a logo, the TM or SM should be designed into the original logo file in a location where it can be easily changed to the registered trademark symbol when the registration process is finalized.

When it comes to e-business, the rules may not change but the landscape does. Enforcing copyrights and trademarks online is an enormous challenge, especially since the Internet is global, and some countries do not honor U.S. copyrights and trademarks. If your livelihood relies on protection of your names or your work, you should invest in a lawyer familiar with cyber law before publishing anything online.

▶▶ TEST DRIVE

Examine your current resources and determine what types of grassroots marketing makes the most sense. Can you or your staff afford to do the following:

- Create a concise and compelling signature file to place at the bottom of all e-mails?
- Spend time reading message boards and blogs and crafting appropriate posts to convey your company message?
- Identify the blogs and bloggers who might be interested in promoting your company or product and developing the appropriate relationship?
- Craft effective press releases and pitches and send them to the right people in the proper format?

Basic Communications and Marketing Online

The Nature of Internet Community

Internet community is often an organic outgrowth of like-minded people communicating through message boards, e-mail lists or any other online tool that allows them to "congregate" and start a dialogue. The Internet tools facilitate group communication in a relatively organized fashion, and people's common interests spark discussions.

Providing community-building tools such as message boards does not automatically build a community. There must be a central theme to the board in order to attract and serve community members. There should be some written rules in place to help guide behavior on the board. It also helps if there is somebody on the board to stimulate discussions and keep the conversation going.

Communities for Business

Some ways an online community can be used in business include the following:

- Building a positive brand
- Providing timely customer service
- Facilitating peer-to-peer support
- Conducting an online focus group
- Fostering customer loyalty

Message boards and online communities are just one of many communications tools that can achieve these things, but they are more complex than sending e-mails and more time-consuming than maintaining a basic Web site.

Types of Boards

Just as with e-mail lists, there are three main ways message boards can be operated and maintained:

➲ Fully moderated discussion boards
➲ Unmoderated discussion boards
➲ Fully moderated announcement-only boards

As a business owner, you are more likely to use full moderation, meaning all messages are first screened by you or your staff before being approved for publication on the message board. When you build and host a message board or forum, you want to minimize potential liability issues that come from inappropriate or incorrect information disseminated through the board.

Having control over the content, however, is a double-edged sword. Control helps minimize anything offensive or potentially harmful from being posted on your boards. **However, the more you control the content, the more you can be legally seen as a publisher of information, whether it actually came from you or from a visitor to your site.** This can expose you to some unexpected liabilities.

Hosting message boards for business can be fraught with issues in addition to legal ones, including the time and money it takes to maintain the boards, keep the discussions going, weed out unacceptable posts, and get measurable benefits from the content and interaction on the boards.

Business Benefits of Communities

Like any Internet-based tool, message boards offer the means to do something online. Just using those tools doesn't necessarily guarantee you'll get the results you want. Having message-board technology and tools doesn't mean you automatically have an online community. Cultivating an online community doesn't mean you will get tangible business benefits from it.

Knowing that the success of an online community as a business tool is variable and can be limited is important when you weigh the time and expense of building one. If you have the resources to put into an online community, however, you may eventually gain measurable business results.

Brand Building

Offering a forum for customers and potential customers to gather and discuss topics relevant to your company, products, or services could have a positive effect on your brand. Because the nature of online community is to participate and to participate often, community members tend to return to message boards on a regular basis.

And That's an FAQ

Developing an FAQ section is an effective way of answering the most common customer questions before they can even be asked. FAQs appear on a Web site in many different formats; most often, they are formatted as a long list of questions followed by the answers. When there is too much information to contain on a Web page, FAQs can be stored in a database. The way the content is displayed once it is pulled from a database can vary. The key is to be organized and to link the answers to the appropriate questions. Adding a search function to a large FAQ can create an invaluable customer service resource.

When you install a message board system on your Web site, pay special attention to how your company name and logo appear on the board. Make sure you customize the look of the boards to include your logo and the right design and colors so the boards match your site.

You not only want visitors to sense that the message boards are an integrated part of your site, you also want them to know that they are provided by your company. In marketing and advertising, repetition is key to influencing potential customers. By visiting your message boards over and over again, potential customers are repeatedly exposed to your brand, logo, and company name—but only if you properly brand your boards.

Customer Service

You can strengthen your relationship with your customers by allowing them to ask questions and responding promptly. Using a message board, customers can post questions, and you or a company representative can then respond to those questions. Those questions and answers are automatically archived.

Customers and even company employees can access archived conversations at any time, creating a knowledge base or database of knowledge and information. The message board becomes an interactive and continuously updated frequently asked questions (FAQ) section that can be accessed around the clock.

Peer-to-Peer Support

In some cases, customers or clients can offer support to one another if you provide them the forum in which to do so. The term for this interaction is peer-to-peer, or P2P. Peer-to-peer support can happen easily when the products or services are technology oriented. Techies tend to congregate often to discuss technical aspects of software or hardware and are willing to interact directly with company representatives to resolve issues.

If you are offering a product or service that is not technical, the results of peer-to-peer support can vary. Often the best way to build a community where members support one another is to find a common theme that is peripheral to what you offer.

For example, if you sell a baby product such as a diaper changing kit, the message board probably would not grow into a vibrant online community solely discussing your product or diaper changing, although this could be one conversation. A better approach is to create a message board for new mothers to exchange tips about relevant issues, including diaper and diaper changing, feeding, and baby hygiene. By broadening the approach to include multiple related themes, you provide more opportunities for discussion, which in turn builds and sustains the online community.

Using the example above, by giving new mothers a forum where they can ask their questions and get real-life advice from other mothers, you create a valuable resource that can be accessed any time of the day or night. By also including an expert moderator in the forum, you provide community members with educated advice as well as subtly communicated marketing messages when appropriate.

Getting Feedback

Those same customers or clients who have gathered at your message boards and formed an online community can also serve as an online focus group for your company. You can survey community members via the message board for honest and immediate feedback. For example, you could ask your community of new mothers direct questions about your product, the diaper changing kit, to find out exactly what they think. Be prepared for candid answers that might not always be positive.

By openly inviting frank and direct feedback, you can generate a lot of good will among customers. By taking it one step further and acting on the feedback by making actual modifications to your product or service, you foster even greater customer appreciation and loyalty. And you end up with a better product or service.

Be careful when marketing your online community. If you aren't prepared to devote the resources needed to manage it, you should not spend the extra time and money to send people to it.

Use the URL

How do you get customers to your message boards? You can start with marketing them on your company Web site. You can also print the URL of your site or your online community directly on your product packaging and on all your marketing materials. You may want to have one URL for the community and another for your site. For example, if your company site URL is www.xyzcompany.com, your online community could be at www.xyzcommunity.com.

Proper Community Administration

The best online communities are the ones where the administration or management is practically invisible. The last thing most people want is to participate in a community where they feel Big Brother is watching them. Therefore, building and maintaining an online community requires a subtle touch.

Seeding and Weeding

Online communities often form organically. Your online community is like a garden. In order to help your garden to grow, you have to plant seeds and also weed the soil. In the case of an online community, the soil consists of the theme and topics discussed within the community. Reaching the right audience with the right topics is the perfect starting place for community building.

The seeds include both conversation starters and conversation stimulators. When you open your forum, the last thing you want people to see is an empty message board. At a minimum, you should post welcome messages in the various topic areas.

The basic types of conversation threads you may want to start when you first debut your message board include these:

1. An introduction to welcome new members and let them introduce themselves

2. A technical support section where members can ask technical questions about using the message board

3. Topic-related sections, with each section covering a different topic

4. A private section, where only members who are invited or who have been screened can post for privacy reasons

5. An open section, where anything goes regarding conversation and it is not necessary to stick to a specific topic

Besides welcoming people to the community, you can post provocative questions and encourage others to respond. The best seeds are the ones that trigger a flurry of discussion by tapping into people's opinions and varied experiences.

When there is a lull in the conversation, plant another seed that either comments on or recaps what has already been discussed or that introduces a new idea that can bring people back to the conversation.

Weeding an online community is a delicate job. More importantly, before you weed and remove inappropriate posts, you must first establish the rules of the community and spell out what is appropriate and what is not. When you have put rules in place that can be easily accessed through a link within the forum, you can always point to those rules when you have to remove a post.

Removing posts may require some damage control. Simply removing the post and pretending nothing has happened can cause a rift within the community. Addressing the issue immediately, openly, and honestly, then pointing to the written rules of the community is usually the best way to handle deleting posts.

Make sure to archive any posts you delete from the public forum and keep them in a safe place. You never know what issues could arise from the deleted post or from the act of deleting the posts, so you should keep a record of every action you take on the board as the moderator. By the very nature of message boards, public posts remain archived so you don't need to make any extra efforts to store them.

When Editing Is a Bad Thing

Never edit somebody else's post. Online communities consist of real conversations between real people in their own words. Typos are to be expected. Improper grammar is forgiven. Don't attempt to control the minutiae of your community. Take a hands-off approach, other than seeding and weeding, and you'll have a lively, thriving online community.

Policies and Policing

When it comes to managing your online community, written internal policies are important because consistency is key. The last thing you want to do is to contradict yourself or to change the rules of the community because you forgot what you did last time. Handling community issues the same way each time helps build trust between you and your community members.

Keeping an eye on the community and the conversation threads takes a considerable amount of time. In order to properly police the community, however, you need to take that time. Encourage members to report violations of the community; most members will do this automatically, even without instruction.

Relying on the community to totally police itself, however, is not responsible management. You need to make the effort to manage it for both the health of the community and to reap the most business benefits.

Legal Responsibilities and Liabilities

Building, hosting, and managing an online community can create some legal issues for your company. There is a fine line between your role as the host of an online community and the publisher of content, whether or not you have actually created that content. Where your responsibility starts and ends when it comes to online communities is something a lawyer who understands the Internet can help you determine.

Hosting Versus Publishing

Hosting encompasses not just providing a platform for discussion but can also include providing the server space and services to provide Web sites and other e-commerce business activities, such as the services an ISP offers. Under the Communications Decency Act, the host (or ISP) is protected from content posted on the host's site until the host learns of any offensive or libelous content. If you are only providing the forum where people can post, and you do not modify anything that is posted, you could be considered a host.

Publishing online means you broadcast someone's work, words, or posts, whether you edit them or not. Publishing can be different from hosting if you take an active role to edit the content that others post on your blog or message board. Under the law, it is unclear where liability begins for the online publisher.

If you are hosting an online forum or blog and change something that someone else has posted, you may put yourself and your company at risk. Because no statement is better than an offensive statement, deleting a questionable post is better than trying to fix it. In the course of editing posts, avoid making the statement offensive or libelous or you assume some responsibility for that post.

The determination of whether a post is offensive or libelous can be affected by where you do business or where you host your Web site, message board, or blog. What might be acceptable in a big city may be totally unacceptable in a small town.

It is essential to include your terms of service on your Web site to help limit your liability, as described on page 83. These terms of service can specify what posts are acceptable and what are not. Alternately, they may state that you, as the host, have the right to make that determination without the input of others. Terms of service can also explain how you will handle unacceptable posts.

Protecting Online Publishers

Congress passed the Communication Decency Act of 1996 (CDA). The provision protecting ISPs, however, remained (47 U.S. Code Section 230). Section 230 states that "No provider or user of an interactive computer service shall be treated as the publisher or speaker of any information provided by another information content provider." This section protects ISPs from content on their site posted by others and can offer you protection if you allow others to post to your message board or blog. Still, if you know about libelous or incorrect information posted by someone else, as the host, you must remove it or risk becoming liable yourself.

Disclaimers and Terms of Service

In addition to internal policies for managing an online community, you should develop rules about how community members are expected to behave, what you will and will not do to manage the community, and where the responsibility for content on the message boards lies. As a whole, these rules are generally called the terms of service or terms of use. They include disclaimers, disclosures, and many other provisions.

For instance, if you decide you will not be responsible for the potentially erroneous information community members may provide, you should post a disclaimer that reads as follows: "XYZ Company, Inc., is not responsible for any content posted to this board that is not posted directly by XYZ Company employees."

A disclosure can be used when you want to make clear that your company supports an online community, particularly when it may not be clear because your logo or company name is not prominently featured on the message boards. A disclosure in this case could read as follows: "XYZ Company, Inc., provides funds and resources to host and maintain this forum."

Posting disclaimers or disclosures is one of the most effective ways of minimizing your legal liabilities when it comes to an online community you have built and maintained. Nevertheless, you should seek out the advice of a lawyer before posting disclaimers or disclosures on your site to make sure they are legally sound.

Disclaim and Disclose

A disclaimer is a legal limit meant to reduce exposure to certain liabilities. A disclosure is when you reveal information to make sure your customers understand your expectations.

Defining the Terms

Every site should have a terms of service section that includes the following:

Limitations of liability: You and your company do not automatically assume responsibility for activities or posts in the online community.

Jurisdiction for legal action: This specifies where your company is located or where the Web site is hosted.

Venue for disputes: This establishes where any court proceedings or mediation should take place in the event of legal action taken against you.

Whether mandatory arbitration would apply: This explains whether any lawsuit brought against you would first go to mediation or arbitration.

Limitations on copyright infringement: This specifies that you are not responsible if someone else commits copyright infringement in your online community.

Restrictions on the posting of obscene or illegal materials: This defines what can and cannot be posted within your online community.

Limits on the age of posters: This limits your legal liabilities, though it also limits you from having teens or children posting within your online community.

Some other statements that you might see in a terms of service section include these:

Conditions and restrictions on use: A visitor can be blocked by you, the blogger or board host, at your discretion.

Registration and privacy: If registration is required to access or comment on the blog or message, a privacy statement explains how you'll use the visitor's information.

Member and user conduct: This defines responsibilities of the visitors, especially if they are posting comments, and should include a list of prohibited conduct.

Disclaimer of warranties: The blog or message board is provided as is, with no warranties made by you or your company.

Disclaimer regarding third-party content: This limits your responsibility as host or blogger regarding links to someone else's content.

Statement of ownership: This states that content posted on the boards or blog is owned by you, and by posting, members agree to these terms.

Acceptance: By using the blog and blog-related services, the visitor agrees to the terms and conditions you have provided.

Courts around the world enforce terms of service even if you include the link to these terms at the bottom of your Web pages which some people might argue is not clearly visible. To make the agreement to the terms more binding, you can add buttons at the bottom of the terms that say "I Accept" or "I Do Not Accept" and allow visitors to actively accept the terms. To make your terms even more effective, you can request some identifying information from visitors, such as their name and e-mail address, in order to match them up with their acceptance of the terms.

The Benefits of Registration

While some Web-based communities allow anyone to post a message on a blog or message board, most require users to register in order to access the board, whether their posts are anonymous or not. A registered user's actions can be traced, and users who have submitted identifying information may be more inclined to use a forum responsibly. Many forums, however, allow people to also register anonymously in addition to posting anonymously. Deciding whether you will allow anonymous posts is an important step to determining the nature of the online community you are building. A lawyer who understands the Internet can help you develop a strategy in order to limit your liability.

Challenges of Community Management

The main thing to remember when thinking about online communities is that they are organic. Trying too forcefully to control an online community can backfire. While your goals may be to leverage an online community for your business, the community members may have different ideas.

Overall, a sense of trust must be established and never violated between the community host and the members. By stating clear guidelines or rules, by acting consistently in response to community situations, and by being open about issues faced by your company and within the community, you can help to build and maintain that trust.

Speed of the Internet

What happens if you break the trust established between you as the community host and your community members, who are either your customers or your potential customers—for example, by deleting someone's post or banning someone from the service without a clearly communicated process or explanation? There's a popular saying among e-marketers: "Good news travels fast on the Internet. Bad news travels faster."

From an e-business standpoint, anything you do online can affect your business quickly and not always for the better. If there is a dispute or a misunderstanding within your online community, word of the situation can spread almost instantly across the Internet. And because your company's name is attached to the forum, your reputation can be damaged.

When you build an online community as an e-business venture, you are involving other people—usually people you do not know—in the running of your business. Other people can be unpredictable, which means you could be exposing your company to potentially negative situations. **Your online community members are not under your control, no matter how many rules and guidelines you put into place.**

Being prepared for the worst is a smart idea in any aspect of business, but it can be especially valuable with e-business. Here are some of the legal issues you could encounter with an online community, each of which would require a strategy and plan:

- Somebody posting something libelous about somebody else
- Somebody posting something libelous about you or your company
- Somebody verbally attacking other community members
- Somebody posting somebody else's copyrighted materials
- Somebody linking to inappropriate Web sites
- Somebody giving erroneous information that someone else acts on, leading to illness or injury
- Somebody using your online community to carry out illegal acts

You have the obligation and duty to delete inappropriate posts from boards within your online community. But unless you monitor the boards around the clock, seven days a week, there is a good chance that many community members will see an inappropriate post and even distribute it before you can remove it.

The speed and ease of Internet communications can suddenly make a small problem bigger than you imagined. You need advice from a lawyer to help write disclaimers that allow you a reasonable amount of time to remove materials posted on your site and to advise how to anticipate and handle any situations you might encounter while running an online community on behalf of your company.

Are You Incorporated?

Many small business owners often start as sole proprietors using an assumed business name, known as a DBA (for "doing business as"). A DBA designates you as the party personally responsible for the operations of your business. Incorporating a business, on the other hand, is a way of limiting your personal legal liability. Also, if you want to sell all or part of your business, it is easier to sell stock in a corporation than to sell a partnership or sole proprietorship. If you are not incorporated and host an online community, someone can potentially sue you for problems that arise within the forum or blog you host. Incorporation limits the suit to the corporation. However, the law doesn't provide absolute protection. Consult your lawyer and accountant to see what form of business is best for you.

Anarchy Online

At times, an online community can get completely out of hand. Members, usually out of a series of misunderstandings, begin attacking one another verbally. The attacks can be brutal and can have a powerful affect on the community members, not to mention the reputation of your company.

If community members seem out of control and are unwilling to stop their inappropriate attacks, there may come a time when the only viable solution is to shut down the message board entirely. In some instances, closing a community is not controversial, such as when there is little or no interaction and few or no members participating.

| Inside Track | Weblogs.com Kills Blogs |

Software developer Dave Winer found out the hard way about the emotional side of online communities when he chose to disable nearly 3,000 blogs he was hosting. The blogs were initially hosted on the servers of his former company. Once he left, he offered to host the blogs for free as part of his site Weblogs.com. In mid-2004, Winer disabled the blogs he hosted. He later claimed he made the decision based on technical issues—hosting the growing number of blogs was too much for his personal Web server to handle. According to some accounts, he did not give notice to the bloggers, many of whom who had formed a tight-knit community.

When he stopped hosting the blogs, word spread quickly. One blogger at Halley's Comment (an invitation-only blog hosted by Blogspot.com) titled a post "Blog Murder" and started her description of the incident by asking "Is there a reason why Dave Winer just killed 3,000 blogs . . . ?" WiredNews.com noted that some bloggers were "screaming that the shutdown is a 'serial blog murder.'"

Dave Winer defended himself by saying that he agreed to honor requests for copies of the blogs he had hosted. He also said that he didn't receive many requests, leading him to believe that many of the blogs he removed were inactive. Still, had he notified bloggers in advance, suggested alternatives for hosting their blogs, and used all available communications methods to spread the word about the impending shut down, perhaps the negative press could have been avoided or at least limited.

When you have a thriving community that runs amok, closing down a community becomes a drastic measure that may have some negative repercussions. Being prepared for any backlash that may come from closing down a community is critical.

TEST DRIVE

Determine if you are willing to take on the liabilities and challenges of building and maintaining an online community. Are the risks worth the rewards? Ask yourself these questions:

- ⮎ How can I use an online community to benefit my business?
- ⮎ Can I develop an internal company policy on how to handle situations that arise within an online community?
- ⮎ Have I crafted a terms of service agreement?
- ⮎ Have I written a privacy policy?
- ⮎ Have I established a crisis communications plan to handle any negative situation that might arise?
- ⮎ Have I decided on a theme for my online community and the potential members I would like to target?

Building Your Online Presence

PART **3**

Deciding on a Domain Name

As you begin to plan your Web presence, in the form of a Web site or blog or both, the first step is to reserve a domain name. The Web consists of a number of top-level domains (TLDs) commonly known as suffixes—.com, .org, and .net are all TLDs. On each TLD, individual Web sites are distinguished by an identifying number known as an IP address. IP addresses consist of a series of numbers and dots, such as 10.201.98.01. Like license plates on a car, no two sites have the exact same IP address.

It would be very difficult to navigate the Web if you had to remember the IP address for all the sites you wanted to visit. For that reason, it is possible for Web site owners to define a domain name for their site that consists of letters, numerals, and a few special characters such as hyphens. The domain name acts like a "vanity plate" address that masks the IP address for a Web site. When users types a domain name into a Web browser, they are automatically redirected to the matching IP address and its corresponding site.

Domain Name Distribution

When domain names were first being assigned, the only publicly available TLDs in the United States were .com (company), .org (organization), and .net (network). Others that existed but were not generally available included .mil (military), .edu (educational institution), and .gov (government). Eventually, the DNS system allowed companies to offer new TLDs such as .us (United States), .ws (Web site), .biz (business), and .info (informational site).

Good Domain Names

Choosing a domain name that makes sense for one's business and is effective for e-business can prove challenging as so many names have been taken. Domain names can be an asset for any business, and some people have made a business of reserving as many domain names as possible in order to sell them for a profit. Picking the right domain name is an important aspect of successfully doing business online.

So what makes a domain name good for business? The best domain names have the following characteristics:

ᴑ Short
ᴑ Memorable
ᴑ Easy to spell
ᴑ Easy to pronounce

The best domain names end in .com because that is the suffix most people associate with the Web.

Worst Names

Knowing what makes a good domain name means that the opposite characteristic is sure to make a domain name less effective, or in some cases, virtually useless:

ᴑ Too long or hyphenated
ᴑ Hard to remember
ᴑ Hard to spell
ᴑ Hard to pronounce

Using hyphens in domain names has become almost inevitable because names without hyphens are harder to come by. Some people go immediately for the hyphenated name, often because they believe using a phrase without hyphens is confusing. Depending on the phrase, the name could be harder to interpret and hyphens could help. Too many vowels or consonants in a row can make a domain name harder to read. But ultimately, hyphens make a domain name harder to communicate and harder to remember. Compare these domain names:

Without Hyphens	With Hyphens
www.iateapie.com	www.i-ate-a-pie.com
www.johnknowshow.com	www.john-knows-how.com
www.abccompany.com	www.abc-company.com

People will spell a domain name based on what they think they hear. If the spelling is even slightly different from how a domain name sounds, people will inevitably visit the wrong site. The more a domain name creates barriers to people finding your company's Web site, the less effective it is.

<table>
<tr><td>Inside Track</td><td>Domain Name Downfall</td></tr>
</table>

In 1995, I reserved my first domain name that would eventually be used by the Internet company I founded early that year. I called my company Cybergrrl Internet Media so reserved the domain name Cybergrrl.com. The spelling was my idea. I felt that Cybergirl sounded like a little girl and Cyberwoman was boring. I opted for Cybergrrl thinking that the two r's added a little attitude. Little did I know the impromptu decision on our first domain name would become a problem.

Within a year, I discovered that people—especially women who were our target audience—had a hard time finding our site because they kept keying in Cybergirl.com. I decided to obtain Cybergirl.com and redirect people to Cybergrrl.com. Unfortunately, not only was it taken, but it pointed to a porn site. No wonder I was receiving irate e-mails every week complaining about the "naked women."

As the media began writing about my company and Cybergrrl.com, newspaper editors and television producers would, at the last minute, change the spelling to Cybergirl.com, sending more people to the wrong site. On the radio, if listeners heard "Cybergrrl.com," they would inevitably jot it down as "Cybergirl.com" and visit the wrong site when they got to their computers.

Even though we had registered Cybergrrl as a trademark early on, each cease-and-desist letter we sent to the porn company asking them to stop using a name that was confusingly similar to our trademark went unanswered. We were never able to obtain Cybergirl.com or prevent the porn company from using it. My early decision to choose a domain name that was cute rather than effective cost our company tens of thousands of dollars and even hurt the company's reputation.

Obtaining Your Domain Name

To register your domain name, you need to go through a domain name registrar, that is, a company with the rights and ability to assign you a unique domain name. Because there is a good chance the domain name of your choice is taken, you should come up with at least half a dozen viable alternatives. You can reserve as many domain names as you want so it is a good idea to get more than one, but be strategic.

Planning Your Domain Name

Reserve not only the name you actually want but also any alternative spellings you think people might key in by mistake. If you are able to get the .com, also try to get .org and .net so nobody else—such as your competitors—can. While you are at it, you may also want to reserve other suffixes including .biz, .info, and .tv.

A strategic list of domain names to register might look like this:

- Cybergrrl.com
- Cybergrrrl.com
- Cybergirl.com
- Cybergrrl.net
- Cybergirl.net
- Cybergrrl.org

- Cybergirl.org
- Cybergrrl.tv
- Cybergirl.tv
- Cybergrrl.biz
- Cybergirl.biz

You can end up spending a lot of money coming up with variations of domain names. By being strategic, you can limit your expenses.

Register Early and Often

If the name you've chosen is available, you may want to register it immediately so nobody else gets it, but you still should take one more step before using the name. Do a trademark search to make sure that your domain name of choice does not infringe on somebody else's trademark. A fast search on the Internet can give you some preliminary idea of what is fair game, but it may be better to order a trademark search through Thomson CompuMark (www.thomson-thomson.com). The cost ranges from about $400 to around $1,000, but the results are more definitive than other searching methods.

Checking on a Name

Before you try to register your domain name, check if it is available. You can do this at any registrar's site by typing the name into the search field on their home page, usually the first step in the registration process. The results page will tell you if the domain name is available or not. If not, the page may show available names or list suggestions of alternative names.

After registering your domain name, you may also want to trademark or servicemark it. You can do this through a lawyer but it is also possible to register it yourself through the U.S. Patent and Trademark office (*www.uspto.gov*). This Web site guides you through the registration process. The filing fee for trademarks or servicemarks ranges from $275 to $325. A trademark covers products, and a servicemark covers services.

ICANN

The Internet Corporation for Assigned Names and Numbers (ICANN) is a non-profit corporation that oversees a number of Internet tasks, including managing the assignment of domain names and IP addresses. ICANN also manages the introduction of new top-level domains. In 2006, ICANN signed an agreement with the U.S. Department of Commerce to move closer to fully managing the Internet Assigned Numbers Authority (IANA). In its first year of operations, ICANN introduced several new top-level domains including .travel and .jobs. Much debate has ensued about whether ICANN should become more international and not have close ties to the U.S. government. ICANN has a governing board; in 2006, its fifteen members represented six continents.

Registering Domain Names

When you are ready to register your domain names, use a reputable domain registrar that charges less than $20 per domain name. That means you'll be spending less than $200 per year for six to ten domain names. Your Web programmer or the company hosting your Web site can point the excess addresses to your main Web site, an additional $100 or so. More traffic to your Web site means more money, so investing in domain names can pay for itself within the first year.

Finding the Right Web Host

You can quickly and easily register your domain name directly through any reputable registrar at their Web site. Alternately, you can opt to have the company that will host your Web site register it for you. The hosting site may provide the registration service for free or for a small fee.

Web host providers, or Web hosts, are companies that provide Web site hosting services. ISPs, companies that offer services such as Internet access and e-mail, can also offer Web hosting.

Web hosting means the company owns and maintains Web servers—specially formatted computers dedicated to the Web twenty-four hours a day, seven days a week. **In order for your Web site to show up on the Web and be accessible to others, the site must reside on a Web server.** Think of a Web host as your landlord. You rent space from them to store your Web site files and make them accessible on the Web.

National or Local

When selecting your Web host, you should consider whether to go with a national or a local company. A national company can offer the following:

1. Lower prices or better bundles of services for the price
2. More experience handling larger sites and sophisticated services
3. Greater reliability because they have more at stake
4. More longevity, meaning they'll still be in business a few years from now
5. More likely to have customer service and technical support available around the clock, seven days a week

While the above is often true with the most reputable national ISPs or Web hosts, lesser-known or new companies may not meet these standards. Also, not all national companies are good businesses even if they have been in business for a long time. Check references to see how their clients feel about their services, and look for any red flags such as special low prices that sound too good to be true. They often are.

A local provider can offer the following:

1. More accountability; part of your community, so may try harder to provide the best service
2. Slightly higher fees because of lower volume, often offset by more personal customer service and technical support
3. More flexibility to create a service plan that best suits your needs
4. Better responsiveness because they have fewer clients to manage
5. Less reliability because they have less clout with the bigger providers of Internet connectivity

Going local can also be a personal choice; you may prefer to do business with a company in your own community.

From Computer to Web

You or your Web designer may have your Web site files on a regular computer. Eventually, however, the files that make up your Web site must be transferred or uploaded to a Web server. Transferring the files is most commonly done through file transfer protocol (FTP), using dedicated FTP software.

Web Hosting Services

In general, Web hosts are in competition for your business, so their rates tend to be comparable. Many Web hosts offer flat monthly fees to host sites. The most common services offered for a flat Web hosting fee include these:

⮕ Web space hosting: Providing the space on and access to a Web server

⮕ Domain name hosting: Setting up your domain name to point to your Web site

⮕ E-mail accounts: Providing multiple e-mail addresses with your Web site hosting account

➲ Web traffic logs: Furnishing you with either monthly traffic reports via e-mail or access to daily or on-demand Web-based reports

➲ Technical support: Providing a toll-free number and twenty-four-hour technical support

Some Web hosts may charge extra for some of the services above instead of providing them as part of a package. Look for providers that bundle at least these basic services or you may end up paying too much for your Web hosting.

The price for Web hosting may also increase if you request additional services, such as these:

1. **Domain name forwarding:** Setting up additional domain names to point to your Web site
2. **Databases:** Managing large quantities of information or to make information searchable on your site
3. **ColdFusion or ASP:** Producing Web pages whose content is pulled from a database
4. **Shopping carts:** Creating an online shopping experience
5. **Secure servers:** Allowing for secure shopping transactions to protect customer credit card numbers and personal information
6. **Additional bandwidth:** Handling higher-than-normal traffic volume

Web Host Selections

While price is certainly one of the first ways you narrow down your choice of Web hosts and types of services is another, also screen providers by the following:

Reputation: Search the Web and blogs for mentions of the company to get a sense of what others think about them.

Testimonials: Ask for contact information for other companies whose sites they host and get feedback.

Service: Visit other Web sites hosted on their servers to ensure you can access them easily and quickly.

Accessibility: Ask if they guarantee that you will be able to access their servers at any time and if not, what concessions they offer such as a discount on that month's rent.

Responsiveness: See how long you are on hold when you call to speak to a customer service or tech support person, and then measure how quickly they respond to your queries.

Reliability: Ask about their down time—how often have their Web servers gone down in the past few years, for how long, and what they did to compensate their customers.

Security: Find out what measures they have taken to ensure their Web servers are secure and safe from hacking.

Backup: Get a detailed explanation of how their Web servers are backed up including the equipment used, how frequently it happens, and if they guarantee the safety of your Web files.

Web analytics: Find out what kind of Web analytics or Web site traffic tracking solutions they offer and how frequently you can access the data.

For some of the above criteria, work with an Internet consultant to assess the services a host provides and make sure they are up to the current standards. You should also check and alter any service agreement you may sign with a Web host to best protect your Web site assets. There should never be a clause stating that the Web host holds any ownership over the files you upload to their servers.

The Technical Side of Hosting

If you have a basic Web site, hosting is simple, and the cost is lower. If you plan to have interactive features or an online store, you have more at stake and should carefully assess your Web host. If you are not technically inclined, a good Internet consultant can help you sort through the more complex aspects of choosing the right Web host. Knowing some of the basic technology and lingo can help you make a better decision.

Shared Servers

The most common type of Web hosting is on a shared server. Your Web site is hosted on a Web server along with a few or many other sites. Your files are contained within a password-protected environment, and theoretically you should not be able to access anyone else's files on the Web server and they should not be able to access yours. For the most part, breaches of Web sites hosted on the same server are uncommon.

Shared server arrangements should be affordable because all customers share the costs of the server. If a Web host guarantees a low number of other sites on a particular server, they may charge more for hosting. More sites on a single server could affect the speed of your site loading, but the effect should be negligible. A reliable Web host will make sure that any sites using more bandwidth are notified and may be moved to a different server to avoid affecting other sites sharing the server. Shared servers usually provide a maximum amount of space, such as 1 gigabyte.

Co-Location

Co-location is the more expensive alternative to sharing a server. You purchase a Web server (at a cost ranging from $1,000 to $5,000 or more, depending on the technical specifications) that is located on the premises of a Web host that offers co-location services. Their technicians are responsible for the physical hosting and maintenance of the server. Your company is responsible for the software and files on the server.

Reasons to co-locate include the following:

1. **Your site requires the installation of software** or technology that is not allowed on a shared server.
2. **Your developer needs more access than a Web host allows** on a shared server in order to implement essential aspects of your site.
3. **You are sensitive to security** and would prefer not to have your site files hosted on a server outside your company.
4. **You have noticed a lag time on a shared server** that affects the functionality of your Web site.
5. **Your site is receiving an enormous amount of traffic,** and your Web host suggests moving to a co-location package.

6. Your company is making a major investment in its site, and you expect a significant return on investment.

Choosing co-location is most often a technical or financial decision. If your site has greater technical needs, co-location can be a logical solution. The additional costs of hosting your site on a co-located server may also help you to achieve more through your site, which in turn can generate more income, making the investment worthwhile.

Access to Technologies

Your Web developer can make sure the Web host you choose provides the right technology based on how your Web site is programmed. Most interactive Web sites are made up of other programming languages in addition to basic HTML. Some other programming used on Web sites that could affect the Web host you chose include these:

➲ ColdFusion
➲ ASP
➲ Perl

➲ PHP
➲ Flash and Shockwave
➲ Real or Windows Media

Your developer should make sure your Web host allows chosen programming languages or software to be used on their servers and that the developer has the proper access to use those languages. Without the right access, your developer will not be able to properly build the interactive features of your site.

What to Look for in an Internet Consultant

The term Internet consultant can be a catchall for someone with Internet savvy, usually someone with more than just a single area of expertise. Skills can include the following:

1. Web strategy: Analyzing, assessing, and planning your company's approach to the Web

2. **E-business consulting:** Encompassing all elements of the Internet and not just the Web
3. **Web development:** Programming or project managing
4. **Web design:** Designing Web graphics and user interface
5. **Content development:** Developing content and a content strategy for your company Web site
6. **Database programming:** Specialized programming and development using databases for Web sites
7. **Internet marketing:** Using the Internet and Web to market your company, products, services, and Web site

A good Internet consultant clearly defines what she or he can offer then establishes relationships with others to provide ancillary services. Be wary of anyone who claims to do it all. Problems typically arise when a technical person without any design experience tries to design a site or a graphic designer without sufficient programming skills tries to create an interactive site.

Established Web development firms have a well-rounded staff that can handle all aspects of Web strategy, programming, and design. Independent Web developers may be more cost effective, but make sure they belong to a freelance team to deliver the services you need.

Finding Your Consultant

To find a qualified Internet consultant, Web developer, or Web designer, you can cast a wide net or take a more narrow approach. Some of the best ways to find an Internet consultant include the following:

- ⮑ Referrals from trusted vendors, clients, or colleagues
- ⮑ Local Internet, computer, or software user groups
- ⮑ Chamber of commerce or other professional organizations
- ⮑ Local universities or community colleges, especially design schools
- ⮑ Google search for your criteria (location, services, industry niche, etc.)

Top-notch Internet consultants are more likely to find their clients through positive word of mouth than through advertising. A warm lead or referral from someone is a far stronger testimonial for a consultant's qualifications than a paid ad.

If you happen upon a Web site for another company that is particularly appealing to you, don't hesitate to contact someone at the company and ask who developed that site. Most people are happy to share the name of their consultant, especially if your company is not one of their competitors.

While you are looking around the Web for sites you like, don't forget to check out the Web developer's own Web site in addition to the sites she or he has developed.

Checking Qualifications

Hiring any vendor requires a screening process to ensure you are working with the right firm or individual. The best way to screen Web developers is to take these steps:

Get a recommendation first. Ask around to discover which developers have a good reputation, or ask people whose sites you like for the names of their developers.

Peruse their online portfolio. Look beyond the home page designs of their client Web sites and click into the sites and test features.

Speak with their references. Even though they'll only give you a list of satisfied customers, ask questions and get impressions from more than one source.

Review their contract or terms. Ask to see a boilerplate contract to get a better sense of what they offer and how they work.

Check their credentials. Find out what skills they have, training certificates they've acquired, and memberships they hold in relevant organizations, such as industry or trade groups, the local chamber of commerce, or the Better Business Bureau.

Not every skill a Web developer possesses is technical. Look for soft skills as well: the ability to communicate well, without a lot of jargon, and the patience and willingness to review everything with you until you understand it. Anyone who throws around technical terms and seems put out when you ask questions is not for you. Being comfortable with your Web developer is important, especially if you are not working with an Internet consultant as a middleman.

If your budget is limited, you may think of turning to a friend or relative to save you money. Unless this person has the credentials, experience, and portfolio to back up claims of being a Web developer or Internet consultant, you may be putting your business at risk. If you decide to go with someone you know and feel confident about his or her abilities, sign a proper contract for the job. No matter how good the friend or close the relative, business is business, and both of you have to protect your interests.

The Right Designer Makes the Difference

Whether your developer does Web design or she works with an experienced graphic Web designer, it's critical to have someone who excels in Web site interface design and who works with images for the Web. The last thing you want is a developer who's a poor designer, leaving you with a site that looks unprofessional and doesn't achieve your business goals.

Spending a Little Extra

The old adage, "You get what you pay for," holds true when it comes to Web design. You may end up paying more in the short term for a highly qualified Web designer, but you'll save money in the long run. The skills and benefits a good Web designer can offer you include these:

- Interface strategy
- Web site architecture planning
- Interface design
- Site navigation development
- Image optimization

Most skilled Web designers started by learning traditional design techniques, giving them a good foundation for Web design. But not all graphic designers who work in print can translate those skills to Web design. If you work with a graphic designer for your print marketing materials, he might be able to work with a Web developer and, with the proper guidance, come up with an effective Web site design. In general, however, a print graphic designer is not the best choice for Web design work.

Moving Forward

No matter whom you decide to hire to build your company's Web presence, you first must determine your expectations and communicate them clearly. Later, a capable consultant can help you assess your business goals, translate them into e-business goals, and make additional recommendations to improve upon your initial plans.

Remember that until you sign a contract, nothing said or promised during initial discussions and negotiations is set in stone. Not until you see those things written into a signed contract can you expect them to come to fruition. Before you sign a contract, however, you will have to settle on a price and the terms of the relationship between you and your consultant.

Finding an Internet consultant can seem like a daunting task, but if you take some strategic steps, you will be able to find the right person for the job. Before searching for a consultant, ask yourself these questions:

- ➲ What business goals am I trying to achieve with my site?
- ➲ How will a Web site help my business?
- ➲ What level of sophistication do I want in my site design?
- ➲ What kinds of interactive features should be part of my site?
- ➲ How large or complex a site do I want?

Knowing When the Price Is Right

You have narrowed down your choice of Internet consultants and now need to determine whom you will hire to do the job. You first looked at capabilities. Now you want to see who will propose a price that works within your budget.

Budgeting for a Web Site

There is also no uniform way of pricing out Web site development. Different companies probably have individual methods for putting a price tag on the job.

Most experts say that to determine your marketing budget, you should spend 10 percent of your revenues for marketing. If your Web site will primarily serve a marketing function, you can draw from your marketing budget to pay its construction costs. The more useful you think a Web site will be for your company, the more of your marketing budget you should put toward it.

If your Web site serves other purposes, draw from the corresponding budgets. For example, if your site will enhance customer service, add money from that budget to the portion you've pulled from your marketing budget. **Eventually, you should have a separate e-business budget that covers Web development, Internet marketing, and other online activities.**

More money should go to the aspects of your e-business strategy that could generate income, but first you need to spend to determine your overall e-business strategy, establish your Web presence, and market the fact that your company has a Web site. If nobody knows your Web site exists and nobody visits it, you will be hard pressed to achieve any of your e-business goals and will have wasted money.

Pricing Models

Because every Internet consultant determines pricing in a proprietary way, there is no way to definitively establish a pricing model for Web development. However, some pricing methods are more common:

1. **Per page:** This makes sense only if your site will consist of a finite number of static pages; best for very small, simple sites.

2. Per hour: This can become expensive unless the developer gives an estimate of the hours as a guideline or sets a cap to the hours.

3. Per project: This flat-fee approach is possible when all aspects of the Web site are clearly defined, but the process for determining the fee can be nebulous and even secretive.

4. By menu: Some developers establish set fees for various Web site features and add them to a base development cost.

5. A combination: Some developers use a combination of these models to come up with a price for the project and a menu for additional costs that may arise along the way.

Your best bet for getting a good deal on a Web site is to establish a fixed price for the job with a clear list of prices for anything above and beyond the agreed-upon elements of the project. A developer's challenge is to offer a fixed price that covers his time and a series of additional prices that will cover any additional work. As long as both parties know what to expect from one another and the fees are in writing, future disputes can be minimized.

The Cost of a Web Site

How much does a Web site cost? Many variables affect price, including who is building your site and the kind of interactive features you want. A Web site can cost anywhere from nothing to hundreds of thousands of dollars. Realistically, a small-business owner can expect to pay hundreds to thousands of dollars for a site. A static site with only several pages could cost several hundred dollars. An online store with a basic shopping cart system could cost a couple of thousand dollars to build. That same online store could be cobbled together for much less or, if the features needed to be more sophisticated, thousands more.

Internet consultants should clearly define their responsibilities when it comes to working with you on your Web site and e-business strategy. It is up to them to determine how much time the job will take and attach a dollar amount to their work. If their pricing model is clear and straightforward, you will have a much easier time deciding on the consultant you would like to hire.

Price Comparisons

A variety of different pricing models can present a challenge when you are trying to compare proposals from one consultant to another, so you should request a project price from each consultant you are considering. You do not want them to submit solely an hourly rate or a per page cost without a cap on the hours or a sound estimate of the number of site pages anticipated.

Putting Out an RFP

To find a suitable Web developer, some companies put out a request for proposal (RFP). An RFP outlines what you expect from a developer so you should do some strategic planning of your own first. You also must compose the actual RFP in an acceptable format. You can find examples of RFPs on the Web. Using an RFP process to screen qualified Internet consultants creates more consistency about pricing and presentation, reducing variables so your decision-making is more controlled. The trick to a successful RFP process is to get the word out about your request to the right people. Sending it through a local chamber of commerce or a Web developers' organization is a good way to spread the word.

Once you are able to establish a base price from each consultant, take a look at additional costs. Sometimes there are unforeseen costs; at such an early stage, you cannot predict the exact number of pages or features you want on your site. Some of those decisions come later so you need to understand how you will be charged for working on strategies and a plan and not just the site programming and development.

Make note of how the prospective consultants respond to your requests to explain their pricing methodology or to simplify their pricing structure. Work with someone who is willing to be flexible but not necessarily someone who changes her entire pricing model to accommodate your requests. A consultant should be willing to negotiate, but she will also take care not to undersell herself.

Scope of Work and Proposals

Information on price should come to you as part of an overall scope of work or Web development proposal. To get to a proposal of any kind, you usually need to meet or talk with potential consultants and allow them time to learn what you hope to achieve online. Some consultants can give you generic pricing and information about the services that they offer, but you are better served with something more tailored to your needs.

Every consultant has his own way of presenting his skills, services, and methodology for completing a project. You can, however, request specific information from each consultant in order to make your hiring decision. If your job is big enough, you can often dictate how you'd like the project to be priced. With smaller Web development jobs, however, you won't normally have any leverage for dictating terms. Still, a reputable consultant will do his best to work with you and stay within your budget, presenting a proposal that is customized to your needs and not just something from a template.

Components of a Web Contract

Just as every Web developer may price his or her services differently, each will use a different contract. Some may add clauses to a boilerplate work-for-hire contract while others may hire a lawyer to compose the contract from scratch. Some contracts may be only a few pages long while others can run up to a dozen pages or more.

A good Internet consultant will present you with a proposal and a contract that are easy to understand and jargon free. Still, as with any binding legal agreement, there will be language and terms that may not make sense to the layman. If you are easily intimidated by contracts, turn to a lawyer to help navigate any written agreement before you sign anything.

Contract Elements

Most Web development contracts should have some similar elements that pertain specifically to the services that will be provided to complete the job. Some things you might see in a Web development contract include these:

1. **Definitions:** Defines the main technical terms used in the contract
2. **List of services:** Specifies the services to be provided
3. **Fees:** Gives the price or prices agreed upon in advance
4. **Term, termination, and renewal:** Designates how long the contract will last, how and when it can be ended, and how and when it can be renewed for continued service
5. **Intellectual property, proprietary rights, and site policy:** Specifies who owns what when it comes to copyrights, trademarks, and other proprietary materials
6. **Confidentiality:** States what is confidential information for both parties
7. **Indemnification:** Explains who will indemnify whom to protect from legal action

Other non-legal elements often included in a Web development contract that help outline the project include these:

- Invoicing schedule for payments
- Payment and reimbursement instructions
- Estimated timeline for the project
- Specified milestones to reach during the life of the project
- List of assets owned by each party that will be contributed or used for project

Sample Web development contracts are available on the Web. Make sure you include both the important legal clauses as well as the relevant technical and business clauses so both parties are covered and protected.

Modifying and Renewing Contracts

Often a clause in a contract will stipulate how the contract can be modified before the end of the contract term. Some modifications can be made on a contract as edits and initialed by both parties. Major modifying should be done in writing and signed and dated by both parties.

Nondisclosure Agreements

Before you divulge any information about your company to potential consultants, consider having them sign a nondisclosure agreement (NDA). This legal contract, signed by both parties before your first meeting, goes beyond a confidentiality clause in a standard contract. The agreement outlines confidential information that one party wishes to disclose to the other party with restrictions as to how the second party can use the information. If you have proprietary information or are in a highly competitive market and do not want to release trade secrets, NDAs are a good idea. NDAs can be mutual, affecting both parties, or may only bind one party to confidentiality. Keep in mind not everyone will sign an NDA.

Another clause often specifies how a contract can be extended or renewed. A contract should not be automatically renewed unless both parties agree. Web contracts should cover a finite length of time, with the option to renew after the terms of the contract have been met to both parties' satisfaction. Taking the time to assess the completed contract and potentially renegotiate terms of a new contract is a way to protect your investments.

Reading the Fine Print

Be wary of any contract that is hard to read, not just in terms of content but font size as well. Nothing in a contract should be hard to decipher.

Hidden Costs

While most pricing models are straightforward and clearly stated in the contract, some developers may hide other costs in their proposals then include them in the actual contract. At the proposal stage, ask a potential consultant if there are any hidden costs not yet discussed or included in his print proposal.

An honest consultant will include all costs up front in her proposal and not try to sneak in a few more fees in the contract. Regardless, go through the costs portion of the contract carefully. Also look for other clauses that may be tucked into another part of the contract that could affect the cost of the project.

Sometimes the costs are not actually hidden and instead something in the contract could affect the cost of the project. For example, a clause common to many Web development contracts limits the number of revisions a Web developer will perform, usually three. After those revisions, additional fees kick in. If you don't realize this clause exists, and you and your consultant go back and forth revising parts of the site, you will incur substantial costs in addition to the base project fee. Typically, additional revisions are billed out at the developer's hourly rate, and this can add up for each revision over the agreed number.

There may also be costs that are not hidden but are not discussed and come up as the project progresses. An example is the fee for the security certificate or the credit card approval system for your online store or a fee to your bank for setting up a merchant's account so you can accept credit cards. An experienced consultant will anticipate these costs based on previous jobs for other clients.

Not all costs of building a Web site will come from the Web developer. Some can come directly from vendors, such as the security certificate fee and the merchant account fee. Your consultant should outline these ancillary fees and specify who should be paid. Some consultants will include these fees in their total project cost. If that is the case, they are responsible for making those additional payments.

Understand or Eliminate

Before you sign anything, make sure you understand everything. **Don't accept the statement that a clause is "unimportant."** No clause in the contract is unimportant. Your response should be, "If it isn't important, let's remove it from the contract."

Case of the Hidden Costs

In 1995, my company was hired to create the first Web site for a doctor who was an internationally bestselling author of diet books and diet products. The doctor was eager to sell his new line of diet supplements and foods online. With my business partner and technology director, we priced out building an online shopping cart for the doctor's health-center Web site. Our price was reasonable, we thought, and by today's standards dirt cheap at just over $1,000.

I remember sitting in a conference room at the health center with the doctor. He turned to me suddenly and asked, "Why are you charging more than $1,000 to build my site when I got this contract from another company offering to do it for a couple hundred." I could feel my face turning red, but I maintained a calm demeanor and asked, "Can I see their contract?"

The doctor obliged. Sure enough, the company was offering to build a similar site for just a few hundred dollars. I scanned the contract terms, and my eyes landed on the fine print—a few sentences in a tiny font that explained that in addition to the low monthly fee for hosting the doctor's Web site, the company was going to charge for "bandwidth." I pointed this out to the doctor and explained he was about to sign a contract that sounded cheap on the surface, but if he were to get any traffic to his Web site, he would be charged additional fees. Using the figures in the contract's fine print, my business partner and I calculated that the low monthly Web hosting fee suddenly turned into hundreds of dollars per month if his site received a small number of visitors and thousands of dollars per month if his site was successful. "I see," the doctor said with a wry smile, reached for our contract, and signed on the dotted line.

If the consultant cannot explain or justify a clause, cross through it. If you modify anything in the contract by hand, make sure both parties initial the change. If there are numerous modifications on each page, ask the consultant to go back and incorporate the changes so you have a clean version of the contract.

Ownership Is Everything

A common question when negotiating and contracting with a Web developer is "Who owns what?" The contract must spell out what the assets are and who owns them. Some typical assets defined in a Web development contract include the following:

- Proprietary code (not HTML)
- Interactive features
- Database programming
- Database content
- Web site content
- Photographs and graphics
- Audio and video

Owning the Code

The HTML code of a Web page cannot be copyrighted or owned by you or your Web developer. Anyone can visit your completed Web site and copy the HTML code of your Web site using their Web browser. All they have to do is go to View on the top menu of their browser and select Source or Page Source. The HTML code of that particular Web page will appear in a plain text format. If someone wants to copy the code of your page and paste it onto his page to use on his site, he can. He cannot, however, copy any graphics, photographs, or content—text, audio, or video—from your site without your express permission.

Spelling Out Ownership

Some Web developers will license interactive features to you for use on your site. These are programs they have developed before working with you, often for other clients. The programming for a unique interactive system or engine can be copyrighted and therefore is owned by the creator. The content you put into the engine, however, can be owned by you.

Some examples of interactive features in which the programmer might own the programming but you would own the content include these:

1. **A Web-based calendar system:** They own the system (or engine), but you own the event information entered into and displayed on the calendar.
2. **An e-postcard engine:** They own the engine, but you own the images and content that make up the e-postcards.
3. **An interactive message board:** They own the board system, but you own the content, possibly including the content others post on the board.
4. **A quick poll engine:** They own the program that produces instant polls on your site, but you own the content of the polls.
5. **A Web-based content editing system:** They own the system that allows you to easily edit the content of your site, but you own the content.

Your consultant may ask you to sign a licensing agreement for the use of her Web-based software. She may give you use of the software license-free, or she may include the licensing fees in her proposal.

Ownership Disputes

Despite the best of intentions, there are times when a disagreement or dispute comes about regarding ownership of assets pertaining to a Web development job. A common situation is when a Web developer creates custom software to the business owner's specifications. The business owner is paying for the developer's time and labor. Who owns the software? The business owner claims he either owns or co-owns the software because he came up with the idea and specified how the software should work. The developer claims she owns the software because without her technical capabilities it would be nothing but a concept.

Before engaging a developer to build a program based on your specifications, draw up an agreement as part of the contract outlining ownership for the custom software. There is no single right way to designate ownership; you should come to a mutually agreeable arrangement.

When there is a dispute over ownership that is not covered in a signed agreement, each party may seek the assistance of a mediator or a lawyer to help settle the dispute. Unfortunately, during the time the dispute is being handled, the developer may disable the software, rendering it useless until an agreement has been reached.

Kill Fees and Out Clauses

The out clause and kill fee clause can be helpful if things don't work out with the consultant. An out clause outlines how and when either party can break the contract without penalty. A kill fee specifies how much money the consultant will get even though the contract has been broken.

If you break the contract, you should be responsible for paying the developer some portion of the cost of the site to pay for her time and labor up to that point. If the contract is broken due to a breach on the part of the developer, however, you shouldn't have to pay her. You can add a clause to your contract that states that if the contract is broken because of a breach by the developer, then you will not owe the kill fee or that the kill fee will be greatly reduced.

Determining Kill Fees

A kill fee is usually a percentage of the overall cost of the project as specified in the contract. The percentage is typically 10 to 15 percent of the total cost when the cost is in the thousands. Often, a consultant will want 25 to 50 percent of the total cost when creating a much smaller site. Sometimes, a kill fee will be a larger percentage for a less costly site and smaller for a more expensive site. This sliding scale can be outlined in the contract.

Breaking the Contract

Terminating a contract often occurs in a murky area where both parties are most likely dissatisfied and probably blaming each other for breaches that make the business relationship untenable. The key to a smooth contract break is a well-written contract that anticipates the possibility that the relationship may end abruptly.

The contract should have a clause that instructs how and when to break it. Most commonly, contracts must be terminated in writing from one party to the other. Legally binding contracts cannot be broken by telephone and shouldn't be broken by e-mail. A certified letter is still the best method of terminating an agreement.

When Things Go Wrong

There is no way to predict every possible way a business relationship between you and a Web developer could go wrong. Trying to cover all the possible scenarios is a good idea but can make for a very long contract. Still, failing to include some specifics about what could justify the end of a contract may cause more trouble in the long run if something does go wrong.

Breaching a Contract

A breach of the contract is the failure to abide by the contract terms. Either party can be responsible for a breach. Here are some of the most common breaches that result in a broken contract:

The Breach	Business Owner	Consultant
Failure to complete project as scheduled	-	x
Causing unnecessary delays	x	x
Infringing on copyright	x	x
Misleading on cost of project	-	x
Going out of business	x	x

As a business owner, your contractual responsibilities to a Web developer may include the following:

- Providing enough time and information to perform the job
- Turning around decisions in a timely manner
- Sticking to the timeline set forth in the contract
- Providing additional time for delays you cause
- Submitting changes and comments in writing

The best way to ensure you will not breach a contract is to be prepared before you meet with a Web developer, to communicate clearly and in writing, and, when coming up with timelines, to give yourself more time than you think you need so you don't cause unnecessary delays.

Legal Remedies

Most contracts include a clause that says if things do go wrong and there is a dispute between the parties, both parties agree to mediation as a means of coming to terms. Mediation can be a less costly way of settling a legal dispute, helping to prevent the parties from going to court in a formal lawsuit.

▶▶ TEST DRIVE

You've found the Web developer with whom you'd like to work, but now you need to get down to the nitty-gritty and agree to the cost of the project and terms of the contract. Some things you should ask yourself before you sign anything are the following:

- ➲ How will I budget for the costs of Web development?
- ➲ What are my plans for covering costs of Web site maintenance?
- ➲ When do I want the project completed?
- ➲ What concerns do I have regarding the cost of the site?
- ➲ What concerns do I have regarding the contract?
- ➲ What clauses will I need in the contract to protect my interests?

Web Sites for Marketing

The most common reason to build a Web site for your business is to market something—your company, your products, your services, or even you. Often the first Web site a company builds is strictly for marketing purposes: to have a presence online that tests the waters to see what works and what doesn't work.

Putting up a marketing site is a sensible way to start, but don't miss the opportunity to have the Web site work for you. You don't want people to simply visit your site once and leave. You want to be able to capture data, measure interest, and generate leads that will translate into sales.

Avoiding Brochureware

Many small companies put up a Web site that is nothing more than their print brochure thrown online with minimal strategy. The term used for this static and ineffective site is brochureware. Some business owners feel that all they can afford is a single static page with their contact information and some marketing content written for a typical three-fold brochure.

Brochureware is a waste of time and money. Before putting your print brochure online as your Web site, consider these arguments:

- ➲ The content of a print brochure will most likely be too wordy for the Web.
- ➲ The layout of a print brochure may not work well on a Web page and will need to be redesigned.
- ➲ Your print brochure does not need to be navigated as a Web site does, so more planning is needed to develop the site's structure.
- ➲ The images in your brochure will need to be resized and optimized for the Web.

In general, a print brochure is flat whereas a Web site should be thought of as multidimensional. Developing a Web site is vastly different from designing a print brochure.

You can use your print brochure as a starting point for your Web site. A good Web developer can take a brochure and rethink the design and content to make a basic but effective Web site that is still consistent with the look and feel of your brochure and other marketing collateral. In some cases, companies actually create their print collateral after their Web site design is established, using the planning process and final results of their Web site to determine their overall branding.

Ways to Market Well

A basic informational site has limited marketing value for your company. Consider adding features and elements that will turn a basic Web site into a proactive and interactive marketing tool. At the very least, implement a feature on your Web site's home page so visitors can subscribe to an e-newsletter. This feature is the most basic form of permission marketing, getting people to give you permission to send them information via e-mail.

Understanding Viral Marketing

Viral marketing, like permission marketing, is a strategy well suited for the Web. The Wikipedia (*www.wikipedia.org*) definition of viral marketing is "marketing techniques that use pre-existing social networks to produce increases in brand awareness, through self-replicating viral processes, analogous to the spread of pathological and computer viruses." The Internet enhances word-of-mouth delivery of information, particularly through the use of e-mail.

How It Works

Think of viral marketing as you having a virus (an idea, a product, a Web feature) that infects others, and they in turn infect more people. Viral marketing works when you have something that generates enough interest that other people want to spread the word about it.

The Internet is the perfect place to get viral because of the fast and easy nature of communicating via e-mail. One e-mail message from you could be quickly and effortlessly passed along to other people when one person forwards your e-mail to people he knows, and they, in turn, forward the same e-mail to their contacts.

Common examples of viral e-mail messages are the jokes, images, poems, urban legends, and heartwarming stories that are forwarded by e-mail to dozens of people at a time because the recipients feel compelled to share them. Other people forward these e-mails because they have struck a chord. Many of these messages are forwarded along because e-mail makes doing so incredibly fast and easy.

Kings of Viral Marketing

The free Web-based e-mail service, Hotmail.com, implemented one of the most successful yet most basic examples of viral marketing. The company needed an enormous number of subscribers to establish a viable business model, that is, to make money. In order to grow their number of subscribers, they placed a small text "ad" on the bottom of every e-mail that each Hotmail subscriber sent, something to the effect of "Get your private, free e-mail at http://www.hotmail. com." The message linked directly to Hotmail.com's Web site. Millions of people subscribed to the free service, many finding Hotmail.com by clicking on the link at the bottom of an e-mail they received. Microsoft later purchased Hotmail.com in a stock swap deal that was estimated at over $400 million. Not a bad return for a simple viral marketing message!

Tell a Friend

Creating a compelling and valuable e-mail is the easiest way to get started with viral marketing. If you have an e-mail newsletter, for example, fill it with useful information that could appeal to many people. Your list subscribers may forward your e-newsletter to others. Putting a statement in your e-newsletter as obvious as "Please pass this along to a friend or colleague" can encourage others to hit the Forward button.

Your Web site is the perfect place to implement other viral marketing features. One such simple feature is the "Tell a Friend" or "E-mail This Article" feature. Most Web-based publications implement this feature through a button or link at the top or bottom of each article they publish online.

From Scope to Hallmark and Beyond

Anyone who has been using the Web since the mid-1990s may remember one of the earliest uses of e-postcards by a major company. Procter & Gamble was one of the first big corporations to experiment with the Web for marketing. They developed a system by which people could send "kisses" through their Web site. The recipient would receive an e-mail with a link saying that someone had sent her a kiss. Clicking on the link would lead her to the Web site marketing the mouthwash Scope, and the visitor would see a big graphic of a lipstick kiss with a greeting and marketing message pertaining to Scope. At that time, most people didn't seem to care that the message was commercial. They were willing to send kisses to everyone they knew, driving traffic to a company's marketing site for a product. In those days, though the marketing didn't even have the name "viral marketing," it clearly was. These days, one of the most popular uses of e-postcards is sending e-cards through companies such as Hallmark. The Hallmark.com Web site contains an extensive selection of free electronic greeting cards, most of which are animated with sound. The site also carries e-cards for sale as well as print cards that can be ordered or mailed directly from the company. Hallmark uses the free e-cards for the viral effect by encouraging the recipient of a card to send a card to someone else. This viral act is encouraged with a button at the end of every card to "Send a Hallmark Card." A popular example of a company not in the business of sending e-cards but using them to drive traffic to their site is CareerBuilder.com whose ad agency developed Monk-e-Mail (www.monk-e-mail.com), a hilarious card-builder using monkey images and digitized voices to "speak" messages to recipients.

When someone clicks on the "E-mail This Article" button or link, he is presented with a small Web-based form where he can enter his e-mail address as well as the addresses of friends or colleagues he thinks might be interested. An e-mail is sent to each recipient, usually containing the article headline, the first few sentences of the article, and a link directly to the Web page containing the full article.

An example of getting the most out of the "Tell a Friend" feature can be found on Amazon.com. On every product page throughout the site, customers can "Share This Product" with others. Recipients receive an e-mail with a message letting them know that their friend or colleague thought they might be interested in the product with a link back to the exact page on Amazon.com, where they can instantly order it themselves. Amazon.com shoppers are marketing Amazon's products for the company and not even getting paid to do it.

Your Web developer can implement a "Tell a Friend" feature on your business Web site. First, you need to determine what you have of value that visitors may want to tell others about. If you have a lot of useful content on your site, an "E-mail This Article" button makes sense. If you have an online catalog, a "Share This Product" button should work well for getting your shoppers to encourage others to visit your site and buy something.

Web Sites for Customer Support

In addition to marketing, a Web site can be a valuable customer service tool for your company. The fact that a Web site is online twenty-four hours a day, seven days a week, 365 days a year makes for an effective support tool, but only if it contains information that can directly serve customer needs.

Building a Better Resource

Providing customer service to your customers through your Web site can help you to achieve a number of goals, including these:

- ➲ Building customer loyalty
- ➲ Encouraging positive word of mouth
- ➲ Reducing customer calls that require staff response
- ➲ Attracting new customers
- ➲ Closing a sale

To make a Web site truly customer-service oriented, you should evaluate your customer's needs based on the kinds of questions they ask. Whatever you may do offline to help a customer, think of ways you can translate those actions onto your Web site.

Features for Support

While many customer service features do not require a staff person on the other end to make them work, some do. As a business owner you need to weigh both the short-term costs of building the features and the long-term cost savings of implementing them.

Some common customer-support features that can be integrated into a company Web site include the following:

- Auto responder
- FAQ
- Searchable databases
- Fill-in forms
- Calculators
- Live chat support

An auto responder is a non-Web-based feature that can send an automated e-mail response to an e-mail inquiry from a customer. The most effective auto responders give a timeframe for response and encourage the recipient to read the company's FAQ. A FAQ can be summarized in an auto responder e-mail, or the e-mail can link to the FAQ on the company's Web site to lead customers to likely answers to their questions. Often they will find the information they need in the FAQ, but if not, at that point staff can be in touch with them.

Using searchable databases, you can give customers or potential customers access to large amounts of information about your products and services and allow them to search that information by topic or keyword. **Any large amount of data can be managed effectively through the use of databases that are integrated into Web sites.** You can make those databases searchable with a typical search field place on a Web page—often the home page of a site—that allows visitors to search keywords and more easily find the information they need.

Fill-in forms, templates, and calculators can be used in a variety of ways. For example, an insurance agent can prequalify a customer for a loan using a fill-in form that can be submitted anytime. A printer can have a customer create a template for business cards that can be easily downloaded and printed. A mortgage company might include calculators on its Web site so customers can calculate relevant costs.

A more advanced customer support feature is live chat support. While live chat support does require staff on the other end of the computer responding to requests, because of the nature of Web-based chat, it is possible for a staff person to field several inquiries at once versus one phone call at a time.

Customer Relationship Management (CRM)

Customer relationship management (CRM) is the process by which companies manage their relationships with their customers or clients by capturing and analyzing customer information. According to Wikipedia (www.wikipedia.org), there are three types of CRM: operational, supporting customers with a sales or service representative; collaborative, directly communicating with customers through self-service tools; and analytical, analyzing customer data. Using Web-based features to provide automated customer service tools would be considered collaborative CRM and could include FAQs, e-mails with auto responders, and peer-to-peer online forums.

Web Sites for Selling

Not every business needs to sell something online. However, if you are selling products or services, in most cases this can be done effectively through a Web site. Building a sales site by adding to a marketing site doesn't always work. You are better off redesigning the entire site with selling in mind rather than tacking on an online store as an afterthought.

Best Features for Sales

On any site where you are selling something, make clear what you are selling. If visitors to your site cannot see immediately that you have products for sale or that they can hire you, your Web site is missing the mark.

A major but all-too-common mistake for product companies is failing to put images of their products on the home page of their site. Be obvious. You can't sell something through your Web site if people don't know you are selling something, much less what you are selling.

Some of the features on a sales Web site that make it more effective include these:

- ➲ Crisp, fast-loading images of products
- ➲ Concise descriptions of products or services
- ➲ Easy and prominently placed ways to purchase a product
- ➲ Clear pricing (or a way to contact for pricing)
- ➲ A seamless, straightforward shopping cart system
- ➲ Clearly stated privacy, security, and return policies
- ➲ Customer service features and customer support

Selling services through a Web site most often translates to marketing yourself and your services on your Web site and encouraging people to contact you to hire you to perform those services. Though it does not usually mean taking payments for services through your Web site, it could.

Shopping-Cart Experiences

Regardless of what you sell online, products or services, make sure the moment a person goes to make a purchase, the technology is invisible, meaning the shopping experience is as painless as possible.

The most basic shopping cart experience starts with a person deciding to purchase a product. The person should be able to take these steps:

1. Select the number of items he'd like to purchase.
2. Click a button to buy the product.
3. Arrive at the shopping cart page, where he has the option to change the number of items, delete items, go back to shopping, or go to checkout.
4. Select "Checkout" and be brought to a screen asking for contact, shipping, and payment information.
5. Submit information to make the transaction; at this point, the purchase is totaled for review.
6. Review his entire order and edit as needed.
7. Approve the purchase with the click of a button.
8. Receive an e-mail verifying his order.

Some additional features that can be added to the shopping-cart experience but also add significantly to the cost of building the online store include the following:

➲ **Registration:** Lets a customer register and submit some or all of her contact and credit card information to be saved for future purchases

➲ **Wish list or favorites:** Allows a customer to save her favorite items to purchase easily later or to save a wish list

➲ **Past purchase history:** Remembers a customer's past purchases to create a reference or a shopping list for purchasing them again

➲ **Recommendations:** Makes recommendations for other products to a customer based on their previous purchases

➲ **Personal shopper:** Allows a customer to submit personal preferences or specific needs to receive custom recommendations and links to relevant products

For security reasons, many online stores will not store complete customer credit card information.

The Fully Functional Web Site

A Web site is only good when both the front-end design and back-end programming of the site work together to create a seamless experience for the user. Unless you own a technology company, the technology should be invisible to someone who visits your Web site.

Front-End Functionality

The front end of a Web site is also called the graphical user interface, or the interface or GUI (pronounced "gooey") for short. Some of the elements of a Web site's interface that need to be considered in order to design an effective Web site include these:

1. The Navigation Bar or Nav Bar consists of buttons or links across the top, left side, or right side of a Web page and allows the user to navigate the Web site.

2. The color combination, including background color and font colors, can drastically affect the usability of a site.

3. Web site designs can end up too boxy because the designer doesn't know how to vary the shapes and the easiest shape to render on a Web page is square.

4. The amount of space between text and images can make a Web page seem clean and orderly or crowded and chaotic.

5. Whether using photographs or illustrations, the graphics on a Web page should complement the text and draw the eye to make a point or encourage an action.

6. Most Web sites use columns, usually two or three, to space out and organize text and images.

The Web site's interface is not only important in making a Web site appear professional, attractive, and appealing but also in making it useable. Working with an experienced Web designer helps ensure your Web site is more than just the elements of an effective Web site but that those elements are well executed and designed to achieve specific business goals.

Back-End Transparency

In the same way that the front-end design of a Web site should be invisible to the user and help facilitate a site's functionality, the back-end technology used to make the site interactive should be equally transparent. Technology or programming that can help make a site more functional and interactive includes the following:

Java is used to produce standalone applications or mini applications called applets, such as a Web site advertising tracking and ad banner rotation program.

Javascript is used within HTML to create functions, such as pull-down menus or mouse-over changes, in which placing the cursor over a graphic changes that graphic.

Databases are used to store large amounts of data (text, images, audio, video files); these can be integrated into a Web site and searched.

PHP or Perl are programming languages for Web features such as submission forms, surveys, and message boards; they are often used to create dynamic content or functionality on a site by interacting with databases.

Macromedia Flash or Shockwave are most commonly used for animation and interactive Web-based games, entertainment, and presentations.

ColdFusion or Active Server Pages (ASP) are used to create dynamic, interactive Web pages either by interacting with databases or drawing elements from a Web server.

Because HTML code is more like the building blocks of a Web site, it is limited in what contribution it can make to a site's functionality. Therefore other programming languages and software must be integrated into a Web site or into the HTML to make most interactive features on a site work.

Web Pages That Suck

Believe it or not, there is actually a Web site called Web Pages That Suck (www .webpagesthatsuck.com) created over a decade ago by Vincent Flanders, an author who speaks about Web design and usability issues. The philosophy behind the site is that you can learn good Web design by analyzing badly designed sites. Web Pages That Suck includes articles and checklists to help you assess your own site as well as links and commentary on other sites that do something wrong. This includes bad color combinations to long scrolling pages to what Flanders calls "mystery meat navigation," where navigational links are difficult to understand or even hard to find.

Web Sites Gone Bad

Determining what makes a Web site bad versus good can be very subjective. One person's idea of a beautiful design is another person's idea of horrible. A business Web site should be judged as good or bad by determining if it is effective or ineffective at achieving your company's goals. That said, there are some basic Web design rules to make a good Web site versus a bad one.

Design Chaos

A well-designed Web site balances all of the elements of design to create not only a visually pleasing page but also one that gives the right amount of weight to the most important features and content of a site. **Knowing how the human eye responds to visuals is key to creating an interface that appears uncluttered and clear versus out of control.** Here are some common design mistakes that can create pure chaos on a Web page:

- Using too many different colors on a page
- Using clashing colors, such as a red font color on a black background
- Using too many photographs or too many images on a single page
- Using images and photographs in too many sizes or shapes
- Using unnecessary animations on a page

Before approving a Web site design, ask yourself, "Can I get away with less?" If the answer is yes, pare down, use things sparingly, and reduce page content—both text and images—to the bare essentials. The overall design of a site should never distract from the business goals at hand.

Information Overload

The kiss of death for most Web sites is too much content on a page. A vast amount of content within a Web site can make it a valuable resource, but that content should be displayed in appropriate amounts and organized formats.

Here are some common Web content mistakes that can bog down or clutter up a Web site:

- ➲ Using too much text and images on any given page
- ➲ Using full pages of text without any variation in layout
- ➲ Using too many font sizes or font faces on a page
- ➲ Using all capital letters for text or centering all text
- ➲ Using long scrolling pages of text without easily accessible navigation tools

The adage "too much of a good thing" can be applied to bad Web sites. Most Web sites that don't work well—from a technological standpoint, from a business standpoint, or both—are often overdesigned or overprogrammed. Conversely, the adage "less is more" can be a mantra to help keep Web development and design under control.

▶▶ **TEST DRIVE**

Before embarking on a Web development process, make sure you know what your Web site will do for your company then determine the best way to do it. Some things to consider include the following:

- ➲ What will my Web site marketing accomplish for my company?
- ➲ How can I integrate viral marketing tactics into my Web site or marketing e-mails?
- ➲ How can my Web site provide customer service to save the company time and money?

Download Time Is Key

Learning how to build a Web site is probably not the best use of your time when there is other business at hand. However, it can be useful to know some basic techniques of Web design when speaking with your Web developer. Knowing how something is done can help to demystify the process to make it more difficult for a Web developer to mislead or overcharge you.

Rules of the Load

Whatever you do on your Web site, however it is designed, make sure each page downloads quickly. That's key to having a site that is accessible to not only customers but also potential customers.

As more and more people are getting online via faster connections such as ISDN, DSL, and cable modem, rules for the size of files on a Web page becomes less of an issue. Knowing your audience is an important step toward figuring out what kind of load you can put on a visitor's computer. Keep in mind that people in rural parts of the country or in other countries may not have the same high-speed connection you might have at your company.

Here are some basic rules to keep in mind about Web page load:

1. Your home page should load in fifteen to twenty seconds (in a perfect world).
2. Keep each page size to an average of 250KB for high-speed connections and 50KB for slow connections.
3. Each image or other file loading on a Web page should average less than 100KB.
4. Limit the number of files that need to load on each page, such as Java applets, animation, and audio or video files.
5. Limit any special effects on your home page that could prevent someone with an older Web browser or slower connection from accessing the rest of your site.

A slow-loading home page can turn people off and send them away before they actually enter your site. You should test the speed of your Web site pages on a variety of computers, operating systems, Web browsers, and modes of Internet access.

Here's an example of Web page download speeds depending on the speed of Internet access:

Connection Rate	Download Time
14.4K	179.02 seconds
28.8K	89.51 seconds
33.6K	76.72 seconds
56K	46.03 seconds
ISDN (128K)	14.10 seconds
T1 (1.44 Mbps)	1.22 seconds

As you can see, a Web page that loads within fifteen seconds on an ISDN connection could take almost a minute to load on a 56K dial-up modem.

Test Your Site

There are a number of free Web site optimization and testing services available online that instantly measure the download time of your Web pages. Since the home page load time is most critical, test that first at sites like Websiteoptimiz ation.com or SiteReportCard.com. Keep in mind that some of these free analysis sites may be older and might give you a review or advice based on slower Internet access speeds. Still, it is helpful to get some quick technical feedback on your home page download time to determine if you need to reassess the images and files embedded on the page. Some companies also sell software that tests Web page loads.

Having Multiple Sites

One solution some companies employ to address the issue of download time and customers accessing the Internet at different speeds is to create two separate sites—one for high-speed connections and the other to be viewed on slower dial-up connections. The main downside to multiple sites is that it can be a cumbersome and expensive tactic for smaller businesses.

If you decide you'd like to create two different sites, your home page becomes the gateway to both sites. You should include a basic marketing statement about your company, then give the visitor the choice of entering the high-speed or low-speed site by clicking on a link. Make this gateway page simple and fast-loading; it defeats the entire purpose of having two separate sites when a person has trouble accessing the gateway page.

Understanding File Sizes

The way file sizes are measured can be confusing. There is a byte, a kilobyte, a megabyte, and a gigabyte. Learning some basic file sizes can help you understand whether your graphics, images, audio files, or video files are too large and will be difficult to download.

Define Size

Here is a conversion chart for the most common file sizes to help them make sense:

Bit: The smallest unit of measurement in computing; valued at either 1 or 0. Not commonly used to designate a file size because it is so small.

8 bits: Equals 1 byte.

1,024 bytes: Equals 1 kilobyte (KB), the unit most commonly used to designate image or smaller audio file sizes.

1,024 kilobytes: Equals 1 megabyte (MB), the unit more commonly used to designate audio or video file sizes.

1,024 megabytes: Equals 1 gigabyte (GB).

An easier but less exact way of measuring file sizes is rounding the numbers down to 1,000 so the conversion would be as follows:

➲ 1,000 bytes equals 1 kilobyte.
➲ 1,000 kilobytes equals 1 megabyte.
➲ 1,000 megabytes equals 1 gigabyte.

Another way to look at this is that 1 billion bytes equals 1 million kilobytes that in turn equals 1,000 megabytes or 1 gigabyte.

Bigger Bytes

There was a time when megabytes were considered very large units of measurement. Then came the gigabyte, 1,000 times as big as a megabyte. There are already terms for even large units of measurement. The next size up is a terabyte (TB) equal to 1,024 gigabytes. The U.S. Library of Congress claims to have about 20 terabytes of text, and the Web site Ancestry.com claims that it has 600 terabytes of genealogical data, including data from the U.S. Census dating from 1790 to 1930. Terabytes are followed by a petabyte (PB), exabyte (EB), zettabyte (ZB), and then a yottabyte (YB). According to Wikipedia, back in 2003, Google had between 2 and 5 petabytes of hard-disk storage.

Data Transfer Sizes

While files are measured in bytes, the speed of an Internet connection is measured in bits. A kilobit is a data communications measurement that equals approximately 1,000 bits and measures the amount of data that is transferred in one second between two points, such as between a Web server and a personal computer. The abbreviation for kilobits is Kb. To measure the speed of data transfer, we use the abbreviation Kbps, or kilobits per second. When talking about Internet access speeds, here is how kilobits are designated:

➲ 14.4 Kbps equals 14,400 bits per second.
➲ 28.8 Kbps equals 28,800 bits per second.
➲ 56 Kbps equals 56,000 bits per second.
➲ 128 Kbps equals 128,000 bits per second.

Modem speeds are written with a "K" such as 14.4K, 28.8K, 56K and 128K.

Graphic Files 101

While there are many graphic file formats in graphic design, including bitmap (.bmp), tagged image file format (TIFF), and picture (PICT), on the Web, there are only two that are specific to Web sites: joint photographic experts group (JPEG) and graphics interchange format (GIF).

JPEG Versus GIF

GIFs, pronounced with either a soft or a hard "g," are used predominantly for illustrations, line drawings, graphics, and the like. When converting a standard graphic file into a Web-ready GIF file, the process "throws away" colors and reduces the number of colors in the image to a maximum of 256 colors to reduce the size of the image file. Unlike JPEGs, GIFs can be used in animation files.

Color Modes

Color modes determine the way a file is encoded as a graphic and affect the colors of the file. The most common color modes are RGB (red, green, blue), used for display on computer monitors; CMYK (cyan, magenta, yellow, black), usually used for four-color process printing; HSB (hue, saturation, brightness); grayscale; and indexed color, which is limited to 256 colors and is the only mode used by GIFs and Web colors that are safe for a more limited Web color palette. To convert a graphic file from CMYK to indexed color, first convert the image to RGB color and then to indexed color.

JPEGS were created by photo experts and are more often used for photographs on the Web. Instead of throwing away or removing colors from an image, JPEG files are compressed to decrease the file size without affecting the clarity of the image as much as a GIF.

In addition to being smaller files, the resolution of both GIFs and JPEGs is only 72 dots per inch (dpi). If you are familiar with printing photographs or detailed graphics, you know the minimum resolution for high-quality printing is 300 dpi, and fine printing is done at 600 dpi or higher. Web browsers cannot read images with a resolution higher than

72 dpi. At a low resolution of 72 dpi, images cannot be enlarged and printed out without becoming fuzzy or pixilated.

Designers and developers debate whether GIFs load more quickly than JPEGs. Experiments have rendered mixed results although most people think that GIFs load faster. It is probably more accurate to say that line art or black-and-white photos or illustrations will load more quickly than images containing more colors.

Sizing and Manipulating Graphics

If you want to use images from your printed marketing materials on your Web site, you will most likely have to manipulate and optimize the graphic files.

Here are the basic steps for making graphics Web-ready as JPEGs. Note that these steps are specifically for Adobe Photoshop so there may be some variation in steps depending on the software product you use:

1. **Use a photo imaging software program**, such as Photoshop, to size your image while it is still at a high resolution.
2. **Save the image as a JPEG.** The imaging software should automatically convert the graphic file to a JPEG. The suffix will be .jpg.

Here are the basic steps for making graphics Web ready as GIFs:

1. **Use a photo imaging software program,** such as Photoshop, to size your image while it is still at a high resolution.
2. **Convert the file from RGB color mode to indexed color mode.** In Photoshop, select Image, then Mode, then Indexed Color.
3. **Select Palette.** Choices include Adaptive, Uniform, Web, or Custom. Adaptive is the more common choice.
4. **Select Color Depth.** The standard selection is 8 bit/pixel or 8 bits of color information per pixel.
5. **Select the number of colors.** At 8 bit/pixel, the number of colors is 256. You can select fewer to decrease the file size, but it will affect image clarity.

6. You have the option to select Dither: Diffusion, None, or Pattern (for Mac OS or Web palette). Dithering mixes pixels of available colors to fill in missing colors. The simple choice is None.

7. Save the image as a CompuServe GIF. The suffix will be .gif.

Grayscale images are easily converted to either JPEG or GIF without additional settings choices. If you have a color image, to convert it to grayscale, you'll need to discard color information. Then save the image in the file format you prefer. GIF is an appropriate file format for grayscale or black-and-white images. For photographs, you may still want to use JPEG files to maintain more clarity.

The Art of Web-Page Layout

There is no one right way to lay out a Web page, but there are general rules for design, both offline and online, that should be taken into consideration when organizing a Web page layout. Knowing both the basics of good design and also the differences between print design and Web design is important for a Web designer.

Copyrighting Look and Feel

The look and feel of Web sites and software can be protected from copyright infringement only when the parts of the site or software interface that have been copied by someone else are actually recognized as protected under copyright law. A famous example of a look-and-feel dispute came about when Apple Computers sued Microsoft claiming that the Windows operating system copied the Macintosh operating system's look and feel. They lost the lawsuit because a judge found that in an original agreement with Microsoft, Apple had given Microsoft a license to use certain elements they now claimed were copied. The judge declared other elements Apple claimed were owned by them were not copyrightable.

The Politics of Pink

Back in 1995, my company created Femina.com, the first searchable directory for women's-issue Web sites. Because I was the sole Web designer in the company at that time, it was up to me to design the site. Colored background on a Web page was a relatively new HTML feature—up until then all pages had been gray—so I decided to use a light pink background on every page of the site. My choice was based solely on the fact that my favorite color was pink. I began receiving hate e-mail from women who were offended that I created a Web site for women using the color pink. I was told that the site was demeaning and stereotyping women. The women e-mailing me were the very ones whom I was trying to serve with a useful resource. I stubbornly held onto the original design because I thought, "This is my company, my site, and my favorite color." I failed to put the customer first. I also failed to take feedback constructively and apply it to improving the site. Finally, I put my ego aside and changed the background color to white. I never heard another complaint, and Femina.com went on to become the top searchable directory for women's issues Web sites.

Look and Feel

When you speak with your Web developer, you may hear her talking about the look and feel of a Web site, another way of talking about the GUI. She is referring to both the appearance and the functionality of a site. **The look of a site encompasses more than just the design but also the way text and images are laid out, colors and shapes used, and even the font faces.** The feel of the site involves how a user interacts with links, buttons, menus, and other features that affect the user's experience on a Web page.

An aspect of the look and feel of a Web site is usability. Usability means how effectively and efficiently a user can perform certain tasks within a Web site, including how quickly he can navigate it or find things and whether or not he can easily do what he set out to do on the site, such as buy something.

You can measure usability objectively by noting how many errors occur when a person uses your site. For example, if many people abandon their shopping carts when buying something from your site, there could be a usability issue. Or if most people leave your Web site after only viewing the home page, unclear navigation could be a barrier to entry.

Usability can also be measured subjectively by surveying users as to their personal preferences regarding your site. Every person is different about what he or she perceives as easy to use, but if you know your target audience, you can begin to determine if the people you are trying to reach through your Web site might find your site usable or not.

Layout Options

A Web page can consist of vertical columns of varying widths or sometimes even horizontal columns. Some pages use an invisible table in the HTML to position text and images in an almost grid-like fashion, filling in rows and columns of cells. Other pages have a more flowing layout with images appearing intermittently between page text in various positions.

Working with White Space

White space is not blank or empty space. On a Web page, white space is any part of the page that is left purposely unmarked. This includes the margins of the page and space between images, between lines of text, between columns and rows, and between text and images. Less white space makes a page appear more cluttered. Adding more white space can open up a page, giving it a cleaner appearance. Filling up every space on a page, particularly a home page, can render it aesthetically unappealing, decreasing its usability and effectiveness.

Most Web pages have the following elements:

1. **Header of page:** Usually where you identify the name of your company, your name or the name of your site
2. **Navigation:** Links or buttons across the top, left or right side of a Web page that allows visitors access further into the site
3. **Body:** The main content area of the page that can be narrower the more columns used in the layout

4. Margins: When using columns, margins can be created with the use of narrower columns on the left or right side or both sides and can be used for additional content or advertisements

5. Footer: Where you can place text links to the main sections of your site as well as copyright information and links to privacy and other site policies

The most important page layout to plan is the home page. The goal is to choose a layout that is uncluttered but can contain the elements you need and present them in an organized fashion.

Navigation Needs

When it comes to navigating a Web site, many sites use one or more of these common navigation elements:

1. Navigation bars: A cohesive strip or bar containing links to the main sections of a Web site

2. Navigation buttons: Buttons, usually rounded or squared, that are not connected and are instead lined up horizontally or vertically

3. Navigation links: Text links rather than graphics used for navigation

4. Pull-down menus: Vertical menus appear as a pull-down list when clicked on

5. Drop-down hovering navigation: Submenu appears either vertically or horizontally when a cursor is placed over a main category on a navigation bar or button

6. Search box: Box that for larger, content-rich sites enhances the navigation of a site (should not be the sole means of navigating)

Whatever the navigation tool for your Web site, it should be simple, clear, straightforward, and easy to use.

The Psychology of Web Design

In order to design the most effective site that is not only appealing to your target market but gets them to take the actions you want them to take, you need to get into the minds of your customers. What are their preferences? What do they like and dislike on a Web site? How do they use the Web?

On the Web, content should be concise and to the point. Most of the actions you want a visitor to perform on your site—fill out a form, request more information, contact you, buy something—can sometimes be achieved through statements on your site. You need to make sure the design of your site enhances the messages you are trying to convey.

Attracting the Eyes

As people spend more time on the Web, they become accustomed to seeing certain site features in certain locations. A help link or button is often on the top right part of a Web page. A "buy this item" or "add to cart" button is usually to the right of the image of a product. Place action-oriented features where people expect to see them.

The Below-The-Fold Rule

In newspaper publishing, the most important headlines of the day are positioned at the top portion of the front page, or "above the fold" of a newspaper folded in half. On the Web, the same principle applies to Web page design. The imaginary "fold" is at the bottom of a Web page when viewed on a computer monitor before a visitor scrolls to see the rest of the page. Since computer monitors vary in sizes, the amount of a Web page that first appears in a browser window varies. Many Web designers use laptop screens as their guide for page design. All essential information is then positioned toward the upper portion of a home page.

If people are reading from left to right, their eyes will most likely pause at the right side of a Web page before scanning back to the left. If you want someone to subscribe to an e-newsletter, don't place the form where she must submit her e-mail address at the bottom of your Web page. Bring it up higher on the page and place it on the right side of the page versus the left side to encourage more people to subscribe.

Placement is not the only way to attract a visitor's eyes to a key area. Use colors and shapes to attract the eyes toward action-oriented features. An unusual shape such as a star will attract more attention than a rectangle or circle. Something in yellow bordered in red will pop off the page more than something in light blue with a green border.

Understanding how people look at a Web page and what catches the eye is helpful when designing a Web site, selecting colors and shapes, and organizing content and images. Take care not to overdo eye-catching elements as too many can create clutter, chaos, and confusion.

Cues and Hints

Some aspects of Web design are much more subtle than just choosing the right color combinations or the most pleasing shapes. Color and shape can also be used to give a visual cue to the visitor that she has moved to a different section of a site.

There are obvious ways to designate a new section of a site as well as more subtle ways. An obvious way is to give each section a prominent header, such as "About Us" or "Our Services," telling visitors where they are on the site. A subtle way to designate the difference is to change the color of the navigation button. If all the navigation buttons are blue with white letters, when the visitor gets to the "About Us" section, the button can turn to red with white letters. This change may be small, but if it has a subconscious impact on the visitor to let her know where she is on the site, that contributes to the site's usability.

Don't take for granted how changes on a page can impact the way a person perceives where she is on a site or where she should go. A good Web designer knows not only the psychology of how people use Web sites and view Web pages but also the design and technological techniques that can influence how your Web site is used.

▶▶ TEST DRIVE

Although you will most likely be working with a Web designer, there are issues you can determine before hiring someone that can make the Web design process easier. Consider the following:

- ⮞ Will my site consist mostly of text or images as well?
- ⮞ Will the images be mostly graphics or photographs?
- ⮞ In what format are the graphics or photographs and are they accessible so I can provide them to my Web developer?
- ⮞ What colors represent my brand, and what additional colors might I approve of for use on the Web site?
- ⮞ What do I know about my customers and how they use Web sites?
- ⮞ How can I find out more from customers about how they use the Web?

PART **3**

Building Your Online Presence

Intro to Basic HTML

HTML consists of tags that specify how a Web browser should read a page, including text styles, colors, images, and layout. In the early days of the Web, the number of tags were limited, making it easy to learn in less than an hour the tags needed to construct basic Web pages and link them together to build a Web site. Today, HTML is only the foundation of a Web page or Web site, and most sites contain additional programming such as Javascript, Perl, or PHP to create more dynamic pages or interactive features. Also, many sites use cascading style sheets (CSS), which are like templates that carry out a page design across an entire site for consistency. The following information applies to pages designed without CSS. Your Web developer may opt to use CSS instead of straight HTML, however, understanding some basic tags is helpful.

Basic Tags

HTML tags are always contained within pointed brackets (< and >). The first tag on every Web page, for example, is <HTML>, which immediately tells the Web browser that the page is, in fact, a Web page.

When you open several tags in a row, the first tag you open will be the last tag you close. For example, if you open tags such as <P><B><FONT SIZE="1"> then you will close them </FONT></B></P>.

Open and Closed Tags

Some HTML tags open then close while others are simply placed and act without needing to be opened or closed. Tags that open and close will first affect the text that follows. The tag for open HTML is <HTML>. When that particular tag is no longer needed to affect the text on the Web page, it closes: </HTML>. All closing tags have a slash in front of the tag name to designate it is closing or ending the tag at that point.

Every Web page is programmed within the following tags:

<HTML>
<HEAD>

```
<TITLE>
</TITLE>
</HEAD>
<BODY>
</BODY>
</HTML>
```

Here is what these main tags mean:

1. **<HTML>** specifies the page is a Web page.
2. **<HEAD>**opens the head tag. The head of a Web page contains the title and can also contain tags and programming such as Meta Tags and Javascript.
3. **<TITLE>** opens the title tag and is followed only by the title of the page.
4. **</TITLE>** closes the title tag immediately after the title of the page.
5. **</HEAD>**closes the head of the Web page.
6. **<BODY>** opens the body of the Web page. Everything after this will appear on the Web page when viewed through a Web browser.
7. **</BODY>** closes the body of the Web page. Appears toward the end of the Web page.
8. **</HTML>** closes the entire Web page and appears at the very end of a Web page.

Here are some other basic tags you'll see on a Web page:

1. **<P>** and **</P>** designate the beginning and end of a paragraph and add an extra space between paragraphs. Current browsers do not require the close-paragraph tag.
2. **
** places a line break between text without adding an extra space between lines versus using a paragraph break.
3. **<HR>** places a hard rule or a horizontal line between lines of text but is not used much anymore as Web page designs have become more sophisticated.

4. **<CENTER>** and **</CENTER>** are the original tags for centering text. Now alignment for paragraphs is contained within paragraph tags, such as <P ALIGN=CENTER> and </P>.

HTML tags can affect text and image positioning, font sizes, styles, and colors. They can create links between Web pages on the same Web site or can link to pages on other Web sites.

To Cap or Not to Cap

There isn't a hard-and-fast rule that HTML tags should either be in all capital letters or all lowercase letters. For consistency's sake, it is better to select one or the other rather than mixing cases. Using all capital letters for the tags, however, can be helpful to distinguish tags from other elements such as image names (often in lowercase) and URL paths (also mostly in lowercase). Anything that helps to differentiate the tags is easier on the eyes. For example, note how using capital letters in the tag <IMG SRC="images/photo.jpg" ALIGN="LEFT"> helps set apart the tags better than using all lowercase such as <img src="images/photo.jpg" align="left">.

Font Sizes and Styles

A page of text can be made more legible by the use of varying font sizes and font colors and faces. Don't use too many font faces or sizes on a single page, though. Use sans-serif fonts for headers and serif fonts for the majority of the text on the page. Also don't overuse bold—<B> and </B>—or italicized—<I> and </I>—text. Reading bolded or italicized text on a computer screen can be difficult.

On the Web, even though there is a tag to underline text—<U> and </U>—it is better not to underline any text that is not a link to another page or site. Most people who have used the Web for a while expect underlined text to represent live links on a Web page.

Some other tags that affect the size of the text are called headers. Headers are used like headlines on a page. They will increase the size of a font, bold it, and place a line break before and after the text to set it apart from the body text. Most Web designers refrain from using headers anymore because they tend to look clunky on a page. The larger font, bolding, and placement of the text can be achieved with other tags or by using graphics.

Header tags include the following:

<H1> and **</H1>**
<H2> and **</H2>**
<H3> and **</H3>**
<H4> and **</H4>**
<H5> and **</H5>**
<H6> and **</H6>**

The most commonly used header tags these days are H2 and H3.

Another way to affect font size is to specify either an exact size such as <FONT SIZE="1">. This opens the font size as "1," which specifies a 10-point font. The tag </FONT> closes it. You can also use a tag that tells the Web browser to read the font as plus or minus several points above or below the browser's default font size.

If a person has her Web browser set with a 12-point font size, "+1" means that the browser will display the font size as 14 point. Using "-1" in a font tag means the browser will display the same person's default font size as 10 point. You can increase font size incrementally by using +2, +3, etc. or decrease it by using "-2" or "-3," but for good Web design, don't make a font on a Web page too big or too small.

You can change the font face or font type using <FONT FACE="helvetica, arial"> to open it and specify which font faces to use and </FONT> to close it. You can list several font faces, and a person's Web browser will display the first one that can be found on his computer.

If your Web developer is using cascading style sheets, there is an entirely different way to designate the font size and face.

Embedding Images

There are a number of ways to embed an image into a Web page:

<IMG SRC="photo.jpg">: This embeds an image in the HTML page (in this case, the image is called "photo.jpg") without any alignment or text wrap designations.

<IMG SRC="images/photo.jpg">: This embeds the same image but uses a path to retrieve the image from a different directory (one called "images").

<IMG SRC="http://www.mysite.com/images/photo. jpg">: This embeds an image into a page on one site when the image actually resides on another Web site.

<IMG SRC="images/photo.jpg" ALIGN="LEFT">: This image tag has an alignment designation so that the image appears on the left side of the page and the text wraps around it on the right side.

<IMG SRC="images/photo.jpg" ALIGN="RIGHT">: This image tag has an alignment designation placing the image on the right side of the page with the text wrapping around it on the left side.

The path you insert into the tag to tell the browser where to find the image should most often lead to a directory on the Web server that hosts your Web site. Linking to images located on other sites could violate copyright, so always ask for permission before linking to someone else's image.

Linking Pages

One HTML tag that is a little different from the rest but is also one of the most "powerful" is the link tag that creates an HTML link out of either text or a graphic. The first part of the tag specifies where the link should go and is opened with <A HREF="page.html">. The tag is then closed or "anchored" with </A>. The text or image in between the opening and closing tags becomes a link. Below are examples of how you would write the HTML to make the following statements link to Web pages in various locations. If you viewed this list as a Web page, each line would appear as a link.

<A HREF="aboutus.html"> This links to the About Us page in the same directory.**</A>**

<A HREF="company/aboutus.html"> This links to the About Us page in a directory called "company."**</A>**

<A HREF="http://www.othersite.com/aboutus.html"> This links to the About Us page on another Web site.**</A>**

<A HREF ="http://www.othersite.com/aboutus.html" TARGET=NEW>This links to the About Us page on another Web site and opens a new browser window to display the page.**</A>**

When you link to other people's Web sites, you are not required to ask permission, but it is always a good idea. The Web is all about linking, networking, and relationships, so letting someone know that you've linked to her or his site could result in a return or reciprocal link that in turn could drive more traffic to your Web site.

Web Colors

The palette of Web-safe colors, meaning the colors that can be properly read by a Web browser and that will show up on various computer monitors, is limited to 256 colors. You cannot avoid some variation in color depending on the computer, the monitor, and the display settings.

Fonts can be displayed in different colors by opening the tag <FONT COLOR="red"> and using </FONT> to close it. A font tag can contain more than one style designation, and color can be one of those, such as <FONT SIZE="1" FACE="arial, Helvetica" COLOR="red">.

Color can also be used as the background on a Web page and is expressed as <BG BODYCOLOR="red">. For greatest legibility, using a light background with dark text is much better than a dark background with light text. Still, a Web browser will display any color you specify if you use the proper code although that same color may appear different depending on the quality of the computer monitor.

Not all colors can be written out in a font or body color tag, but the most common colors you can spell out include the following:

<FONT COLOR="white">white**</FONT>**
<FONT COLOR="black">black**</FONT>**

```
<FONT COLOR="red">red</FONT>
<FONT COLOR="green">green</FONT>
<FONT COLOR="blue">blue</FONT>
<FONT COLOR="aqua">aqua</FONT>
<FONT COLOR="yellow">yellow</FONT>
<FONT COLOR="brown">brown</FONT>
<FONT COLOR="gray">gray</FONT>
<FONT COLOR="pink">pink</FONT>
<FONT COLOR="magenta">magenta</FONT>
<FONT COLOR="purple">purple</FONT>
<FONT COLOR="violet">violet</FONT>
<FONT COLOR="brown">brown</FONT>
<FONT COLOR="orange">orange</FONT>
```

Another way to express specific colors in HTML is to use hexadecimal numbers. Hexadecimal (HEX) numbers include the # symbol in front of them. For the Web, twenty-four-bit colors are made up of three parts, RRGGBB, meaning the red component, the green component, and the blue component.

Hexadecimal numbers actually use both numbers and letters.

Here are some examples of hexadecimal numbers that represent colors on the Web:

- ➲ #000000: Black
- ➲ #FF0000: Red
- ➲ #0000FF: Blue
- ➲ #00FF00: Green
- ➲ #FFFF00: Yellow
- ➲ #FFFFFF: White

The Web has many hexadecimal charts, such as those at *www.html-color-codes.com*, and RGB-to-hexadecimal converters, such as those at *www.inquisitor.com/hex.html*, to help you select the right color and the proper HEX number. Keep in mind that just because you can find the right HEX number for the color you want, not every computer monitor will read the color in the same way.

Overview of Advanced Web Programming

Beyond the basics of HTML, there is still a great deal of programming used to build your Web site. Keeping up with the latest technology information is a challenge even for Web developers who build sites for a living. A cursory knowledge of the technology can help you better communicate what you want and need to use for your Web site.

XML and DHTML

Over time, HTML became too limiting for Web developers so new specifications for programming Web sites were developed by the World Wide Web Consortium (WC3), a group of companies involved with the Internet and Web. Extensible markup language (XML) is one of the specifications and is a markup language for documents that contain structured information, meaning both content and a role for that content. Content can include words, images, and sound. Content can have different roles such as the role of a footnote or the role of a caption. Most documents have a structure.

Where HTML tags are fixed, XML doesn't really consist of tags but is a system to describe markup languages so XML can define a tag then define the structural relationship between it and other tags. XML is "readable" by both humans and by machine.

The most important thing for you to know about XML is that it is used in both Web and database development. Most small businesses building a straightforward Web site will not need to use XML, but if customization is needed for a site, XML can come in handy. For the business owner, however, XML should be invisible.

If a Web developer emphasizes that he programs in XML, he is probably trying to demonstrate his technical prowess. It is more important for a Web developer to be able to use XML when a site warrants it and then to program it to be invisible to the non-programmer. In content-oriented Web sites, for example, the developer should build a content management system (CMS) to hide the XML so a non-programmer can edit the Web site content without having to worry about the HTML, XML, or any other markup or programming language.

Dynamic HTML (DHTML) is an extension of HTML that can make a page more dynamic using style sheets and Javascript. DHTML can be used to affect the following:

1. **Cascading style sheets (CSS),** which can be used for such things as creating a watermark on a Web page (an image that stays in place while text flows over it).

2. **Text can be modified or made to change dynamically.** For instance, text could move to another location on the Web page when a cursor is placed over it.

3. **Events are things that happen after an action.** For instance, a dialogue box with a message might pop up when you click on a Submit button.

4. **Forms such as input forms can be made easier to fill out.** For instance, after filling out your mailing address, clicking a button automatically makes it the billing address.

5. **Images can create effects** such as mouse-over images, changing the size and position of an image, or other animated effects on an image.

6. **Links can affect links** by making them blink, shake, change the text, space out letters in the text, or even change banner ads each time a page is refreshed.

A good Web programmer should be familiar with the standard and most commonly used programming and markup languages.

CGI Scripts, Perl, PHP, and Javascript

If a programmer is old school, she may be familiar with or common gateway interface (CGI) scripts that help trigger actions or perform functions between a Web page and a Web server. These scripts are most often written in a programming language such as PERL, C, or C++. For example, CGI scripts can be used to power Web forms. Once a person fills out a form on a Web site and hits the Submit button, the CGI script can then trigger actions such as these:

1. Submitting the contents of the form to the Web site owner via e-mail
2. Submitting the contents of the form into a database
3. Bringing up a page with a message such as one reading, "Thank you for filling out this form"
4. Pulling data from a database and publishing them on a Web page

PHP is a programming language often used in lieu of a CGI script to develop Web-based software applications in order to help create dynamic content on a Web site. PHP is compatible with many different types of databases and open source, meaning that the program is open to modification and improvements by other programmers.

Javascript is an open-source scripting language that adds interactivity to a Web site. Javascript can interact with HTML and be used to create features as basic as navigation buttons that change color when moused over or more complex features, such as forms that automatically check for errors or that calculate numbers for a total.

ColdFusion and ASP

Like CGI scripts and PHP, both ColdFusion and ASP help integrate databases into Web sites. ColdFusion is a development tool that has its own markup language separate from HTML. ASP stands for Active Server Pages, which are dynamically created HTML Web pages: The browser requests the ASP, and the Web server delivers an HTML page. You can recognize Web sites created in ColdFusion because the pages have .cfm at the end instead of .html. Active Server Pages are recognized by .asp at the end of each page.

Shockwave and Flash

Shockwave is a technology developed by Macromedia, Inc., that can add multimedia features to a Web page including audio, video, animation, and games. It works on both Macintosh and Windows-based computers. Other Adobe products need to be used to create a Shockwave "object" that is then referenced in an HTML page to pull up the object. Director is the authoring tool for Shockwave objects, and the program Afterburner is then used to compress the objects.

In order for users to see, hear, or interact with the Shockwave object, they must have a Shockwave plug-in loaded into their Web browser. These plug-ins or "add ons" to Web browsers are available free from the Adobe Web site. Flash is a multimedia authoring technology that is owned by Adobe and although originally used to create vector graphic animations, it now includes video and other graphics. Flash sites or elements also require a special plug-in to be viewed.

Basics of Search-Engine Optimization

Search engines operate through the use of software programmed to scour the Web, gathering URLs and Web page data then storing them in a database using an automated indexing system. The software that collects Web site information can be referred to as robots, bots, crawlers, or even spiders.

Search engine optimization (SEO) involves strategic planning of Web design, particularly from the standpoint of the HTML. The goal is to make it easier for search engines not only to collect the Web page data for their databases but to lift the right data so the indexing of the Web site or page is accurate. **The way a Web page is designed and the manner in which the HTML of that page appears can influence the way the page is described in the list of results for a search conducted on a search engine.**

Because search engines automate the gathering, archiving, and indexing of Web pages, the software may not always retrieve the most descriptive information about the page. When a Web page is programmed without considering SEO, the search engine's software may be unable to locate the proper content. Knowing even the basics of SEO can help ensure that your company's Web site is properly indexed in the most popular search engines.

Keeping Up with Search Engines

Everybody wants his Web site to come up first on search engines, meaning that when a potential customer conducts a search using particular keywords, the company's Web site is the first link at the top of the search results page.

While it is possible that your company's Web site will come up first when someone searches for your exact company name, it's less likely the site will show up in the top results from searching relevant keywords that describe what your company does.

History of Web Search Engines

In 1993, a student at MIT, Matthew Gray, developed the first Web crawler, called the World Wide Web Wanderer for Wandex, the first Web search engine. The first crawler-based, full-text search engine, Webcrawler, examined and indexed all the words on Web sites. Around the same time, Carnegie Mellon University released Lycos. Other search engines followed soon after including Infoseek, Northern Light, AltaVista, and Inktomi. At the time, these sites differed from Yahoo! by using software to index Web sites instead of humans. Google became popular around 2001. Yahoo! eventually implemented its own search engine technology in 2004 to compete with Google.

For example, if you own a travel agency called Jane Smith and Associates Travel, chances are good that anyone searching for your company's name on a popular search engine will see a link to your company Web site on or close to the top of the page. If, however, a person searches for "travel," there is little chance your company's name will show up, even on the first ten search results pages. The reason is because there are so many other companies out there offering the same or similar services in the travel sector. The competition is fierce for those top listings or first few search result pages.

If, however, your travel agency has a specific specialty, such as booking travel for single parents traveling with children, you've increased your odds by emphasizing this aspect of your business on your Web site and even in your Web site's HTML. If someone searches for "travel agency single parent with children," your company Web site is much more likely to show up at least on the first search results page.

Search engines constantly evolve as their creators develop new ways of refining searches. Some search engine companies license their search engine software to other search engine companies or some may purchase smaller companies' search engines, so one can never be sure which search engine is using what system. Trying to stay on top of the near-daily changes of search engine functionality is a full-time job, one that was taken on by the founder of SearchEngineWatch.com, an in-depth daily look at search engine developments that is a resource for understanding and leveraging search engines for marketing purposes.

Page Design for Search Engines

A good Web developer will know that there are certain aspects of Web design that can affect the way search engines automatically index a Web page or Web site. The most common obstacle search engine robots or spiders face is with tables that are used to form the main structure of a Web page. Many Web pages are laid out using HTML tables to place images and text in any position on a Web page instead of the standard flush left of regular HTML tags. A search engine, however, will often lift the first text it can find within an HTML page and access text within tables last.

If your company Web site, for example, uses HTML tables to contain the majority of the content on the home page of your site, the most critical information about your company may be less accessible to search engines. If your company site contains a few text links at the top of the home page outside of the HTML table such as "Contact Us," "Privacy Policy," and "Site Map," it is possible that the search engine will lift that text and index your Web site's home page accordingly. Therefore, when someone searches and finds your company's Web site in a search engine, the description might read "Contact Us Privacy Policy Site Map" instead of a proper description of your company.

There are simple techniques to assist search engines in properly indexing the site, including meta tags, title tags, ALT tags, and comment tags. While none of these HTML tags is a guarantee of higher listings in search engine results, they can improve the way in which your company site is listed in many of the search engines. Again, since search engines constantly change the way they index sites and deliver results, there is no guaranteed way to improve search engine placement other than either paying for the placement or spending an excessive amount of time— or paying someone else to spend time—optimizing your site for search engines and submitting and resubmitting your URL to the most popular search engines currently online.

Using Meta Tags

Meta tags are used at the top of the HTML source code of a Web page to feed search engine crawlers or bots specific keywords, site description, and other relevant information. Meta tags are commonly placed within the "head" of the HTML document or between the <HEAD> and </ HEAD> tags at the top of the page. While meta tags are not visible on the Web page itself when viewed through a browser, they are visible within the HTML source code of the page.

A number of components make up meta tags, including author (where you can designate the author of the page) and robots, where you can expressly allow search engine bots to index your Web page or prevent them from indexing the pages. The two most common parts are key-words and description.

Keyword Tags

The keywords meta tag, with sample content, looks like this:

```
<META NAME="keywords" content="freelance writer, writing,
speaker, women, woman, aliza sherman, cybergrrl, webgrrls,
femina, PowerTools, Internet, e-business, e-marketing, entrepre-
neur, business">
```

To create a keywords meta tag, select approximately twenty-five words that best describe your company, the business you are in, and other relevant descriptive words that might be used by a potential customer when searching for a company like yours. Some sites may use more than

| Inside Track | The Case of the Infringing Meta Tags |

If a direct competitor of your company puts your registered trademarks or service marks in its meta tags—such as your company name or trademarked product name—the company is infringing on your marks. There have been precedents for companies successfully getting their competitors to cease and desist infringing on their trademarks on Web sites, including meta tags.

In the case of Horphag Research Ltd. v. Larry Garcia, dba Healthierlife.com, Horphag owned the trademark Pycnogenol, used to market a pine bark extract product. Healthierlife.com, a direct competitor, sold a competing product called Masquelier's. Garcia of Healthierlife.com not only used Pycnogenol repeatedly in his Web site's meta tags, but also throughout the text in his site referred to his company's product as "Masquelier's: the original French Pycnogenol" and copied some of Pycnogenol's literature verbatim. Garcia also used the trademark Pycnogenol on other sites to create links to his own site.

The court found in favor of Horphag because the use of Pycnogenol throughout the Healthierlife.com site was deemed confusing to visitors who might be searching for Pycnogenol and mistakenly go to Healthierlife.com instead. The court also awarded the plaintiff "substantial attorneys' fees and costs to plaintiff as compensation for the costs incurred in pursuing its trademark infringement claim."

Garcia was deliberately using his competitor's trademark to boost his rankings on search engines and to attract his competitor's customers, not through competitive business strategies but through deceptive e-marketing tactics.

twenty-five keywords, though most search engines only accept the first fifteen to twenty-five, depending on the search software. Place the keywords in order of relevance and importance.

Description Tags

The description meta tag, with sample content, looks like this:

<META NAME="description" content="Aliza Sherman is a motivational speaker, Web pioneer and expert, author and freelance writer, marketing and public relations consultant.">

Try to keep your description to a single twenty-five-word sentence. Search engines usually only take the first twenty to thirty words. Find a way to make your description twenty-five words to ensure the whole thing is used. Use some of your keywords in the description to emphasize those words and increase the chances of your site coming up when those keywords are used in a search. Do not, however, repeat a single keyword over and over again thinking it will trick the search engine software into assigning your site a higher placement on a search results page. Most search engines will automatically exclude a site from their databases if there is excessive keyword repetition in the HTML code.

A search engine such as Google often lifts the meta tag description verbatim and uses it on its search results page. For example, when the above meta tags were used, a Google search on "Aliza Sherman" returned the following result:

ALIZA PILAR SHERMAN: Author, Speaker, Web Expert
Aliza Sherman is a motivational speaker, Web pioneer and expert, author and freelance writer, marketing and public relations consultant.

www.mediaegg.com/ - 7k - Cached - Similar pages

Viewing the Source

One easy way to learn HTML is to view the HTML source code of other people's Web sites. While looking at a Web site through a browser, go to the top menu and select View, then Source or View Source. A separate text file will open on your computer to reveal the HTML. You should be able to recognize some basic tags and even learn how to program more complex tags such as tables. HTML code is not copyrightable so you can copy HTML from another site and paste it in your own. Do not include copyrighted content or images.

Title, ALT, and Comment Tags

The title tag of an HTML page is placed within the <HEAD> and </HEAD> tags, usually before the meta tags. The title of the home page should say something other than "Home Page" or the URL. If you are creating your own Web page and using a template or basic Web authoring software, you may not know how or be able to specify the title of your home page, much less any other page on the site. It is better to have control over the title tag for search engine optimization purposes.

The Importance of Title Tags

The title tag of your company's site should include your company's name (or the site's name, if it is different) as well as either some keywords or a brief descriptive statement that is shorter than the meta tag description but includes some of the important keywords.

Many sites fail to take full advantage of the title tag, and their search engine listings are less clear. In other cases their listings don't even make sense. While the title tag on pages beyond the home page can include a description of the actual page, such as About Us or Our Clients, it is still better to include the company name and a few keywords along with the individual page title.

An example of a homepage title might read like so:

<TITLE>ALIZA PILAR SHERMAN: Author, Speaker, Web Expert</TITLE>

The title from a subsequent page, such as a page about books written by the author, could be written like so:

<TITLE>ALIZA PILAR SHERMAN: Author, Speaker, Web Expert: Books by Aliza Sherman</TITLE>

The title tag content does not appear within the actual Web page when viewed through a browser but instead appears on the title bar or the bar across the top of the browser window, usually a gray bar. If your title exceeds the width of the title bar, the entire title may not appear on the bar, but a search engine may still pick up the complete title and include it in its database and listings. Failing to use strategic titles on the pages of your Web site is a lost opportunity to reinforce your company name and important keywords to improve your search engine listings.

Advantages of ALT Tags

ALT tags are placed within an image tag to describe the image. These tags are useful for two reasons. First, software used by the visually impaired will read these tags rather than vocalizing "image" each time it reaches an image tag. Second, search engines may also index pages or images on pages based on the ALT tags. The following demonstrates how ALT tags can appear with image tags:

> <IMG SRC="logo.jpg" ALT="John's Pet Shop logo">
>
> <IMG SRC="images/dog.jpg" ALT="Dog at John's Pet Shop">
>
> <IMG SRC="http://www.mysite.com/images/owner.jpg" ALT="John Smith">
>
> <IMG SRC="images/staff.jpg" ALIGN="LEFT" ALT="The staff at John's Pet Shop">
>
> <IMG SRC="images/storefront.jpg" ALIGN="RIGHT" ALT="John's Pet Shop storefront">

Don't place your company name in every single ALT tag if it isn't relevant. Be careful about repeating any keyword too many times, even in ALT tags.

Inserting Comments

A comment on an HTML page is only visible in the HTML source code and not on the Web page viewed through a browser. The comment is meant to be hidden text, often used by programmer to comment on or claim credit for the HTML code. While some Web developers question the effectiveness of adding comments for search engine optimization, using comments sparingly can be helpful.

Comments are written in this manner:

<!--This is a comment.-->

The text between <!-- and --> is "invisible." When using comments for search engine optimization, put the twenty-five-word description from your meta tags in a comment somewhere within the text of the page. The sample meta tag used earlier would be inserted into a comment like this:

<!-- Aliza Sherman is a motivational speaker, Web pioneer and expert, author and freelance writer, marketing and public relations consultant.-->

Remember the rule about being careful with repetition or risk being banned by some of the more popular search engines.

▶▶ TEST DRIVE

Although you may not be doing the HTML programming for your company's Web site, you should do some strategic thinking before debuting your site. Spend some time developing the following:

- ⮑ Up to twenty-five keywords to be used in the meta tags that are relevant to your business
- ⮑ A twenty-five-word description of your company and site to be used in the meta tags
- ⮑ A title to be used in the title tag of the HTML of your site's home page and subsequent pages
- ⮑ Appropriately descriptive ALT tags for the images included on your Web site.
- ⮑ An appropriate comment to use on the home page

PART **3**

Building Your Online Presence

Serving Your Audience

One of the foundations of good business is the knowledge that the "customer is king (or queen)." If you take a customer-centric approach to your Web site strategies, you are more likely to have success not only serving current customers but also attracting new ones. When planning your company Web site or even a Web site redesign, first understand whom you are trying to reach and what you are going to do for them via your site.

Identifying Your Market

Before you went into business, you most likely identified the type of customer or client you wanted to reach. You chose marketing tactics to best reach them based on what you knew about them.

When you use the Internet to enhance your business, you need to re-examine your target audience and determine how a Web site will affect your relationship with them. Here are some questions you should ask:

- Is your target market online?
- How does your target audience use the Internet?
- How are your current customers or clients using the Internet?
- How can you use your Web site to attract your target market?
- How can you use your company Web site to better serve your existing customers or clients?

Chances are good that your target market is online. Shopping online continues to increase, growing by 33 percent in 2005 (according to Ecommercetimes.com). Still, most people are using the Internet for communications and for research, including research on products and services.

If you have clients or customers, you can use the following methods to survey how they use the Internet:

- Ask them to answer a survey by mail.
- Ask them to fill out a survey on site.
- Survey them over the phone if they call in.
- Survey them by e-mail if you have permission to e-mail them.
- Ask them in person.

Often the quickest and most affordable way to find out how your customers are using the Internet is to ask at every appropriate opportunity.

The Number of People Online in the U.S.

According to an August 2006 report from Nielsen/NR, 69.3 percent of the population in the United States is using the Internet—or about 207,161,706 people—up from 44.1 percent in 2000. The United States is tenth in terms of Internet penetration, with Iceland, New Zealand, and Sweden coming out on top. The FCC reported that the number of subscribers to high-speed broadband Internet service jumped 32.3 percent to 42 million lines between June 2004 and June 2005. The United States was twelfth regarding the number of broadband subscribers, most likely because other countries subsidize broadband services and their populations live in more accessible regions, according to *InternetWorldStats.com*.

Effective Surveying

When asking your customers if they are online and how they use the Internet, also find out about their needs and their expectation of how your company can fill those needs. Keep the survey as short as possible, usually ten questions or less. Use strategic questions that will provide you with information that can help you better serve your customers.

In e-business, you can place online surveys on your Web site or even use them before you have a Web site of your own. While it may seem easy to survey customers via e-mail if you have their permission to contact them, it is harder to tally survey results. You can manually enter the responses into a spreadsheet but there are more efficient methods.

If you have a Web site, add a survey to it in which the responses are stored in a database to be sorted automatically based on specific criteria. Sites like SurveyMonkey.com or Zoomerang.com offer free surveys (with some limitations, such as a limit of ten survey questions and 100 responses per survey). They also offer fee-based surveys with additional features including unlimited surveys, questions, and archives of surveys.

When surveying, several kinds of questions can be useful in different ways:

Multiple-choice questions with one choice allowed per question: Good for determining responses from a pre-determined set of answers. By limiting the number of choices respondents can select, you can learn the most popular answers to your questions.

Multiple-choice questions with unlimited choices allowed per question: By allowing users to select all the options that apply to them, you can get a more detailed profile of the customer.

Yes-or-no questions: Allowing users to either choose yes or no can give you a more definitive response, but in many cases, yes or no isn't the right answer. You can provide additional response options, such as maybe or undecided, but you risk getting answers that may not provide you with useful information.

Open-ended questions: These are good for getting more personalized responses and details that you may not otherwise think of when crafting your questions. The challenge of open-ended questions is reading through the responses and extracting usable information.

When using open-ended questions, you can limit the number of characters allowed in the response field to help manage the length of the answers. A mix of the different types of questions is usually most useful and yields the best results.

Matching a Design with Business Goals

Once you identify your target market and better understand what customers want from your company and from your company's Web site, revisit your business goals to make sure they are in sync with the customers and potential customers you are trying to reach. There are many reasons why people want to implement e-business tactics, but the first reason should be to better achieve business goals.

Evaluating Your Goals

You should not have to drastically change your company goals in order to integrate the Internet into your business. You may, however, need to modify or reprioritize goals in order to get the most use out of the Internet.

After conducting a survey of an appropriate audience, take a look at what you have learned. The priorities customers identify as important to them may differ from what you thought they were.

Some business goals that can also be e-business goals include the following:

Goal	Short Term	Long Term
Announce a new product or service.	x	-
Build your company brand.	-	x
Provide up-to-the-minute information to your audience.	x	
Strengthen your company's relationship with customers.	-	x
Attract new customers to your company.	x	x
Encourage site visitors to request more. information	x	x
Obtain permission from site visitors to e-mail them.	x	x
Attract more people to your Web site.	x	x
Provide customer service through your Web site.	x	x

Your company Web site should be designed to achieve your business goals. A Web site built just to be a presence online or because your competitors are online will fall flat as an effective e-business tool.

Choosing a Suitable Design

There are specific Web site designs and features that can best achieve some of the more common business and e-business goals. For example, if publishing timely information is important, a blog format may be appropriate instead of a more common home page design.

To better communicate with and strengthen your relationship with customers, you can integrate forms into your site, either on the home page or through the use of prominent links on the home page that lead to Web-based forms. Customers can use these forms to do the following:

- ➲ Request more information
- ➲ Submit feedback
- ➲ Subscribe to an e-newsletter
- ➲ Apply for something
- ➲ Provide personal data

A catalog-style Web site design allows you to provide product or service information in an organized fashion. If images are essential to your business, a gallery-style Web site design with thumbnails that are clickable to larger images can better showcase photos or artwork.

Select a design or style for your company Web site that facilitates doing business. While it may be tempting to choose a design that is flashy and high-tech, the audience and the goals you are trying to achieve may warrant a more subdued site.

What Should You Put on Your Site?

Although it is easy to put almost anything online with the right tools or budget, the decision of what should go on your Web site should be strategic. In some cases, the more you put on your site, the better resource you are providing to customers. In other cases, using just enough images or information on your Web site to attract customers and get them to want more can be equally effective.

Assessing Your Assets

Before you build a Web site, evaluate the information and images you currently have available to put online. What you put on your Web site usually falls into several broad categories:

- ⇩ Company background
- ⇩ Product or service details
- ⇩ Credibility enhancers
- ⇩ Customer service
- ⇩ Relationship builders
- ⇩ Interactivity
- ⇩ Viral marketing tools

Not every site has to have every feature listed above. However, successful sites usually have most or all of them.

Making Your Assets Work

Once you know what kinds of information and assets you have that can be used on your Web site, figure out what categories they fall into. Company background can include company history, philosophy, and mission as well as biographies of key staff. Product or service details can be as simple as a list or as complex as a catalog. Credibility enhancers can include customer testimonials, press clippings, and white papers. An online press room can be a great credibility enhancer.

Customer-service features can include FAQs, feedback forms, support forums, and even live support in a chat or instant-message format. Many customer-service features can also be relationship builders in addition to communications tools such as e-newsletters.

Many customer-service features also fall under the interactivity umbrella. Interactive features should allow the site visitor to interact with the site, with your company, or with one another. They can range from calculators and quick polls to more complex programs, such as a three-dimensional dressing-room feature that allows the user to try on clothing virtually.

Anything on the site that is easy to pass along to others—particularly via e-mail—or about which visitors are impelled to spread the word can be considered a viral marketing feature. The three-dimensional dressing room may be so engaging that people will tell their friends about it. An e-newsletter can be forwarded with ease to a friend. Publishing e-postcards that people can send or putting "Tell a Friend" on the site's Web pages can encourage visitors to lead others to your company Web site.

Mapping Your Site

While there are sophisticated programs available to map your Web site during the planning process, even using a pen and notepad to sketch out some ideas is a good way to start. A good Web developer should be able to take your rough ideas and turn them into a more strategic and cohesive vision. But until you know what you want, you will have a hard time communicating it to your developer.

Using Flow Charts

A useful visual exercise to help you plan out your site is through the use of traditional flow charts. You can invest in a low-cost flow-chart program, or your computer may already have a simple one installed. Some people use Microsoft Word, Excel, or even PowerPoint to create basic flow charts.

Providing a Site Map

Some sites use a site map to explain where content is located. A site map can literally be a visual map or diagram, such as a flow chart, with links leading to the corresponding section of the site. Other site maps are long lists of links to Web pages on the site organized by the same categories the site uses. Not every Web site needs a site map. A site with a dozen pages should not require a separate page to direct visitors to all the information. A well-designed Web site uses clear and logical categories and subcategories to lead visitors beyond the home page.

Each box of the flow chart should be a main page. Start with the home page at the top. The next row of boxes represents the top-level categories that are part of your main site navigation. Boxes placed vertically below them represent relevant pages to that category or section. Boxes placed horizontally below them represent subcategories.

Here are several ways to illustrate a Web site using flow charts. There is no single correct way to develop a flow chart for a Web site as long as you are able to accommodate the various levels and layers of your site in the diagram. In some cases, a site diagram may extend across multiple pages or larger format paper.

An Eye to the Future

As you map your Web site, imagine where you'd like to see your company in a year, three years, even five years.

Your diagram can include phases for Web site development. Phase one includes what you'd like on your site in the immediate future. Phase two should be where you'd like to go within the next year or so. Phase three can include longer-term plans once you reach certain milestones with your Web site, such as reaching a specific number of customers or clients or a specific amount of sales revenue from Web site sales.

E-business doesn't happen in a vacuum. **Whatever you plan to do in business affects what you do online and vice versa.** Planning ahead, even if the plan is just theoretical, can help ensure that you start building your Web site in a way that anticipates and accommodates growth and expansion.

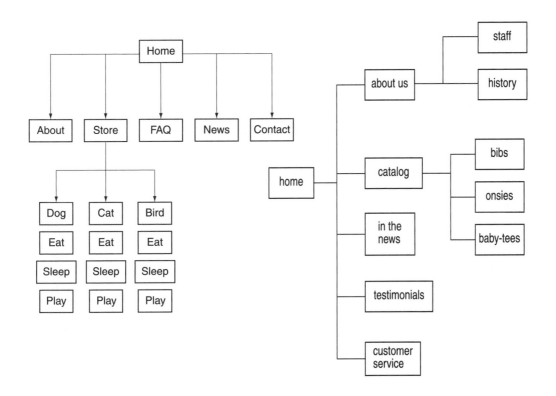

Writing for the Web

Often, the main Web asset for a company is content. Online content often needs to take a different form than content in traditional print materials such as annual reports, marketing brochures, company fact sheets, product information, and press releases. Once you have identified and located content that you'd like to include on your Web site, evaluate the best way to put that content online.

Leveraging Content

One major challenge when sorting through company content is determining what should go online. Some common content you should consider includes the following:

1. **White papers** in a searchable archive of summaries, with full documents available in PDF
2. **Press releases** in an online press room sorted by year and other relevant categories, such as company division
3. **Marketing brochures** or links to PDF files of the brochure for download
4. **Product information** can be included in an online catalog, with additional information such as ingredients, instructions, and other details in pop-up windows or as downloadable PDF files
5. **Bios and photos of staff members** and other shorter documents as HTML pages with links to longer documents, such as annual reports
6. **Rate sheets** or text encouraging people to contact you for prices

To ensure your company site is useful to customers and potential customers, consider developing a resources section where you can provide information, tools, and links to other resources. Using the Web as a place to archive vast amounts of data can prove valuable to others who need access to the information. When your site becomes useful, it is likely to be visited more than once. A fundamental goal for any company Web site should be that a visitor actually bookmarks it so she or he can return again.

Presenting Content Online

Regardless of how much progress has been made on computer monitors, reading online is still challenging to some, difficult for others, and annoying for the rest. Computer monitors have a flicker rate—that is, the monitor may seem to display a steady and solid projection but in fact the screen is flickering at a rate faster than eyes can detect. The flicker rate of a monitor can cause, at a minimum, eyestrain and headaches. This is why less content online is often more effective.

Links to Other Sites

Linking to other sites is a common practice on the Web, and lists of links can be considered content. If your goal, however, is to keep visitors on your site or returning to your site, you must link strategically. Compilations of links can be useful resources on your site, but try to confine these links to a resources section or links page. Your Web developer can program every link out of your site to open a separate browser window so after a person closes the new window, your Web site remains on their screen.

Unless you are specifically in the business of publishing content, you should explore different ways of publishing company information online beyond text on Web pages. Some of the ways to publish content online include these:

1. Straight text on a page, breaking up the text with font styles, bulleted or numbered lists, generous white space, images, and other techniques
2. On multiple pages, using either a table of contents gateway or page links at the bottom of each page to signify the number of pages and give immediate access to them
3. Pop-up windows that open when a link or button is clicked
4. Excerpts with links to PDF or Word documents, though PDF files require that the user has downloaded a copy of Adobe Acrobat Reader in order to read the file

5. Using interactive features such as a quiz or poll to present the content in a more dynamic way and incorporate user input to produce new results

6. Within a multimedia feature such as audio, video, and/or animation

Determine what content in your site lends itself to more creative presentations beyond straight text on a page. Your Web developer can help you assess content and provide creative suggestions for presentation as well.

▶▶ TEST DRIVE

When you are in the initial stages of planning your Web site, even before you have met with a Web developer, ask yourself some key questions to be better able to communicate your expectations:

➲ Who is my target market, and what do they want from my company?

➲ What type of Web site or site features will best serve my customers?

➲ What are the most important things I hope to achieve for my business through my Web site?

➲ What assets do I have, including content and images, to publish on my company Web site?

➲ How can I make the information I'm presenting on my company site more dynamic and interactive?

➲ What can I publish or create online that will be of value to my customers and encourage them to bookmark my site?

Roles and Responsibilities

During the Web development process, the Web developer should clearly define the process of building a Web site. Knowing in advance what is expected from all parties involved helps the process go smoothly.

The Web Developer's Role

Some of the developer's responsibilities include the following:

- Developing a realistic timeline for the project
- Managing the resources to complete the project on time and within budget
- Overseeing or implementing the technical steps of site development
- Handling quality control for the work rendered
- Providing regular updates to the client
- Involving the client in a regular approval process

A Web developer's role is not to manage your company's staff. There should always be a point person at your company who can funnel information to and from the developer.

The Business Owner's Role

Some of the things you should handle include the following:

- Outlining any deadlines that need to be met for business reasons
- Directing appropriate company resources toward the project
- Overseeing the progress of the project
- Providing honest feedback at each step of the process
- Updating the developer with new information that may affect site production
- Giving thorough reviews and prompt approvals of materials submitted by developer

If you make important business decisions before the Web site development process begins, you can save time and money and provide your developer with consistent, thoughtful input. A Web developer should not dictate how you should run your business but should make suggestions about how e-business can help your company run more efficiently or effectively, based on your business goals.

The Development Site

Whether you are building your company's site for the first time or are redesigning an existing one, your developer should set up a development site. The development site should reside on a Web server and be kept private with password protection. If you have an existing site, a development site resides in a separate location to avoid confusion between the different versions. Development sites are accessible for review and approval purposes to anyone working closely on the project. Until the development site has been tested and approved and is ready to go live, the existing site remains online and untouched unless there is a clear business reason to take it offline.

Timelines and Milestones

You and the Web developer should establish timelines and milestones—that is, points along the way when certain things need to occur before the process can move forward. Web site development needs strategic project management just like any other project.

Setting Realistic Timelines

There may be business reasons for your company Web site to be online sooner than later. You need to communicate specific internal company deadlines to your Web developer immediately. A developer bases timelines for a project on resources, her own current workload, external deadlines from a client, and a realistic assessment of how long each task will take given her previous experience and overall expertise.

A challenging aspect of setting up a realistic timeline for the development of a Web site is unforeseen events that cause a delay or interruption of the process. Another major challenge is often client delay. Some Web developers include a clause in their contract that protects them from penalties if a missed deadline is due to client delays. As the client, you must be aware of your critical role in keeping the project on track, on time, and on budget.

Establishing Clear Milestones

The Web developer usually suggests the project milestones based on her knowledge of the typical steps of the Web site development process. As the client, you can question or suggest modifications to the milestones, but any changes you make—such as shortening a timeline and increasing the complexity of a milestone—could hinder the overall process.

Milestones vary greatly from project to project. Here is a sample timeline with milestones for a Web site redesign:

Date	Task Completed
Month 1	Assemble a team Old site assessment complete Initial strategic meetings with client Develop plan to present to client
Month 2	Strategic meetings continue Plan approval by client Begin implementation of plan
Month 3	Build development site Freeze period on old site
Month 4	Beta testing Client approval of site Soft launch
Month 5	Official launch

As each milestone is reached, you and the developer should sign off that you both agree the milestone was met. This process of agreement can help prevent disputes along the way or at the completion of the project.

Using Planning Software

Software exists to make the planning and management process easier. Because Web development often takes many steps and requires at least several people working on the project, any tool you can use to better manage the process is good practice. Your Web developer may use project management software that can be licensed to you. She may also have a proprietary project management system for Web development. You can use a project management tool for managing your internal company resources. Software such as Microsoft Project and Basecamp can be useful for managing Web development projects.

Beta Testing

During any Web development process, most developers will insist on structured beta testing of the site. If yours does not, you should request it. Beta testing is most commonly used in computer game and software development but is also effective for Web site development. In software development, the alpha stage is when the product is first created, and the beta stage is when the problems and bugs are identified and fixed. The same process occurs with Web site development.

A beta test for Web site development takes place when online users try out a site or site features and provide feedback about their overall experiences.

Setting Up Beta Tests

There are several important aspects of a beta test that help to make it effective and useful. Keeping your target marketing in mind, a beta test should:

- Use different computer platforms, that is, both Windows and Macintosh machines
- Use different Web browsers on both platforms, such as Internet Explorer, Netscape, Firefox for PCs, and Firefox, Netscape, and Safari for Macintosh

➲ Access the site from different physical locations based on the target market locations

➲ Access the site using different connections including dial-up, DSL or ISDN, and cable modem

➲ Use testers outside of your company and not affiliated with the Web developer

➲ Use testers with varied Internet skills, from new users to more experienced users

➲ Use a testing template for comparison's sake so all testers are answering the same set of questions

The Web developer usually recruits beta testers, but you may be able to provide some testers as well. **Before recruiting beta testers, clearly establish the criteria for testers to cover all the variables that will make the beta test results more comprehensive.**

You can locate beta testers in a number of ways, including these:

➲ Friends, family, and acquaintances, and people they know

➲ Current customers or clients and people they know

➲ Vendors and strategic partners and people they know

➲ People responding to posts or ads requesting beta testers

➲ Beta-testing communities or services

You can find experienced communities of beta testers and companies that offer beta test services online through a Google search. Other ways to find beta testers online include posting appropriate requests within online forums that your target market potentially frequents.

Using Beta Test Data

Establishing a formal beta-testing process with consistent questions and a set timeframe helps make the data from responses more useable. Questions vary for each beta test depending on the project. Here are some types of questions you may consider:

⮑ Demographic information about the tester, including occupation and Internet experience

⮑ Computer, browser, and Internet connection specs

⮑ The tester's familiarity with your company, products, or services

⮑ The tester's first impression of the home page of your company site

⮑ The tester's first impression of your company based on his impression of the home page

⮑ The look of the site, including colors, style, fonts, and images.

⮑ The feel of the site, especially details about the site navigation

⮑ Questions that direct testers to try out specific features such as site search as well as interactive and multimedia features

⮑ Questions that reveal details that a tester might not think of mentioning but that you need to know to make improvements to the site before launch

Leveraging an "Extranet"

An extranet is a password-protected Web site accessible by all parties involved in a business or working on a project. Web developers often set up extranets for their clients that include private forums and even blogs to keep track of communications and site development. Use an extranet to manage documents and files, e-mail correspondence, online discussions, and approvals throughout the entire Web site development process. The extranet becomes an archive of all documents for future review. Ask your Web developer if she can set up an extranet along with the development site.

More often than not, beta testers' responses will surprise you and can reveal new and useful information. You may also learn something from beta testers that can affect the overall site development process. Keeping your overall business goals in mind helps direct you to appropriate decisions. Remember that you are building a site for others and not just for yourself.

The Soft Launch

When a Web site is made available to the public, it has been "made live" or 'launched." If, however, the site is not announced right away, the initial launch is considered a soft launch, the stage after beta testing but before an official launch. A soft launch can also happen in stages as new features are added to the site.

Lifting Password Protection

While your site is in the development stage, it should be password protected not only to prevent the public from accessing it before it is ready but also to keep search engines from indexing the site. Even if you don't actively submit your company site to search engines, they may automatically index any Web page that is not behind password protection.

You can deter search engine software or robots from indexing your site by using a robot meta tag along with the description and keywords tags. The robot meta tag can either invite search engine robots to enter a site and index Web pages or specify that it should not enter.

To keep a search engine out, use the following meta tag:

<meta name="robots" content="noindex,nofollow">

Once you have officially launched your site when you want your site indexed, you need to change the tag as follows:

<meta name="robots" content="index,follow">

"No index" robot tags do not guarantee all search engines will leave your site alone, but it is likely that for the most part, search engines will acknowledge the tag and not index your site. Your Web developer could also use a protocol on the Web server to exclude robots and specify what parts of the Web site can or cannot be indexed using a robots.txt page.

The only way to guarantee search engines stay out of your site is to implement password protection. Once a site is indexed on a search engine, it is easier for people to find it.

Working Out the Bugs

Often the actual launch takes longer than expected. Don't be alarmed if your Web site is not immediately available or if portions don't function properly. There may be an initial down time between site approval and confirmed site launch.

Using a development site can help limit the bugginess of a newly debuted site. Because it should have been fully functional at its development location, theoretically it should still function at its live location. Still, human or machine error can lead to some temporary loss of functionality.

If you have an existing site that is live and using your company's domain name, the new site you move to the same location should be accessible with that domain name. However, if you are moving the site to a new Web server, there may be additional and unavoidable down time while the domain name is pointed to the server. The process by which a domain name becomes completely accessible to all computers and servers on the Internet as the servers replace the old location information with the new information is called domain name server (DNS) propagation. It takes up to seventy-two hours for your domain name to propagate and lead people to the correct site on the right Web server.

Even with the best-laid plans and a flawless process of bringing a site online free of any errors, unforeseen problems can arise. Knowing that there may be up to a few days of downtime can help you prepare for any issues that might arise from your site being inaccessible.

The "Coming Soon" Page

While Web developers differ about whether or not to use a "Coming Soon" page as a placeholder for a pending Web site, there are ways to make this page a useful tool for your company. Rather than simply putting a message that says "Coming Soon," include your company logo and contact information. Integrate a way for visitors to submit their e-mail addresses or fill out forms with their own contact information so they can be notified when the site officially launches. You can build a substantial e-mail list to be used later for site marketing purposes. Let people know they are signing up for your e-mail list to receive future announcements.

The Official Launch

The official launch of a site happens with an appropriate amount of fan-fare and concerted effort to let people know the site is online. The official launch should be a distinct item on the project timeline and should remain fixed unless both parties agree it needs to be moved forward or back.

Assessing Readiness

There is only so much testing you can do before a site goes live. The one thing you may not be able to duplicate in the beta test phase is large amounts of simultaneous site users. Your Web developer, however, should be able to create a program to hit a Web site multiple times over a period of time to try to simulate heavy site traffic. What she cannot do, however, is create a program to go through a site the way a person might, meandering, changing his mind midpurchase, coming back to the site and completing a purchase, and other variations.

By now, you should have verified the following:

- The home page loads quickly on a variety of Internet connections.
- The images on the site all load completely; there are no broken images.
- The links on every page function; there are no broken links.
- The site's search function works properly.
- The interactive and multimedia features work as you expect.
- All bugs and errors identified during testing have been fixed.

Opening the Virtual Gate

Some of the ways you can bolster your official launch include the following:

- Change robot tags.
- Distribute online and offline releases.
- Send out e-mail announcements.
- Make announcements in online forums.

"Add to Cart" buttons prominently can make a big difference in closing a sale.

Product description: Offer as much content as you can to describe your products, even beyond the usual information such as color and size options. Include customer reviews, media reviews such as *Consumer Reports*, ingredients, or materials, and link to complementary products or accessories to make shopping easier.

Product pricing: Make pricing decisions for products you are selling online before you begin building your site. If your products cost the same online as they do in the store, remember customers also have to pay shipping. If you don't sell products offline, you should check out your competition online to see how to price your products competitively.

Selling online requires more than just decisions about technology. Examine how your company does business or how you want to do business, and bring those qualities and aspects of your business online in the most effective, professional, and strategic way.

Mail Order or Catalog Companies

Regardless of the technological progress made with online stores and catalogs, there are still fundamental business issues that need to be addressed in order to successfully sell online. If you've already been selling by catalog or mail order, the main issues you need to address include the following:

1. **Inventory systems integration:** Examine how the online inventory system will integrate with your offline system.
2. **Taxation:** Apply the tax where your bricks-and-mortar store or business is located.
3. **International shipping:** If you did not ship internationally in the past, consider how you will handle—or prevent—international orders.

4. **Product presentation:** A Web-based catalog requires a more complex design to produce a good online shopping experience.

5. **Managing growth:** Adding online sales to your business can increase sales incrementally or more rapidly, and you need to be prepared for the additional business.

If you are going to sell online, you should examine how it will affect all aspects of your established business.

Bricks-and-Mortar Companies

If you've sold products in a store but never through a catalog, here are some things you need to think about:

1. **Shipping options:** Provide a number of options for your customers including USPS, UPS, and FedEx.

2. **Taxation issues:** Because you have a real-world presence, you should charge taxes based on your location.

3. **Packaging and handling:** If you've never shipped products, you need to find the best way to package items so they arrive intact and undamaged.

4. **Handling returns:** Be prepared for a greater number of returned items as people making purchases online won't have the benefit of seeing the product in person.

5. **Exchanges:** If a customer wants to exchange an item, there will be shipping costs incurred. You need to determine who will pay for them—you or your customer.

If you've never sold products before, you can start selling them online with minimal investment, but you will still need to address issues of inventory storage and management as well as fulfillment and distribution.

Choosing an E-Commerce Solution

There are numerous options for setting up an online store. In addition to third-party shopping-cart services, online store builders, and online marketplaces, you can also purchase or license software and use it to build your online store or catalog. It's critical to select the right package based on your e-commerce needs as well as the resources you have to build and maintain the online store.

Boxed E-Commerce Solutions

While there are companies that still sell off-the-shelf storefront software that you can purchase and install, many companies are turning to Web-based solutions or to delivering their software through the Web.

Some companies that offer online shop builders also offer shopping-cart software or storefront software products although you can still find companies offering standalone storefront software in a box. Storefront software companies include the following:

Provider	Software	Web-based Solution
X-Cart (*www.x-cart.com*)	x	-
Storefront (*www.storefront.net*)	x	x
LiteCommerce (*www.litecommerce.com*)	x	-
Volusion (*www.volusion.com*)	-	x
CoreSense (*www.coresense.com*)	x	x

Most providers opt to offer their store-building solutions online with Web-based tools rather than boxed or downloaded software. The convenience of Web-based solutions for your company is less to download or install and more plug-and-play tools that are easy to use. With Web-based solutions, you don't need your own team of techies to manage the software. A reputable provider should offer round-the-clock technical support.

Reviewing Solution Options

Some of the main factors to consider when choosing an e-commerce solution include the following:

1. **Scalability:** The system should support growth and not require switching to a new system.
2. **Flexibility:** You should be able to customize and manipulate what you need based on company goals, not be locked into a limited set of options.
3. **Modular:** If you want to start with fewer features to test the waters then add enhanced features later, the solution should allow you to pick and choose features.
4. **Registration:** If you want to allow customers to register with your site, pick a solution that has this system built in.
5. **Easy to use:** Tools for editing and updating your online store should be graphical and easy to use, even for a non-programmer.

Remember that if anything is missing from the solution you use, you will have to hire a programmer to add it or you may have to switch to a different system to get the features you want. Making the right decision at the start can help avoid a costly and time-consuming migration to another solution.

▶▶ TEST DRIVE

If you are not in the mail-order business, there are many issues you will need to think about before you begin selling online for the first time. Consider the following:

➲ What are some of my favorite online stores?
➲ What features make online shopping there a better experience?
➲ What features would work on my site, and what e-commerce solutions provide them?
➲ Will my online store be developed in-house, or should I hire a Web developer?
➲ How will I integrate my online store with what the company does offline?

PART **4**
From Marketing to Selling Online

Setting Up Processes and Procedures

Before you open your online store or begin taking online transactions, you should make sure you are e-business ready. Doing business online will overlap your offline business processes, so be sure you are prepared to address new issues that come up.

The Way Things Were

While you probably have been using e-mail for general business correspondence, chances are you are not conducting any major business tasks primarily through e-mail. Without a transactional Web site, chances are your main sales interactions with customers or clients take place in one or more of these ways:

➲ In person
➲ By telephone
➲ Via fax
➲ By mail

You may also be accustomed to paper documentation, whether written notes, faxes, copies, or other printed matter. And you probably have a paper filing system to keep track of a lot of business dealings. This is not to say that your company does not use computers or have an online filing system as well, but chances are you are not digitizing your paper documents and filing them electronically.

If you are not doing business on the Web, doing business electronically may be limited to a few areas such as online banking and placing orders from vendors online. **You will probably need to change the way you organize information once you launch a transactional Web site.** Online businesses generate a great deal of electronic documents, from e-mails to orders, feedback, and requests. Being prepared for the shift in communications forms will help to make the transition from real-world business to e-business.

How E-Business Changes Things

When you have a Web site, you'll find that customers who take the initiative to do business with you online in turn expect you to conduct business with them via e-mail. Sales transactions should not take place through e-mail because e-mail is not secure, but if a customer e-mails you, he'll expect to receive an e-mail in return. You need to be ready to meet this expectation by assigning appropriate resources to monitoring and responding to customer e-mails generated from your Web site.

Transactions and communications through your Web site will be electronic messages and documents. While there is a temptation to print everything as you receive it, examine whether that is the most efficient and cost-effective way to process and archive the information. Businesses should have a balance of paper and electronic records. The backup of electronic records, however, is not invariably a printed copy of every e-mail and every order you receive.

As your company moves from mostly offline to a significant amount of online business, you should have the following in place:

1. **Company computers with the current operating system and software** to be able to properly access your Web site and any electronic systems related to the site.
2. **An automatic backup system** for company computers that doesn't rely on people remembering to back up their computers.
3. **A secure offsite backup system with a third-party provider** to conduct regular backups of your company data.
4. **A system for archiving electronic communications and transactions,** usually contained in a database attached to the Web site.
5. **Training and technical support for staff** who will be dealing with new business and communications coming from the Web site.

There may be a learning curve for staff to get up to speed with the new technology and systems. With all the planning in the world, there may be moments early in the adjustment process when errors are made or confusion ensues. A reliable technology backup system can reduce the negative impact of human error, and good training and technical support can reduce confusion.

Fulfillment and Distribution

When you decide you are going to sell online and you have already been selling by mail order offline, chances are you have your fulfillment and distribution systems in place. Your main concerns are to make sure online orders integrate properly with offline orders and get to the right people to fulfill and ship customer orders.

If you are selling and shipping products for the first time, you have several methods to choose from, including in-house fulfillment and distribution, drop shipping, and using a third-party fulfillment house.

Doing It In-House

If your product list is small and you anticipate a small number of orders on a regular basis, you could opt to stock the inventory, package, and ship products to customers straight from your company. This method is referred to as the inventory model. Some benefits of the inventory model are these:

- ➲ Full control over the product until it leaves your company
- ➲ Quick response to customer orders based on the system you have set up
- ➲ Shipments you send are branded with your company logo and materials without fail
- ➲ Control over packaging materials and the quality of packing
- ➲ Control over the customer-service experience

The tradeoffs for having absolute control over inventory include some significant disadvantages:

1. Inventory that doesn't sell quickly takes up space, and that can cost you money.

2. Ordering too much stock in anticipation of major sales days such as holidays may incur costs that cannot be recouped.

3. Fulfillment takes tremendous committed resources, including people to locate stock, package it carefully, arrange shipping, and be on hand for customer service.

4. Computer systems in-house must mesh with your Web site, so you may require a major investment to get computers up to speed and personnel trained.

5. Your Web site's shopping-cart system may need to be more sophisticated to help automate processes that your company does not have in place.

Doing everything in-house means you are responsible for everything from storage space to packaging materials, tracking packages, handling returns, and dealing with all kinds of customer inquiries.

The Drop-Shipping Option

Drop shipping is a method of shipping whereby you identify manufacturers or distributors of products you want to sell and make an arrangement with them to fulfill orders from your Web site. You may be able to save time and money by going the drop-shipping route. Some of the benefits include these:

1. The manufacturer handles inventory so you won't need to spend money stocking up on products.

2. Inventory is stored at the manufacturer's facility so you won't need to invest in storage space.

3. The manufacturer is experienced in packing the products, which will reduce breakage and damage from improper packing.

4. The manufacturer takes care of shipping so you don't have to set up your own shipping systems.

5. Some manufacturers will ship products in packaging branded with your company logo and information so customers don't need to know you didn't ship it.

Drop shipping can have problems as well, though being aware of them might alleviate them. Problems and issues include the following:

1. You have less control over response time to orders because your control ends when the order has left your Web site or company and is in the hands of the manufacturer.

2. You have less control over the shipping process, and a manufacturer may forget to include your branded packaging materials, leading customers to call the manufacturer for customer service, if needed.

3. You have less control over customer service, especially if the customer calls the manufacturer by mistake. The manufacturer may not treat your customer the way you'd like.

4. You have less than real-time inventory updates because it may be more challenging to integrate your Web site with someone else's inventory system.

5. You see less profit from sales because you will lose some of your profit margin paying for drop shipping.

You may be able to establish excellent relationships with manufacturers and work out a seamless inventory system. You may also find manufacturers who hold customer service in as high regard as your company does. Drop shipping can work well if all those factors are in place and if the cost of drop shipping doesn't take away your potential for making a profit on sales.

Using Third-Party Fulfillment Services

Fulfillment services, also called fulfillment houses, are another way of distributing products to customers. If you've ever ordered from a catalog company, chances are they use a fulfillment house if they don't handle the inventory in-house. Fulfillment houses can usually do all or some of the following:

➲ Stock inventory
➲ Take orders
➲ Pull products for orders placed

➔ Package products
➔ Ship packages
➔ Handle customer service calls

Fulfillment houses can completely customize their services so your customers get the impression they are dealing directly with your company. Using a fulfillment house eliminates inventory integration issues with your Web site as long as they have a working system for taking online orders in place. Make sure the fees a fulfillment house charges won't cut too deeply into your profit margin.

Deciding between keeping the inventory in-house, using drop shipping, or enlisting a fulfillment house is more a business decision than an e-business decision. However, if you are planning to sell products on the Web and you have never done so, you must do your homework before starting to build your online store to take all aspects of systems integration into account.

Privacy and Return Policies

Posting a privacy policy on your Web site is good business practice. It will raise a visitor's level of confidence as she or he is considering providing you with personal information. Having a return policy already established for returns on online sales is critical to handling returned product in a consistent and timely manner. While the privacy policy is easy to develop based on existing templates and actual examples online, return policies require more thought, as the way in which you handle returns can affect your company's bottom line.

Developing a Privacy Policy

At a minimum, a privacy policy should outline how your company views Web site visitor and customer privacy, including why you want their personal information. Because of existing laws in the United States relating to children and the Internet, the privacy policy on your company's Web site should also mention compliance with COPPA.

Here are other things that you can put into your privacy policy:

1. A statement about who owns the Web site
2. A breakdown of visitor information gathered or tracked
3. A breakdown of the ways visitor information is gathered, both voluntary and involuntary, such as tracking Web traffic patterns or purchasing habits
4. A breakdown of ways visitor data is collected, such as through e-newsletter subscriptions, message board registration, feedback forms, and so on
5. A statement outlining the use of cookie files placed within a visitor's Web browser and an explanation of how it works
6. An explanation of how information gathered is used
7. A statement as to whether or not information gathered is shared or sold
8. A list of what kind of security systems are in place on the company's Web server and site
9. Directions for how a visitor can opt out from anywhere they've submitted their personal information
10. A statement about implied consent stating that by using your Web site, the visitor is consenting to the collection of and use of the information outlined in the policy

Sample privacy policies can be found on reputable Web sites, usually accessible through a text link at the bottom of the home page or every page of the site. You can find additional sample privacy policies through a search engine. To minimize your company's risk, have a lawyer review the policy you've created before you put it on your Web site to make sure you've covered all the bases from a legal standpoint.

Crafting a Return Policy

Every company that sells products should have a written return policy. For companies selling on the Web, that written policy should be posted on the site in prominent locations including on product pages and on pages appearing during the checkout process.

Most online return policies include some of the following information:

1. The length of time allowed for a return to take place (for instance, within thirty days of purchase or of delivery of the item)
2. The amount that will be refunded (100 percent or the full amount less shipping and handling)
3. How the refund will be administered (credited to a credit card or as store credit only)
4. Whether your company or the customer will pay for the cost of shipping returned items
5. What your company will accept about condition of the products returned (for instance, new and unopened only)
6. A statement that only products purchased through your company's Web site can be returned to ensure customers do not try to return items purchased elsewhere
7. How you handle exchanges, including the additional shipping and handling of the new item sent
8. Whether or not you offer a partial refund if the item was opened or if the customer sent it back beyond the stated return timeframe

Child Privacy and Protections

In 1998 the U.S. Congress passed the Children's Online Privacy Protection Act (COPPA) to limit how Web sites and online services collect personal information from children under thirteen, regardless of whether their site is for children or general audiences with a children's section. Some things COPPA requires from operators of Web sites and online services are to "post a privacy policy on the homepage of their Web site and link to the privacy policy on every page where personal information is collected; provide notice about the site's information collection practices to parents and obtain verifiable parental consent before collecting personal information from children; and give parents a choice as to whether their child's personal information will be disclosed to third parties."

A helpful tool for customers who are returning an item is a form on the Web site they can print and fill out that provides you with all the key information needed to properly handle the return.

Using Cookies

A cookie is a text file some Web sites insert into a visitor's Web browser cookie file. It tags the user with information such as their username and password from a registration site, their personal preferences, shopping-cart information, previous purchases, and other records of personal information as well as Web surfing and shopping habits. If you are using cookies to enable certain features on your site such as remembering a password for the visitor, be clear in your privacy policy how, where, and why you use them.

Taxing and Taking Money

At the time of this book's publication, there were no U.S. federal sales tax laws for the Internet. Before you build your online store, speak with a lawyer and an accountant familiar with e-commerce issues to determine the way your company should pay taxes on the online sales generated from your site.

E-Commerce Tax Laws

In 1998, the Internet Tax Freedom Act was established, and as of early 2007 it had been extended through November 2007. The act is meant to encourage business growth by keeping the Internet tax-free.

The general rule for charging sales tax on the Internet is the same as for mail-order businesses. Taxes are charged if the customer is in the same state as the seller. If, however, your company has a retail store in the state where your customer resides, that customer should pay a sales tax (if that state has a sales tax).

Depending on the online store solution you are using, many software packages have built-in tax tables that you can customize based on the current taxation laws, where you are located and where you are shipping. The six states that do not have a sales tax are Alaska, Delaware, Hawaii,

Montana, New Hampshire, and Oregon, although Hawaii has a general excise tax.

Taking the Customer's Money

In order to accept credit card payments on your site, you need a merchant account with a financial institution or service that allows you to process credit card numbers and complete transactions. You can shop around for the most competitive price. Fees are usually based on a percentage per credit card transaction.

Many online shopping-cart solutions provide merchant account services for a fee and facilitate the entire process for you. Others process your transactions through their merchant account and charge you a percentage per transaction. Typical transaction fees range from 1.5 percent to 2.5 percent.

Getting a Merchant Account

Some of the companies that provide merchant accounts or services, called merchant service providers, also help you take payments online through your Web site. A company like Authorize.net provides merchant accounts for both online and offline businesses. Check with your Web host and even see if your domain registrar offers merchant account services. Automated Web-based online store builders such as Yahoo! Merchant Solutions give you the option of either processing transactions through their account or obtaining your own account.

A transaction solution such as PayPal allows payments by credit card as well as a PayPal account for people without credit cards or who wish not to use their credit cards online. A customer can have a PayPal account draw funds from his own bank account, and you can also have a PayPal account and receive the payment directly and later withdraw the funds, transferring them into your own account.

Some credit card processing companies include these:

- CardService International (*www.cardserviceunlimited.com*)
- Charge.com (*www.charge.com*)
- Electronic Transfer, Inc. (*www.electronictransfer.com*)

➲ Merchant Accounts Express (*www.merchantexpress.com*)
➲ Merchant Warehouse (*www.merchantwarehouse.com*)

If you already have a merchant account for your offline business, check with your provider to see what you need to do to use the same account online. Accepting credit cards is a business decision that involves more than the technology. Understanding the additional costs and risks of accepting credit cards is important, so do your homework and make sure you limit your liability.

▶▶ TEST DRIVE

Doing your homework before you actually begin building your online store or catalog can save you time, money, and legal problems. Some questions you need to answer as you prepare to sell online include these:

➲ What processes do I currently have in place for selling and shipping products?
➲ How will what I do online integrate with what I am doing offline?
➲ If I haven't sold or shipped products before, how will I handle inventory, fulfillment, and distribution?
➲ What will my company's privacy and return policies say?
➲ What shipping options make the most sense for both my customer and my company's bottom line?

The Benefits of Registration

Having an online store or catalog can generate revenues for your company. Your online catalog may be an extension of an existing bricks-and-mortar store or print catalog, or you might start selling products online without having a real-world presence. In either case, selling on the Internet can open up new e-business opportunities.

Registration on Shopping Sites

If you allow people to buy online, give them the option of registering as a member of your site. Membership, in turn, should have its privileges. Registering should be beneficial to your customer and should also provide you with valuable customer data that you can leverage to improve sales.

The registration process should be optional but encouraged. You should not require registration lest you lose sales. Reducing barriers to transactions is essential in order to facilitate online sales.

Following are some barriers that may keep customers from buying online:

Required registration: Some customers will not feel comfortable entering their personal, contact, and credit card information into your site if they know it will be stored and are wary of security.

Confusion: Poor navigation can make it difficult to get to products, product information, and purchasing options.

Clunky shopping-cart system: If the shopping-cart portion of an online store is not seamless and easy to operate, potential customers may bail out of a shopping cart before completing the transaction.

Cumbersome checkout: Requiring customers to fill out much more than the minimal information needed to complete a transaction could turn them off.

Hidden prices: Some online catalogs don't show the price of a product until a customer has entered her credit card information. The number of sales will be immediately reduced if a customer cannot see a price upfront.

By offering customers the ability to register, you can reduce some common barriers to transactions.

The Benefits of Membership

To make registration on your site attractive, you first need to overcome a customer's objections to registering. Emphasize your company's privacy policy and security policy to alleviate concerns that customer and credit card data may not be safe. Make sure the registration process does not require many more steps than a regular transaction. You will also need to invest in top-notch security measures to protect customer information.

Next, show how registering with your store creates convenience for the customer. Registering should address some of the barriers of online shopping by expediting the shopping-cart and checkout process so the customer does not have to enter his information every time he makes a purchase.

Develop and offer additional features for your online store that customers can only access as registered members of your site. Enhanced features that add convenience and make shopping easier include the following:

- Purchasing reminders
- Personalized notices
- Shopping lists
- Wish lists
- Personal recommendations
- Gift registries

You can offer additional incentives to encourage customers to become members, such as providing free product samples with their orders if they are registered with your site. Most people shop online for the convenience, so finding ways to make their online shopping experience easier and less stressful can turn customers into members.

Personalization and Customization

Once customers become registered members of your site, you can better target features and services directly to them. Personalization on a Web site means giving users a more familiar experience based on what you know about them and their activities on your site. Customization allows the user to select options and make modifications to your Web site based on her own preferences. **Customization gives the user more control, while personalization is more of a cursory approach.** Together, they can make a big difference in a customer's shopping experience.

Having an e-commerce solution that allows you to save customers' information and present that information back to them for their convenience can strengthen your relationship with them and encourage repeat visits and purchases. When a customer registers on your site, make sure you get her permission to send her personalized notices from your company so you can build an even stronger relationship with her over time.

Getting Personal

The most basic form of personalization online is to address each customer by name when he or she returns to your online store. When customers register on your site, the registration system can place a cookie within the cookie file of their Web browser if they opt to save their log-in information. Even if the customer doesn't opt to save his log-in information through a "Remember Me" feature, when he logs into your site, the system can dynamically publish a greeting on the site's home page including his name. Amazon.com does this effectively, greeting the registered user but also offering a text link that states: "If you are not Jane Doe, click here." The visitor can log out of someone else's account, and he can register or log in with his own account.

Another form of personalization is addressing your customers by name in e-mails you send them. This adds a personal touch, but you should go further by tapping into the information you are gathering from them as they use and shop on your site. The ideal is to deliver e-mails to customers based entirely on their preferences and past activities and by analyzing both to anticipate their needs.

Reminding Customers

Once customers have registered and given you permission to send them e-mails, find ways to remind them of your company, your online store, and your products through automated systems that generate personalized customer service e-mails. A built-in reminder system can increase online shopping convenience and build customer loyalty. The more information they provide you through your site, the more compelled they will be to continue to use your site rather than re-entering their information over and over again on other sites.

Customers Want a Targeted Experience

According to the 2006 ChoiceStream Personalization Survey (*www.choices tream.com*), 57 percent of consumers said they would be willing to provide demographic information (up from 46 percent in 2005), and 34 percent were willing to allow companies to track their clicks and purchases if it resulted in a more targeted Web experience. Sixty-two percent said they were concerned about their privacy on the Internet. Seventy-nine percent were interested in receiving personalized content. The survey does point out that the most interested in personalization are eighteen- to twenty-four-year-olds (62 percent) followed by fifty and over (37 percent).

Reminder systems can include things like the following:

Birthday reminders: Customers can enter the birthdates of friends and families, and the system will automatically e-mail a reminder of the important date far enough in advance to order a gift online and ship it.

Event reminders: Customers can enter the dates of other events, including anniversaries and other occasions for gift giving.

Refill reminders: A useful service to remind customers to refill herbs, supplements, or medicine orders. Customers can also be reminded to purchase items that may run out within a certain time period, such as beauty and bath products.

Shopping reminders: Sites like Drugstore.com automatically send a reminder e-mail at a regular interval, such as monthly, that includes the entire list of the most recent purchases to act as an interactive shopping list.

Reminder e-mails can contain links to specific product pages to facilitate a quick purchase or even give the customer the option of clicking on a link that automatically adds the product she wants from the list directly into a shopping cart.

Lists and Recommendations

Any personalized list that can be accessed by a customer, either via an e-mail from you or within his account pages on your company Web site, can encourage repeat sales. The more interactive sales-oriented customer service features you can add to your site, the more you can provide customers with exactly what they want while also continuing to build up a valuable repository of customer data to not only help you serve each customer better individually but to better serve all your customers as a whole.

Saving Items to Wish Lists

A wish list within an e-commerce system is a feature allowing customers to save items they'd like to purchase in the near or long term. The wish list is a feature they can access every time they shop, either to review it and make a purchase or to add more items to it. **Wish lists act as reminders to customers, allowing them to think about something before buying it.** You are much more likely to get a repeat sale by allowing customers to save items they are thinking about buying than relying on them to remember exactly what they were looking at and how to find it on your site the next time they stop by.

Wish lists can also increase sales by allowing customers to e-mail their wish lists to friends and family so others know what to purchase for them on their birthdays or for other occasions. The ability to share a wish list encourages customers to fill it with items they would like to have in order to make it easier for others to shop for them. In turn, their

Getting Creative with a Shopping Site　　Inside Track

In the late 1990s, my company was hired to design the first Web site for one of the brands owned by a major international cosmetics company. The product line was made with aromatic plants, earth and sea substances, and other natural resources. Entering one of their retail stores was a sensory experience, particularly because of the incredible smells. Because scent is one thing that cannot be pumped through an Internet connection, we had to find ways to create an experience for Web site visitors in keeping with the company's philosophy and playful attitude. Even though we were building an online store, we wanted to find new ways of leading customers to products. We ended up developing several interactive features. The first was a quiz that measured a visitor's stress levels then led them to relaxation products. The second was an interactive reflexology chart—an illustration of a foot in which different regions represented outcomes. A visitor could place her mouse over the toes of the foot and learn that pressing the points were relaxing. Mousing over the middle of the foot brought up an explanation that this was helpful to the heart and lungs. The illustration led visitors to a foot massage lotion and cotton reflexology socks. Another feature was more experiential—a mandala produced in Shockwave that visitors could manipulate with their cursor, stretching the design into various shapes. In the background, meditation music played and would change as the mandala shape changed. Although this feature did not directly lead to a specific product, all the product buttons were available to the visitor at any time. The mandala became a popular viral feature that people told their friends about, sending more potential customers to the online store. Think of ways that features on your site can lead your visitors to products in interesting and engaging ways.

friends and family may visit your online store for the first time and make a purchase. These are new customers whom you can try to convert to registered members and bring them back to shop at your online store in the future.

A more advanced feature of wish lists allows customers to publish their lists on your site so they can be accessed by anyone who searches wish lists by the customer's name. Your Web developer can outline the requirements and costs of adding this type of service.

Making Recommendations

The more data you gather from customers, the more you should be sure the data is stored in a robust, flexible database. Most e-commerce systems are built on a database such as SQL. Once data is in a database, you can manipulate it to provide both you and your customer with more value.

For your customers, the value is that you can provide them with product recommendations based on what they purchased previously. For example, if they purchase a shampoo product from you with a green-apple scent, your online shopping system could recommend a green-apple–scented hair conditioner. This recommendation could be offered in a variety of ways:

1. On the product page, in the form of a recommendation with a link to the corresponding product page
2. On their shopping-cart page before checkout, drawing their attention to a related product and offering them the ability to add it to their shopping cart
3. On the page confirming their completed order, allowing them to save the related product to their wish list to consider purchasing later
4. In the e-mail confirming their purchase, suggesting they check out the related product, including a link to get them to the proper page
5. On the home page, so they can add the related product to their shopping cart if they are interested

Another way to use a database to generate product recommendations for customers is to develop a quiz in which the answers lead to different products. Here's a sample questionnaire:

1. What kind of skin do you have? a. dry; b. oily; c. normal; d. sensitive
2. What kind of hair do you have? a. dry; b. oily; c. normal; d. color-treated
3. What is your hair length? a. short; b. medium; c. long; d. very long

4. What scent do you prefer? a. lavender; b. mint; c. floral; d. unscented

5. What item are you most likely to purchase in the near future? a. hand lotion; b. body lotion; c. shampoo; d. conditioner

Based on the answers submitted by a customer to the above questions, the system can feed the results into the online shopping system to generate recommended products. For example, if the person answers with all "a's," the system can recommend the following products in this order:

1. Lavender hand lotion for dry skin. This item lists first because of the customer response to question 5.

2. Lavender body lotion for dry skin

3. Lavender shampoo for dry hair

4. Lavender conditioner for dry hair

5. Hair accessories for short hair, such as mini barrettes. This corresponds to the answer for question 3.

The quiz or questionnaire format can also be used for gift shopping. A customer buying a gift for someone else can answer questions based on a variety of personality types, such as an outdoors type, a reader, a fashion-conscious person, a pet lover, or a businessperson. Based on the customer's selections, he is presented with gift recommendations for a specific type of person.

Databases can also generate recommendations using the relationships between data. For example, Amazon.com uses sophisticated database systems and relationships between data to provide a variety of automated services, including these:

1. Product recommendations on the home page when a customer is logged in, based on previous purchases

2. Product recommendations on a product page based on what other people who purchased that same product also purchased

3. Related lists created by other Amazon.com shoppers containing lists of items related to the product being viewed

4. A button in the shopping cart to "see more items like those in your shopping cart"

5. A personalized Amazon.com with the customer's name. The link leads to a page with daily recommendations, most popular tags, or keywords based on items previous viewed or purchased, a view of shopping-cart contents, new items related to interests, and customer wish-list highlights.

When recommendations databases go beyond recommending based on specific criteria and integrate the preferences of others with similar interests, the results can be uncannily accurate. The more elaborate the relationships and functionality, the more expensive a database can become.

The Size of Your Database

Unless you anticipate offering only a small number of products to a relatively small set of customers and don't plan on saving a lot of customer data, don't go with the cheapest solution just to save money now. Use a smaller database solution, such as Microsoft Access or MySQL, only if you can get assurances from your Web developer that the data can be extracted from it and imported into something more robust, such as SQL, in case you want to add many more products or your customer base grows beyond your current system. This kind of adaptability for growth is known as scalability.

Using Gift Registries

A gift registry is a handy customer service and retention feature that can help to build customer loyalty as well as expand your customer base. Once a customer registers with your site and compiles products into his registry, he can let others access it to make gift purchases, bringing new customers right to you. Gift registries can come as add-on features offered by your online store builder that can be easily integrated into your online store.

Types of Registries

Online gift registries can be attached to a particular store or, in some cases such as TheThingsIWant.com and MyRegistry.com, can be universal and not store specific, allowing a person to create a registry independent of a particular site. If you are selling your own products online, encourage your customers to create a site-specific registry using your site. While there are a variety of types of gift registries, the following are the most common:

- ⮑ Bridal shower registry
- ⮑ Wedding registry
- ⮑ Baby shower registry
- ⮑ Baby registry

Lists of items wanted for Christmas, a birthday, and other occasions are usually referred to as wish lists and not registries, though they may operate in the same manner. If a person opts to create her own registry on your site, she usually specifies details about the occasion then clicks on an "Add to Registry" button in your online store. The customer's registry should have a unique address and can be password protected. You should allow users several ways of notifying friends and family of their registry, including printable registry cards to mail out, digital registry cards to e-mail, or a form to enter or import e-mail addresses to notify others of the location and password for the registry.

Using Registry Services

These are some companies that offer registry services:

- ⮑ **FindGift.com:** Free, just add HTML code into your product pages
- ⮑ **MyGiftList.com:** In addition to free, also offers private label registries starting at $9 per month or more customized solutions for a higher price

➲ **eWish.com:** Operates on a 5 percent commission basis with a one-time, fully refundable setup fee of $599

➲ **Marcole Interactive Systems (www.marcole.com):** Offers in-store and online retail solutions

The benefit of a registry service is that the solution is low cost and low tech for you. The company providing the service hosts the gift registry technology for you. Usually all you have to do is add some custom HTML code onto your product pages to activate the registry and add the feature to your online store.

Offering Gift Certificates

By allowing customers to purchase and send gifts certificates to people they know, you are providing them with an easy gift choice, and the gift certificate will in turn bring you a new customer. Many online store solutions have a gift certificate feature to easily add certificates as a product at different dollar amounts. You must decide if you want to ship paper certificates or only offer online gift certificates to be redeemed solely at your online store.

Mining Your Site for Data

There are two main reasons to mine your site for data. First, you want to better serve your customer by analyzing and learning what they do on your site, what they purchase, and what they like, so when they visit your site again you can give them a more personalized experience. Second, you can obtain invaluable information about ways to improve your site, identifying what works and what doesn't work and how to not only attract more visitors but more effectively convert them into customers or clients.

Tracking Shopping Habits

There are many ways to obtain the data that can help you better serve your customer and improve what you are doing online, including these:

- Through a form customers fill out
- Through quizzes, questionnaires, or surveys
- Through a registration process
- By adding a cookie to their Web browser and tracking how they use your site
- By tracking the products they've purchased
- By tracking purchasing frequency
- By tracking their propensity toward gift giving
- Through a wish list or gift registry

Regardless of how you gather customer data, make sure to post your privacy and security policy in a prominent and consistent place. Most sites include links to their policies as well as to their sites' terms of use at the bottom of the home page and sometimes at the bottom of every page.

Permission to Mine

In theory, data mining should be an anonymous process. When you personalize a Web site experience for a particular user, his data helps to determine ways you can provide more tailored services. In general, however, data that is compiled and analyzed to determine customer patterns and habits should be tied to customer behavior. Still, many people are uncomfortable being watched when they are surfing a site and often will disable cookies in their browsers hoping to ward off surveillance.

While it is unlikely most customers will give explicit permission to monitor their shopping habits, they give their implied consent based on what you include in your site's terms of use and privacy and security policies. If you are allowing them to register at your site, you can make their acceptance more active by offering them the opportunity to review your policies during the registration process.

In fact, most people don't read terms of use or any policies until they are unhappy with something and are seeking a remedy. Even when you present a policy for them to read, they often scroll through the document and click "I Accept" without understanding what they are accepting. As long as you make efforts to provide customers with detailed information as to how you are tracking their Web browsing and shopping habits, they can choose to read the information and also opt not to visit or shop at your site.

▶▶ **TEST DRIVE**

As you look for ways to create a more personalized online shopping experience for your customers, you can integrate features into your shopping cart system and online store to leverage customer data and provide better customer service. Before enhancing your online store, consider the following:

➲ Have I selected an online store solution that allows me to add on enhanced personalization features as needed?

➲ Should I allow customers to register on my site, and if so, how will they benefit by registering?

➲ What is my policy on the data I gather from users?

➲ Do my terms of use, privacy, and security policies state what information I'm gathering from customers, how I'm getting it, and how I'm using it?

➲ How will I leverage the data mined from my site to improve my site for customers?

The All-Important FAQ

No amount of bells or whistles online can ever take the place of solid, old-fashioned customer service. At the heart of good online customer service is a frequently asked questions (FAQ) document or section on your Web site. Everything else you do online, whether via e-mail or on your Web site, should provide more personal and personalized service to your customers to turn your company's site into a true e-business asset. Because the Web can be both impersonal and personal, you need to go for the personal touch online to effectively serve your customers.

Building Your FAQ

Here are some common steps to building a comprehensive and useful FAQ:

1. Develop questions and answers based on previous customer inquiries.
2. Solicit common questions and answers from staff to supplement your list.
3. Compile e-mailed questions along with appropriate answers.
4. Organize questions and their corresponding answers by categories.
5. Start with a Web page of questions and answers.
6. If your FAQ is more extensive, consider building a searchable knowledge database linked to your company's Web site.

The more you know about your typical customer, the more you can anticipate what prospective and new customers may need to know in order to build confidence and close the sale. A thorough and accessible FAQ on your company site can bridge your customers' support needs, particularly after hours when you and your staff are not available to answer questions.

FAQ Presentation

While there are many ways to present an FAQ on a Web site, the most common format is a list of numbered questions at the top of the page followed by corresponding numbered answers. Early FAQs were formatted as long scrolling pages of text without any links. With HTML, each question can be linked to its corresponding answer. If all of the answers are contained on the same page as the questions, the links will jump down the page to the appropriate answer.

Here is a sample basic FAQ format:

1. How can I be sure my credit card is secure on your Web site?
2. What is your privacy policy?
3. What is your return policy?
4. How do I contact customer support?

1. We are aware of the security and privacy issues surrounding the use of the Internet. As a result, we have taken every precaution, including the use of secured socket layer (SSL) encryption, for the transmission of all data to ensure that our Web site and software is of the highest standard and secure. Read our Security Policy for more details.

2. Your privacy on the Internet and on our Web site is of the utmost importance to us. Please read our Privacy Policy to learn what information we gather and track and what we do with the information.

3. Our standard policy is to accept most returns within thirty days from the date of delivery. You may return most new, unopened items sold and fulfilled by us within thirty days of delivery for a full refund. We'll also pay the return shipping costs if the return is a result of our error (you received an incorrect or defective item, etc.). Items that are opened or returned more than thirty days after delivery will receive a partial refund. Read more about our refund policy on our Refunds Page.

4. To contact our customer support, e-mail support@ourcompany.com or call our toll-free number Monday through Fridays, from 8:00 am to 5:00 pm EST at 1-800-555-5555.

As your FAQ becomes more detailed, you can put answers on separate pages so the list of numbered questions becomes a table of contents. If many of your answers contain links to additional pages, combine the answer with the additional background information on the same new page rather than forcing customers to click more than once to get to the complete answer. Condensing and consolidating information will make your FAQ less confusing and more useful.

Establishing a Response Policy

Because of the speed of e-mail, people have higher expectations for quick responses. Even telephone customer service does not seem to always provide a fast response rate, particularly when a customer is kept holding for long periods of time. Trying to meet expectations of a faster response by e-mail can be a burden on any business. **Knowing how to manage a customer's expectations on your Web site can help reduce the stress of having to respond to every e-mail the moment you receive them.**

While a twenty-four-hour response time is ideal, with limited resources you can still go with forty-eight or even seventy-two hours. By stating that someone from your company will respond personally to an inquiry within seventy-two hours or three business days, you are managing a customer or Web visitor's expectations. Look closely at your available resources for reading e-mails generated from your Web site visitors.

Common Response Rates

By communicating with customers via your company Web site, you can buy yourself some time without giving the customers the feeling that they are on hold. Specify on your Web site, particularly on your contact page or near your contact form, exactly how quickly you will respond.

Here are some additional ways of managing e-mails from your Web site:

1. Having canned answers to common questions that someone can copy and paste into an e-mail rather than typing the same answer over and over again.

2. Including in a contact form a pull-down menu with topic choices such as Questions about Returns, Questions about Products, Question about My Order, and so on.

3. Including in a contact form a pull-down menu to automatically direct the e-mail to a specific person or department such as sales, customer service, and technical support.

4. Setting aside a specific time period each day for someone to respond to all e-mails to the company so the task is not forgotten.

5. Bringing on an intern to help sift through e-mails and prioritize them so the most pressing are handled promptly.

Auto responder

Your ISP or Web developer can set up an e-mail that will automatically go out to anyone who e-mails you through a main company e-mail address. The e-mail response should be short and courteous, letting the customer know your average response rate. Because through an auto responder a customer receives an e-mail response almost immediately after sending his, he gets instant gratification, even if only to learn that you will be getting back to him in a day or two.

Anatomy of a Response

Responses to e-mails generated from your Web site can be handled in a variety of ways, but there are some things you should consider before your Web site is up:

1. **Will you respond using text-only e-mails, or will you use HTML or formatted e-mails?** Text-only is easiest to download and read,

but HTML e-mails are more appealing and strengthen your company's brand.

2. **Will you include excerpts from your FAQ within the e-mail or instead include a link to the FAQ on your company site?** The shorter your e-mail response, the easier it is to read, so a link to relevant questions and answers on your Web-based FAQ allows customers to delve more deeply into information if they so choose.

3. **How will you personalize the response?** Will you use the customer's first name or more formally use a salutation and their last name? You should address your customers via e-mail in the same manner you would on the phone or in person.

4. **How much information will be included in the signature file of the responding e-mail?** Will you give staff member's full name or just a first name, a phone number, or an e-mail address? If you are looking for e-mail to help you manage customer-support functions, you may not want to include a phone number in each e-mailed response.

5. **How detailed a response do you want to provide?** If an answer is more complex, you may want to refer the customer to a phone number or to a specific page on your Web site rather than filling an e-mail with too much text.

6. **How will you handle situations that could create a legal issue?** A lawyer can guide you on avoiding legal issues when using e-mail for customer support.

Your goal when responding to e-mails is to provide a concise and accurate answer or a thorough response to the comment. Keep in mind that e-mail differs greatly from both an in-person encounter with a customer and a telephone encounter in that there is a very clear record of what has transpired between your company and the customer. Using canned, approved responses is easier than trying to come up with responses on the fly, but don't forget to add a personal touch to the note so customers realize there is a real person behind the e-mail.

Early Web Customer Service

Before shopping carts or secure online transactions existed, companies were looking for ways to use the Web to sell their wares online and convince people to use the Web to make a purchase. As an avid catalog shopper, I was immediately comfortable with buying online. My first online shopping experience took place when I decided to buy a unique gift for a friend's birthday. I knew my friend liked brownies, and through a search on Yahoo.com, I located Joan and Annie's Brownies. The site did not accept credit cards online but instead contained an order form that could be printed out and faxed to the company. I faxed my gift order, entering an American Express card number on the form for payment. The next day I received a phone call from my friend thanking me for the incredible brownies. Then my doorbell rang. A FedEx delivery person handed me a box from Joan and Annie's Brownies. Confused, I opened the package to find fresh brownies and a note. The note stated that their company did not accept American Express as payment and requested that I call the company's toll-free number to provide a different credit card for payment. The note ended with an invitation to sample their brownies to thank me in advance for getting in touch with them. I called the company, of course, and paid with a different credit card. I'll never forget the incredible customer service that the company provided with a special (and delicious) touch. You don't need fancy technology to make a Web site work for your company. A Web site is a tool. Doing business well online is based on the same principles of doing business well offline. Good customer service rules.

Managing Web Site Communications

Many small companies initially set up the "Contact Us" feature on their Web sites as an e-mail link. An e-mail link, however, is insufficient to provide quality customer service through a Web site. An e-mail address on a Web site can also be more vulnerable to spam. Putting an e-mail address on a Web site without using a "mailto" link that immediately launches a customer's e-mail program so they can compose their message can be frustrating for the customer. There are better ways to invite customers to contact you beyond a simple e-mail link.

Feedback Databases

A common communications tool used on Web sites is a feedback or inquiry form. The form should be programmed so it does not contain an e-mail address in the code. Programmers can program a feedback form so that the content is either e-mailed to a designated company e-mail account or stored within a database. If the content is sent via e-mail, it can be responded to through e-mail as well. Often when an e-mail is sent to a database, it is also e-mailed to the appropriate recipient. However, responding by e-mail when the message is in a database fails to take advantage of using a feedback database in the first place.

The advantages of a feedback database include the following:

➲ Data is less likely to get lost as an e-mail in somebody's inbox.
➲ Data can be sorted and counted quickly.
➲ With a database, you can run reports to better analyze the types of inquiries and feedback you are getting.
➲ Using a form to feed a database allows you to control the information you get from customers, including their contact information and location.
➲ A database makes it easy to build a Web-based tool to facilitate online communications.

A useful Web-based communications system that can reside within your company's site is one in which a customer can fill out a form that has both fields to fill in as well as pull-down menus to select from distinct lists, such as the specific topic of their communications and where to direct the e-mail. When a customer submits a message through your site, the content of the entire form can be stored in a database. An e-mail message is automatically sent to the person handling e-mail responses to let her or him know there is a new message.

The system can have a password-protected Web page through which your staff can access and respond to the message, also using a Web-based form. The person responding can access a pull-down menu with options for canned responses, as well as a field where he can add a more personalized message and even add links to the company FAQ in the signature. The response e-mail is then sent from the system while all the content of the response is also stored in the feedback database. The person responding can tag the message with additional categories or keywords to make it easier to search and find the correspondence if needed. The system can create a ticket or reference number for each inquiry to help keep track of all communications. The administrative part of this system should allow new categories to be added as needed to encompass all types of inquiries and feedback received through your site.

Content contained in databases can be a real e-business asset. Databases can interface with Web sites, allowing you to have a Web-based form on your site that can search and extract information from the database. So when you manage communications from your Web site in a database, you have the potential to build a valuable resource that can improve customer service.

Building a Knowledge Database

Databases of information gathered and archived are referred to as knowledge bases. The questions and comments from your customers and the responses from your company are assets that can help supplement a standard FAQ or completely replace it. The beauty of a knowledge base is that it continues to grow as communications with your customers continue.

Not everything in a feedback database should be accessible to all customers. The administrative portion of the communications system can include a way to tag each piece of correspondence to either include or exclude it from a search. Using databases to both manage communications and provide other customers with the content helps automate part of the customer-service process, saving time in the long run. Having a database also allows you to better analyze the communications you are receiving and pinpoint potential problems that can be addressed to improve the customer experience.

Support Forums and Live Chat

In addition to phone support, there are several interactive ways of providing customer service on your Web site. Not every company, however, is equipped to handle online forums or live chat as additional methods of online customer service.

Using Forums for Customer Support

Setting up posting boards on your Web site as a customer-service option is the easier part of the process. Monitoring, moderating, and maintaining the forums can be time consuming. Monitoring requires someone to regularly check the forums to see if there are questions that need to be answered. You can set up forums to e-mail staff to notify them when a new post is generated.

Giving and Getting Advice

According to the 2007 Simultaneous Media Study (SIMM) by BIGResearch (www.bigresearch.com), over 90 percent of consumers either regularly or occasionally give advice or seek advice about products and services from others. Most of the people who give advice are also the ones who do their product research online before making a purchase in a store. The most common means of gaining product knowledge for advice givers is through Internet searches. The most common information they are researching online include maps and directions; clothing and shoes; medical information; automotive and truck; and financial services. Don't discount word of mouth as a means of promoting your company offerings.

Moderating means reviewing posts and determining if they are questions that need to be addressed and if they are appropriate to post to the forums. Allowing users to post without moderating can create problems, particularly if the posts are inappropriate. To properly moderate a forum, you need to have guidelines and a decision-making process as to what is appropriate and what will be approved for posting. Maintaining an online forum requires technical ability to troubleshoot any issues with the forum software or programming.

Two benefits of using online forums for customer service are that they do not require immediate attention as does telephone support, and the information can be archived for all customers to access at any time. You can also provide a platform for peer-to-peer support so other customers or users can contribute helpful tips or information. Allowing others to post information, however, can create a liability if the information is incorrect. Therefore, it's advisable to moderate the posts.

Implementing Live Chat

Live online chat support requires more internal resources than online forums, but it can be more efficient than telephone support. An employee can learn to engage in several chats at one time in a seamless manner whereas trying to juggle several phone calls at one time is next to impossible. Once staff is up to speed on the technology, fewer employees are often needed to handle live online chat inquiries than phone inquiries.

Some companies that provide online chat systems include:

- InstantService Chat (*www.instantservice.com*)
- Live Person Business Chat (*www.liveperson.com*)
- LiveChatNow (*www.livechatnow.com*)
- LiveHelper (*www.livehelper.com*)
- LiveSiteManager (*www.livesitemanager.com*)
- Velaro.com (*www.velaro.com*)

While each company has its own pricing structure, in general you pay a monthly fee for live chat support software then pay an additional monthly "per seat" charge based on the number of staff or operators you want to be able to use the system simultaneously. You could pay anywhere from $20 per month to over $1,500 per month depending on the software package and the number of seats. Most live chat support software allows for an unlimited number of operators, but you will have to pay for them as you add them. Some software packages may include a set-up fee.

Assuring Security and Privacy

Established customers will probably be comfortable that they can trust you with their personal information. For new customers, however, particularly those who find you on the Web and are unfamiliar with your company, you need to assure them that you take their privacy seriously and that you've taken the extra steps to back up your claims.

The FTC and Your Privacy Policy

Under the Federal Trade Commission (FTC) Act, if you have a privacy policy, you must follow it or the FTC could pursue you. If you have no privacy policy, you can do anything you want with information disclosed to you by your site visitors. Posting a privacy policy before you ask people to provide you with personal information is good business.

Security Policies

A security policy is yet another written document you may want to have on your Web site to give customers a greater confidence that their credit card numbers and personal contact information is safe when entered into your Web site. Even if you tell them that their information is safe with you, you may want to spell out how you are using technology for security purposes.

Make sure you provide a security system using secured socket layer (SSL) encryption for secure transactions, and mention it in your policy. If you encrypt or scramble customer data within your system, such as their credit card numbers, mention this. If you use a particular software system with a strong reputation in security, mention it. Above all, be honest about your security measures. If you haven't invested in them, don't state that you have or it could cause trouble if something goes wrong with customers' personal data and you've misled them to believe your site was secure.

Respecting Privacy

While it is easy to state that your privacy policy is stringent and that you will not sell or distribute your site visitors' personal information to third parties, sticking with your policy can be a challenge. At times, opportunities arise that seem financially rewarding in the near term. You may receive an offer from an advertiser to buy your list of customer e-mails, for example. Though tempting, you must evaluate the level of trust you are building with your customers. The right solution is to stick to your original policy and find more creative ways to partner with an advertiser other than selling your list. You could, for example, offer the company the opportunity to be mentioned in your e-newsletter as an advertiser even if you had not thought of selling advertising in the past.

You do, however, have the prerogative to change your policies—any of them. When you first develop your site policy statements, one clause should state that your company has the right, at any time, to modify the policy.

TRUSTe Certification

An independent non-profit third-party certification organization is TRUSTe (www.truste.org). Through their Web seal program you can apply to have your privacy policies reviewed and, if you qualify, receive a graphic or Web seal to put on your home page. The seal links back to the TRUSTe site and provides your site visitors with verification of your company's privacy compliance with their strict privacy standards. Price for certification starts around $650 and is based on company revenues. Consumers can also file privacy complaints and TRUSTe works to resolve the issues.

In practice, however, changing your policy could cause a backlash. If you make a policy change, make sure you have a strategy in place that includes the reasons for the change and how to handle any negative response to the changes. Make sure you clearly inform customers about the policy changes either in your e-newsletter, on your home page or What's New section or by making a prominent note at the top of the policy when the change is first implemented to draw attention to the new information. As long as you are honest about your intentions, you should be able to keep the trust you've built with your customers intact.

►► TEST DRIVE

Taking a customer-centric approach to everything you do online should yield better results for your company. To get in the customer's frame of mind, consider the following:

- ➲ How am I keeping track of the questions my customers are asking?
- ➲ How am I listening to my customers and applying what I hear to improving my company's Web site?
- ➲ How is customer feedback having an impact on my e-business strategies?
- ➲ How do I leverage what my customers are saying to strengthen my relationship with them?
- ➲ How am I continually building trust with my customers?

Submitting to Search Engines

Google and Yahoo! are two of the largest companies using the pay per click (PPC) model, where site owners bid on keywords they think people might use in order to find their site or similar sites. The more popular keywords cost more. The word "travel" costs more than "Alaska travel"; "RV" costs more than "RV women" and so on. With a PPC model, you only pay when people actually click on the link to your Web site that appears on the search results page for the keywords you have purchased. **Most search engines charge to place a link to your company's Web site at the top of a search engine results page, usually based on the keywords you have purchased.** Many directories charge to guarantee a listing on their site. Yahoo! receives so many site submissions that they started charging to expedite the listing process. Although they still add sites for free, it can take months to get your site added.

Free Submissions

Submitting your site to most major search engines is still free though many of them also offer premium services for a fee, so you are paying for placing your listing in a favored position in search engine results. For example, Yahoo! offers Search Submit Express for $49 for the first URL submitted. The cost per URL falls the more you submit. They also offer Search Submit Pro, a pay-per-click model, in which the cost varies based on the category. Here are some of the top search engines:

1. **Yahoo!** *(www.yahoo.com)*: Scroll down to the bottom of the home page and click on "Suggest a Site." Choose "Submit Your Site For Free" and sign into your Yahoo! account (free). You can submit a site or RSS feed but will have to authenticate the feed as your own (directions provided).
2. **Google** *(www.google.com)*: Click on "About Google" then "Submit your content to Google" under "For Site Owners." Then click on "Add your URL to Google's Index."

3. **Ask.com** (*www.ask.com*): This search engine does not allow submissions but recommends optimizing your site for search engines.

4. **MSN.com** (*www.live.com*): MSN uses Microsoft technology called Windows LiveSearch. To submit your site, follow the instructions at *http://search.msn.com.sg/docs/submit.aspx*.

The search engine universe continues to consolidate, so there are fewer major search engines that will have a significant impact on your site traffic.

Paying for Site Submissions

There are companies that will submit your company site to search engines and directories for a fee. Some charge to use a Web-based tool that automatically submits your site to search engines. Others charge a fee for search engine submission services they perform for you. Prices start around $25 per URL submitted.

Some of the companies offering search engine submissions services include these:

- ➲ 1 2 3 Submit Pro (*www.websitesubmit.hypermart.net*)
- ➲ AddPro.com (*www.addpro.com*)
- ➲ Submission-Pro (*www.submission-pro.com*)
- ➲ Submit Express (*www.submitexpress.com*)
- ➲ Website-submission.com (*www.website-submission.com*)

Only a handful of search engines are popular and widely used, such as Google, Yahoo!, Ask.com, and MSN. Other search engines are powered by the search engine software created by the popular search engines. For example, AltaVista and AlltheWeb.com use Yahoo! while AOL Search and Netscape Search use Google. Getting listed, however, does not guarantee top placement on search engines. Often the only guarantee is buying placement from the search engines that sell it, like Yahoo! and Google.

Paying for Online Advertising

In many cases, online advertising follows a similar model to offline advertising. Purchasing banners and other graphical ads on Web sites is closest to offline advertising. Buying listings on a directory is similar to buying a listing in the Yellow Pages or another kind of print directory. Buying keywords on a search engine, however, is something that is unique to the Web. Understanding the basics of online advertising can help you determine how best to spend your marketing dollars. Just as in traditional advertising, the more effective ads are often the more costly.

Banners and Web Ads

Ads on the Web are graphics in a variety of shapes and sizes, although some shapes and sizes are more common than others. The most widely accepted standard banner size, for example, is 468 pixels high by 60 pixels wide.

Banners and Web ads can be static or animated. They can even contain rich media, or multimedia features using Shockwave or Flash to make them more interactive. Many people feel that Web banners are passé although they are still in use on most popular content Web sites. Because of the inundation of online advertising, it is hard to get people to click on banners anymore.

The following are the main ways sites charge for a Web banner or ad:

1. **Impressions:** The number of views of the pages where your ad appears.
2. **Click-throughs or click-thrus:** The number of times visitors actually click on the banner or ad to go to your site. Calculated as a cost per click (CPC).
3. **Action:** The number of times a visitor clicks through and then takes action, such as signing up for something on your site. Calculated as a cost per action (CPA).
4. **Performance:** This is different from action in that it measures an actual sale so you pay per sale, either a set dollar amount or a percentage of the sale.

You usually pay before your Web ad appears, based on an agreed number of impressions. However, in the CPC or CPA models, you often pay once you receive a reporting of the clicks or actions. You can also verify the numbers from your end by tracking page views or actions because they take place on your site.

Online Ads and Electronic PR

The main benefit of placing ads online is that the ad can easily be linked to your Web site. With traditional advertising, people must move away from the television or remember your Web site URL after hearing it on the radio or bring their newspaper or magazine to their desk then turn on their computer, get online, and access your site. With online advertising, they can get to you right away.

Getting mentioned in online media outlets has a similar advantage, but not all online media Web sites link out to other Web sites. Take a look at CNN.com, MSNBC.com, and other top news sites. Most of them limit the number of links they have to outside Web sites, and some do not link out at all. Getting mentioned on media Web sites does not guarantee an immediate link back to your site.

When it comes to online advertising and public relations, here are some things to consider:

1. Make sure the message is clear and branded or tied to your company image, logo, or name.
2. Include key information along with a call to action, such as a message to visit your company site.
3. Specify specific pages within your Web site where ads should link to better monitor results.
4. Make sure your press releases include your Web site URL.
5. Keep track of traffic whenever you send out a release or place an ad to see what triggers the most traffic.
6. Measure the results of any marketing campaign as a traffic driver and hone your marketing budget to put more money toward more productive marketing tactics.
7. Modify your marketing messages to improve actions and click-throughs to drive more traffic to your site.

Whatever online advertising and public relations you plan, orchestrate it with your offline advertising and PR efforts. While there are reasons to implement all ads and releases at the same time for a major push, such as when your Web site launches, you also want to spread advertising and PR across an extended time period to keep up the momentum.

Seeding Forums and Blogs

Message boards or forums and the comments sections of blogs are places you can market your Web site, but you must be thoughtful when you do so. When it comes to grassroots online marketing, the seed you plant in public forums should take into consideration the rules and purpose of each forum.

Marketing on Other Boards

Seeding, or posting advertising messages on online forums, is often considered a violation of written or unwritten rules of the online community communicating within that forum. Some message boards do have written rules—often in the FAQ—that explains what can and cannot be posted on the board. Advertising or commercials are more than likely on their forbidden list.

If you post a commercial message on a board it will probably be removed or, if the board is fully moderated, will not even get posted. In some cases, you may experience a backlash from the board's community members, who do not look fondly on blatant advertisements.

If you are thinking of seeding an online forum with a marketing message, there are some steps you should take, including these:

- Read through archived posts to become familiar with the tone of the board.
- Craft a message to post that is informational and useful rather than promotional.
- Include a link to your company Web site where more relevant information and resources exist.
- Include a one-line marketing message, if appropriate, at the bottom of your post as a signature.

Because you may have the ability to post anonymously on a message board or to a blog, you may be tempted to pose as someone else when you post. However, this practice is frowned upon by most online communities. Being straightforward, open, and honest about your identity and your intentions when you post something related to your company, product, or service is much better than posing as a satisfied customer.

Marketing on Blogs

The comments feature on blogs creates an online forum that looks similar to an old-fashioned guest book, where people can post messages that appear one after another down the length of a Web page. While message boards allow for threads or conversations to be grouped or linked and have more sophisticated organizational features, comments in a blog are expected to be in direct response to the corresponding blog post. They can appear immediately unless the blog owner or blogger moderates the comments section.If you are planning to seed a blog with a marketing message, proceed with caution. Many blogs are the platforms for the bloggers who run them, and they may not appreciate you suddenly appearing on their blog with a commercial. When it comes to seeding blogs, on-topic, appropriate, and non-commercial is better. Overall, be respectful of the online community.

Building Links Relationships

Links are the basis of the Web—both links within a Web site leading to other pages within the site and links from one Web site to another, augmenting one site's content and resources by tying into another relevant site. While it is possible that individuals and companies will link to your Web site from their sites, it is far more effective to take a proactive approach to establishing linking relationships.

A systematic effort to obtain links from other sites is called a reciprocal link campaign. A reciprocal link campaign is different from trying to get your site listed in search engines and on searchable directories. You are asking owners of Web sites to create a link to your Web site. In exchange, you usually link back to theirs.

Some things to consider before linking to other sites include these:

⮕ How will linking to other sites create value for your site?

⮕ How can you link to other sites without losing visitors?

⮕ Where is the most appropriate place to link to other sites from your site?

⮕ Will you also include a description or graphic, such as a logo, with the link?

⮕ Will you still link to a site if it does not link back to yours?

Linking to other sites can be useful to your visitors, but the real goal is getting other sites to link to yours. By getting more sites linking to your company site, you are not only increasing the likelihood of people finding your site, but it will also indirectly help improve your search engine rankings on certain search engines that factor in link popularity, measuring the number of popular sites that link back to yours.

Locating Link Partners

The first step to implementing a reciprocal link campaign is to identify the sites you would like to link back to you. Chances are that your list will include large, mid-sized, and small company sites and, in some cases, blogs or personal Web sites. The likelihood of high-trafficked or highly popular sites linking back to your site is slim, or there will probably be a cost involved, but it never hurts to ask.

To figure out what kinds of sites might add a link to your site, take these steps:

1. Use a search engine to find sites that are complementary to your site.
2. Visit each site that sounds promising and see if it has a links page or resource section.
3. Make note of other sites the company links to from their site and add relevant ones to your list of prospects.
4. Locate the contact information, particularly an appropriate e-mail contact such as a marketing person or Webmaster.
5. See if the company has other marketing or advertising opportunities, including banners or other types of online ads.

Use a spreadsheet to keep track of the information you gather from sites, including the site name, URL, contact information, whether or not they have a links or resources section, and some of the key sites they link to from their site.

Who Is Linking to You?

You can find out who is linking to your Web site by using search engines. Instead of searching for your company name, search for links by entering the following text in the search field of a search engine such as Google: link:http:// www.yourcompanysite.com. This should reveal the number of sites linking to you, a list of those sites, and pages where that link appears. Try doing a similar search at other search engines such as AltaVista.com to see if their database turns up additional sites. Consider sending a thank-you e-mail to sites that link to yours.

Establishing Link Relationships

People often exchange links on the Web through text links on a links or resources page. If you haven't yet planned for a links or resources page, add this to your Web site plan if it makes good business sense.

If you decide that linking to other sites is a good idea, there are several ways of looking at linking to other sites:

- ○ Link to them regardless of whether or not they link back to create a valuable resource on your site.
- ○ Link to only the sites that agree to link back to yours.
- ○ Link to other sites with a text link only.
- ○ Link to other sites using a graphic, such as a logo.
- ○ Link to other sites and include text, such as a description.

The most effective link campaigns happen when more sites link to yours or when the reciprocal links are of equal value and placement, meaning if you link to them with a graphic on your links page, they do the same.

Inside Track   Faking a Blog Comment

According to Wikipedia, "astroturfing" describes public relations efforts that "seek to engineer the impression of spontaneous public reactions . . . when in fact the efforts are centrally coordinated." Astroturfing is considered bad form at best and deceptive at worst. In the world of online forums and blogs, if astroturfing is revealed, the companies at the heart of the deceptive seeding efforts are usually lambasted in the press, on Web sites, and even more so on other blogs. In the fall of 2006, beauty blog Jack & Hill (www.jackandhill.net) posted a message accusing a PR firm of posing as "thrilled customers" of their clients' products. Angry about the blog spam, the Jack & Hill blog advised other beauty blogs to be on the lookout for the fake comments. Dozens of bloggers picked up the discussion, linking to the PR company's Web site, directing even more attention to the controversy. The PR company denied any wrongdoing. The previous year, a bread company was in the middle of a fake blog comment and fake blog, or "flog," brouhaha when a chef blogging negatively about the company found a comment on her post that read suspiciously like what she called "corporate propaganda"—a glowing review of the bread company and a link to a fan blog. After the story appeared on multiple blogs, the fan blog suddenly disappeared. The company denied any involvement with the fake comment or fake blog. Apparently an ad agency trying to win the company's business created the fake blog and comment. Bottom line: Faking it online can result in a backlash. Stick with honesty, full disclosure, and transparency when marketing online.

Once you have identified the sites you want to link to your site, compose a short, simple e-mail such as this:

Hello,

I'm the president of ABC Salmon Company located in Anchorage, Alaska. We've launched (or re-launched) our online catalog offering salmon products. We'd like to exchange links with your site because we seem to have complementary businesses, and I know our customers would be interested in what you offer. Please take a look at our site and click on the Links button to see where we'd link to your site. I look forward to hearing from you.

Jane Doe
President, ABC Company

Allow several weeks before you follow up with a second message. When you get a response, make sure you mark the results off on your spreadsheet and carry out the link relationship in the manner you've established with your new linking partner.

Going for Linkbait

Tracking down sites for reciprocal link campaigns is a time-consuming process. Some experts advocate using linkbait to lure people to link to your site. The term linkbait means unique content that you put on your Web site to encourage other Web sites and blogs to link to it. The more value or resources you create on your Web site, the more likely others will link to it voluntarily. Unless you are a content site, however, developing compelling content that attracts links is even more time-consuming than asking a site or blog owner to link to your site.

Viral Link Campaign

You can implement a link campaign that is more viral by coming up with an attractive, cute, or clever graphic compelling enough to lead other sites to lift the graphic and link back to your site. You usually need some kind of theme to carry off this sort of campaign. Then create buttons and banners in various sizes so each site owner can select the one that best fits her or his Web site design.

To implement the campaign, create a page that contains both the graphics and the HTML code in case site owners want to link to your site and use the graphic without having to download the graphic to their own site. From your home page, you can include the graphic with a message to "Click here to put this on your site!" You can then market this campaign to sites that may be interested.

Often sites that have members or subscribers offer graphics that can be downloaded with the HTML code to link back to their site. Some provide code for Flash badges that dynamically update, such as the badge from a company named Twitter that updates with new personal messages from subscribers and the Confabb badge that lists current speaking engagements and conferences.

Setting Up an Affiliate Program

An affiliate or performance-based marketing program is the process whereby you pay a sales commission to other Web sites that help sell your products. Amazon.com popularized the affiliate program by allowing people to set up their Web sites with a bookstore and the books of their choice and providing a system to track the sales generated from customers they referred to the Amazon.com site. There are several reputable affiliate program service providers that offer turn-key solutions to start your own affiliate program, including Commission Junction (www.cj.com), LinkShare (www.linkshare.com), and ClickBank (www.clickbank.com). Depending on which service you use, when you set up an affiliate program, you might be considered an advertiser or publisher, while a site that carries your products through your affiliate program is considered an affiliate (or sometimes a publisher). Ultimately, you are setting up an affiliate program and other sites are affiliating with you by carrying your products or linking to your products from their site for a commission.

How Affiliate Programs Work

Affiliate program service providers usually offer an automated system that allows other sites to become affiliates of your company's Web site. While prices vary with each affiliate program service, you may be charged a set-up fee then pay a small percentage of each transaction, or the service will mark up your price to add on a per-product fee.

Your affiliates are provided with the proper tools and HTML to either list some of your products on their sites or place graphic or text ads for your company and products on their sites. When a visitor clicks on a product, ad, or text link on an affiliate site, that visitor is led to your site or online catalog. The system tracks all customers referred to you in this manner as well as the purchases they make. The affiliate program system not only keeps track of how many sales are generated from each of your affiliates but also helps you calculate and distribute commissions.

Before you set up an affiliate program for your site, you should take the following steps:

1. **Determine the commission you will provide to your affiliates.** Most affiliate systems allow you to input the specific amount you want.

2. **Decide whether you will provide affiliates with text ads, graphic ads, or your logo, and whether they have the ability to link directly to products or just to your home page.** The more options you offer, the more effective their affiliation will become.

3. **Be prepared to develop ad copy for text ads.** The affiliate system you use may offer tips and guidelines for any copy you create.

4. **Be prepared to develop graphics, both banners and other ad shapes and sizes, to be used by your affiliates.** The affiliate system you select should specify what images to create.

5. **Determine how frequently you want to pay commissions to your affiliates.** Most affiliate systems allow you to select monthly, quarterly, or other timeframes.

You can market your affiliate program on your home page, in your FAQ, on your contact page, on the order page of your online catalog, and anywhere else on your site where prospective affiliates may look. Once you sign up, the affiliate program service should also list your affiliate program within its system so potential affiliates can more easily locate your company when they are actively searching for affiliate opportunities.

Pros and Cons of Affiliate Programs

Implementing an affiliate program on your Web site can increase brand visibility and sales for your company. Using an affiliate program service can help make the set-up process more streamlined and automate the maintenance of the program.

Some of the challenging steps you must take when setting up an affiliate program include the following:

1. **Determine the criteria you will use to screen applicants for your affiliate program.** Usually, an affiliate program service provider can outline the best criteria to use.
2. **Screen applicants.** The affiliate system may automate this process to a certain extent, but you will still need to assign this task to someone in your company or take it on yourself.
3. **Develop text and graphics for your affiliates.**
4. **Regularly update the text and graphics for your affiliates.** Establish a schedule for developing new creative ideas based on holidays and events that are relevant to your market.
5. **Monitor your affiliates for proper usage of your graphics and text.** Some affiliate program services may provide basic monitoring, but you may need to assign someone on staff—or take it upon yourself—to visit your affiliate sites to make sure your company's information is current and properly displayed.

While affiliate programs can be automated to a certain extent through affiliate program service providers, no automated system can entirely eliminate the work you will need to do to implement and keep up with the program.

▶▶ TEST DRIVE

As you are thinking about how to attract customers to your online catalog or how to sell more product online, consider:

- ➲ How much do I want to invest in sending out online releases, particular through wire services?
- ➲ How much time do I have to devote to seeding online forums and blogs, and what is the right message for this type of grassroots marketing?
- ➲ How much time do I have to locate and contact sites with whom to establish linking relationships, and where will my links to other sites fit on my company site?
- ➲ How much money do I want to spend on online advertising, and on which sites should I advertise?
- ➲ Do I have the internal company resources needed to set up an affiliate program?

The Online and Offline Mix

You've gone through the planning and the building processes for your Web site or online store. You've conducted the proper beta testing, you did a soft launch, and now you are gearing up for an official launch. There are many traditional tactics for marketing a Web site, including print advertising, television and radio ads, media coverage, and marketing materials. There are also corresponding online tactics to get the word out about your site.

When it comes to e-business, fully integrated marketing involves a strategic blend of both traditional and online marketing tactics, creating the right balance to effectively reach your target market. The more that online marketing tactics complement offline tactics, the more technology is being leveraged to your company's advantage using your marketing budget efficiently to better reach your market. Whatever you do about marketing, keep your customers or prospective customers in mind in order to select the tactics that will best match the way they consume media.

Assessing Traditional Tactics

There is nothing wrong with using offline marketing to direct people to your online presence. Whatever tactics you have been using, you should assess how they are working for you. Some questions to ask include these:

1. **How are my customers finding out about me?** If you don't know whether it was the newspaper ad, direct mail piece, or word of mouth that led them to you or your Web site, ask them.

2. **How am I measuring the response rate to my marketing efforts?** Whether you've used a coupon so you can count how many have been redeemed or invite people to your store on a particular day for a one-day sale, look for ways to gauge the effectiveness of each marketing tactic.

3. **Based on what I'm spending, how much of a return am I getting for my money?** Newspaper and magazine ads can be much more expensive than sending a press release. However, if you know 200 people saw your paid ad while no media outlet

picked up a release you sent over a fee-based wire service, you can assume a better return on the ad than the release.

4. **How much am I paying to attract each potential customer?** Look at the cost of your newspaper ad with a coupon and divide it by the number of coupons brought in to see how much it cost you to bring in each customer. Calculate this cost for all marketing tactics.

5. **How can I make sure my offline marketing efforts are complemented by what I'm doing online?** Look for ways to cross-promote from offline to online and back. For example, reference your Web site in print collateral and mention your offline store on your Web site.

No tactic should be developed in a vacuum. Look at all tactics to see how they fit together, cross-reference, and support each other.

Integrating E-Marketing Tactics

For every offline marketing tactic, there is a corresponding online version. While the offline tactics may be familiar, the online ones may require some research and even consultation with an online marketing expert to get it right the first time.

Mistakes online also cost you money, but because of the quick nature of Internet communications, they can create bigger problems. Good news travels fast online, but bad news travels faster.

Here are some offline tactics and their online counterparts:

Offline Tactic	Online Tactic
Press releases	E-releases
Print collateral	Web site
Advertising	Online ads
Newsletters	E-newsletters
Direct mail	E-mail campaign
PR staff	Online press room
Meetings	Online forums
Partnering	Online networks
Word of mouth	Viral marketing

Just because you have been successfully using an offline tactic does not automatically mean that the online tactic is right for your company or your customer.

The Advertising and PR Mix

When you advertise in traditional media outlets such as newspapers, magazines, radio, and television, you can expect significant costs, including creating the ad or hiring an advertising agency and paying the ad fees. While the cost of online advertising is less than offline advertising, you still need a budget to place ads. With public relations, both offline and online, a significant cost can come with hiring a public relations firm; for this reason, many companies choose to do PR in-house. There really is no such thing as free advertising or free PR because everything comes with a cost—if not money, then definitely time.

Print Advertising

In marketing, the difference between advertising and public relations is in the customer's mind. They know you pay to place an advertisement, but if a reporter writes about your company in a reputable media outlet, the implication is that the coverage is not biased, not paid for, and therefore more credible. Some people think that PR is less costly than advertising, particularly if they send out press releases without hiring a PR firm. With an ad, you pay an upfront advertising fee and have guaranteed placement. With do-it-yourself PR, you pay with your time, and there is no guarantee any media will pick up your story.

With both public relations and advertising, make sure you include your Web site URL. In print advertising in particular, you can create duplicate home pages to be used in each ad you place to help you measure the effectiveness of that ad. For example, you could place an ad in your local newspaper—say the *Cheyenne Tribune Eagle*—and put the following URL in your ad: www.yourcompanysite.com/cte.html. For your sponsorship package on Wyoming Public Radio, your audio ad could contain the

URL www.yourcompanysite.com/wpr.html. Now you can easily tell how effective each ad is in sending traffic to your site by monitoring in your Web traffic logs the number of page views to cte.html versus wpr.html.

Here are some tips for integrating your URL into a print ad:

1. Use the shortest URL possible.
2. Don't bother using http:// if your URL begins with "www."
3. If your URL starts with anything other than "www," such as *http://shop.mycompany.com*, you may want to include http:// in front.
4. Brand your URL by making it more prominent than your company name. If your company is ABC Flowers and your URL is www.abcflowersonline.com, consider using ABCFlowersOnline.com more prominently than your company name.
5. Place something prominently on your home page or the landing page mentioned in your ad that lets people know they've come to the right place, such as welcoming readers of the daily paper where you've placed the ad.

The more prominently you use your Web address in your ads, the more you need to make sure your Web site is an effective e-business tool for your company.

PR in the Mix

Trying to place a news story with public relations is really hit or miss—you have no way of guaranteeing that a media outlet will mention you in a story. With advertising, you pay for an ad and usually for a particular timeframe and even placement of that ad, and it will be there as ordered. Some people find PR to be a time-consuming, frustrating, and thankless process. **However, a good media placement can strengthen your company's reputation far more than any ad.**

First, you should identify the media outlets where you want to send your release based on the audience you are trying to reach. Next, obtain the correct contact information for those outlets—usually through a media source such as Bulldog Reporter or Bacons, either in a directory or through an online account. Media directories are pricey, running in the hundreds of dollars. Once you have all the contact information, compose your release, and distribute it in an appropriate manner. Sending it out is not enough: You have to follow up with the media contacts and convince busy reporters and producers to cover your company or Web site as a news story.

While one way to distribute press releases is directly to editors, producers, and reporters, if you don't have an established relationships with the media, getting your release read—much less your news story picked up—is challenging. You can use services on the Web to send your releases. There are some free press-release distribution tools such as Free-Press-Release.com and 24-7pressrelease.com, but it may not always be clear what media subscribes to or receives releases from free or low-cost Web sites. Still, any form of online distribution can be helpful.

The Bad E-Release

A bad electronic release sent via e-mail is long and forces the reader to scroll and scroll to read it; contains attached files; is sent to the wrong reporter; doesn't display contact information prominently at the top and bottom of the e-mail; and is sent to an e-mail list incorrectly so everyone sees everyone else's e-mail address. Sending a bad e-release could put you on a reporter's spam list to be banned from that inbox forever. Your goal is for the media to welcome your e-mails and releases and more importantly, to read, respond, and report positively about your company.

For better results, use fee-based distribution channels for press releases that can send your release directly to media who subscribe to their services in a format the media is used to seeing and from a source they most likely trust. Some fee-based services for distributing press releases include the following:

- PRWeb (*www.prweb.com*)
- PR Newswire (*www.prnewswire.com*)
- Business Wire (*www.businesswire.com*)
- Marketwire (*www.marketwire.com*)
- Collegiate Presswire (*www.cpwire.com*)
- Internet News Bureau (*www.internetnewsbureau.com*)

There are also regular news wire services such as the Associated Press, UPI, and Dow Jones. For the most part, submitting your release to news wires is like submitting to reporters. They are inundated with press releases and often make decisions on what to report on based on relationships, current news trends, and assignments.

Online Pressrooms

An online pressroom, also known as an online media center, helps the media access information about your company and your Web site. There is no limit to the type of information and kinds of resources you can offer in an online pressroom, but remember this is not a traditional marketing feature of your site. The media are looking for factual information, not marketing jargon and hyperbole about the greatness of your company.

Elements of an Online Pressroom

The materials included in an online pressroom can vary from company to company. First and foremost, your pressroom should be a searchable archive of any media materials you produce. Next, you want to supply the media with the tools to do their job more effectively. Overall, you want to make sure your messages to the media are clear and consistent and that they continue to emphasize your company's overall business goals.

An online pressroom might include the following:

- ➲ Easy-to-find contact information for your company's media relations contact
- ➲ A company history and other fact sheets, available as downloadable Word documents and PDF files
- ➲ Company team bios and high-resolution photos
- ➲ Expert sources listed with talking points and credentials
- ➲ Chronological or searchable archive of past press releases
- ➲ Chronological list of current press releases
- ➲ High resolution images of your company logo and photographs of products
- ➲ Suggested story ideas (news items and trends, not advertisements)
- ➲ Audio and video files, if appropriate and available
- ➲ Links to relevant materials in other sections of your company site

Online pressrooms do not have to be fancy or flashy. They should be easy to use and useful. Reporters are often on deadline so have little time to surf around to find the information they need.

Keep in mind that customers may also access your online pressroom because it is not customary for this area to be password protected. While most customers may not peruse an area marked for the media, make sure you present only information you want available to the general public at any time. Customers are often interested in reading articles about your company, so you can include a separate area on your site called "In the News" with links to articles.

Online Press Releases

Online press releases are usually much shorter than regular press releases. A good length for an e-release is 400 words. The elements of a press release, either electronic or print, are virtually the same and include:

- ➲ A descriptive headline
- ➲ A concise and informative first paragraph answering who, what, when, and where

⮩ Two or three additional short paragraphs with background

⮩ A quote from a company spokesperson that can answer how and why

⮩ Contact information at the top and bottom of the release

In the content of your e-release, identify what makes your company's Web site unique or interesting beyond the fact that it has recently launched. Look for human-interest angles; tie-ins with current events; links to national or regional trends; or service and how-to oriented messages to pique the interest of the media.

Take advantage of links in e-mails by including a link to your Web site within the text of your e-release as well as at the end. You can also include a link that leads directly to your online pressroom so the media can find supporting documents, images, and other tools to enhance your release. Try to avoid attaching files to e-releases but instead link to the additional materials.

Viral Word of Mouth

Getting other people to talk about your company, services, or products is the foundation of grassroots marketing. **The marketing term for powerful word of mouth is buzz, and you can generate buzz offline as well as online.** But online buzz travels faster and wider than offline buzz because of the speed and global reach of e-mail. Also, offline buzz can quickly end up online as people e-mail their friends, family, or colleagues about something they've read, seen, or heard offline.

Viral marketing in and of itself is not a guaranteed revenue generator, but by using it you can get visitors to your site or get members of your e-mail list to drive more traffic to your Web site. The more people you can draw to your Web site, the more opportunities you have to market and sell to them.

Viral E-Postcards

A common viral feature for Web sites is an e-postcard engine, which creates a way for people to send and receive electronic postcards from your Web site. An e-postcard engine is a software system that stores and manages images that are the size and shape of a traditional postcard—usually five by seven inches—allowing visitors to select an image, insert a message, and send a message via e-mail to someone they know. The entire postcard image is not e-mailed, however. The recipient receives an e-mail with a message that she has a postcard sent by someone she knows and a link directly back to the site that contains the electronic postcard on a Web page.

A basic e-postcard engine can be purchased for under $1,000. E-postcards are a natural fit for artists and photographers or anyone who is in the business of creating images that could then be digitized and used as electronic postcards. With proper branding on the card, such as the artist's name and Web site URL, these e-postcards not only drive people to a Web site but can also act as calling cards for an artist's work.

To leverage a viral marketing tactic such as e-postcards, prominent links to the rest of the Web site should lead visitors to an online store, for example, where they can immediately buy a print of the postcard art. Any critical calls to action should be readily accessible from the page where users retrieve the e-postcard and message.

Word of Mouth Marketing Association (WOMMA)

WOMMA is a trade organization for companies that use word-of-mouth marketing. They've produced ethical guidelines to protect both consumers and the industry and work to "promote word of mouth as an effective marketing tool." If you are implementing viral marketing features and looking to stimulate word of mouth about your company or products, refer to their library of articles and resources on their site at www.womma.org. Under Ethics, you can access "10 Principles for Ethical Contact by Marketers," a checklist companies can use to make sure their marketing efforts involving bloggers are appropriate and ethical.

Getting Viral with Monkeys

A popular career, employment, and job-search site, Careerbuilder.com, has launched a viral marketing campaign using e-postcards with a twist. Monk-E-Mail (www.careerbuilder.com/monk-e-mail) allows visitors to pick one of three monkeys then accessorize it in headgear, outfits, glasses, and even put something in its hands, like a cell phone or a sparkler. Next, visitors select one of several options for message delivery: a recorded message, text converted to speech, or a message recorded via phone or computer microphone. The image of the dressed-up monkey then lip-syncs the message the visitor submits. The message is limited to 200 characters, but the postcard packs plenty of humor into just a few seconds, encouraging the recipients to go to the Monk-E-Mail site to send their own messages.

The interactive feature was created by CareerBuilder.com's agency, Cramer-Krasselt, and the campaign launched in January of 2006 to complement the company's "I Work with a Bunch of Monkeys" television ads. The campaign received extensive media coverage including Business Week Online, a number of daily newspapers, *Advertising Age*, and even humorist Dave Barry's blog. Hundreds of bloggers mentioned and linked to the Monk-E-Mail site. According to online marketing review site MarketingSherpa.com, within three months of launch, over 14 million e-mails were sent and played. By September 2006, over 60 million had been played. The first week alone generated more than 250,000 sessions. Success can cost money as the company needed to add 350 more phone lines to handle the record-by-phone feature. A search for Monk-E-Mail on Google returned over 84,600 results seven weeks post launch and 10 million results a year after launch. The right viral idea can generate a great deal of traffic for your company site. Be prepared, however, for the technical issues that can arise if your viral marketing campaign is a tremendous success.

If photographs or artwork are not your line of business, that doesn't mean you cannot use e-postcards as a form of viral marketing. Some ideas for implementing e-postcards include the following:

1. A travel agency might use destination photographs purchased from a travel photographer.
2. A hiking supply company might use paintings of outdoor scenes purchased from an artist.
3. A computer consultant might include quick, useful computer tips on each card.
4. A women's health-care provider could put an important message, such as "Remember to get a mammogram," on postcards with a pink ribbon graphic for breast cancer awareness.
5. A clothing company could commission a graffiti artist to create colorful designs for digital postcards.

The e-postcard system doesn't force people to send actual files to others, though some people—particularly teens—don't mind sending or receiving attached files. The goal of e-postcards is to get other people to drive traffic back to your company site. Most people are more likely to click on a link in an e-mail from someone they know than from a company they haven't encountered before.

Downloading Plug-Ins

If you are creating a file that can be downloaded from your site that requires special software to view or use, place a link on your site to sites where your visitors can download the required software, reader, or plug-in. A plug-in is a small software program that can be downloaded, usually for free, and integrated with a Web browser, "plugging in" to add a new capability. Some common plug-ins are Real or Windows Media that play both audio and video files; QuickTime to play video files; and Adobe Acrobat to read PDF files. The link to a plug-in should be near the links to the files on your site to be downloaded.

Viral Downloads

If you're trying to target the teen market, you could create something that could be downloaded then attached to an e-mail and forwarded along to others. Here are some things that could be downloaded and passed along:

- ➲ Cartoons or comic strips
- ➲ Animation
- ➲ Photographs
- ➲ Slideshows in PowerPoint
- ➲ Audio files
- ➲ Digital video files
- ➲ Small software programs
- ➲ Screensavers

The key to any downloadable file is that it must be compelling in some way—humorous, moving, odd, or unusual—so that the person who downloads it wants to share it with others.

If you are concerned about the liability of allowing others to compose their own messages on your e-postcards, you can remove that feature and allow them to choose from a series of messages you've developed that are relevant and appropriate. The messages should not be commercial but rather be something people would like to share with others.

Television and Radio

The most attractive aspect of online marketing tactics is the way they can be measured more readily than anything that occurs offline. For example, measuring how many people came to your store because of a radio ad is much harder than measuring how many people in a marketing e-mail clicked on a link and arrived at your Web site. Once people are at your Web site, you can continue to track and measure where they clicked after arriving on your page, how many pages they viewed on their visit, and, if you have an online store, even what products they purchased.

Leveraging Broadcast Ads

When you flash your URL on a television ad that usually lasts only thirty seconds, make sure it is short and easy to remember. If a voiceover says the URL or if you are broadcasting it on the radio, make sure what the audience hears will lead them to your site. If your URL or your company name can be spelled in a number of ways, you may want to spell it out, especially on radio. Keep in mind that having to spell your URL can take up precious time on a radio ad.

You can circumvent some of the confusion from misspelled URLs by anticipating the misspellings and reserving those extra domain names and having them point back to your company site. For example, if you own the Hotel Baranoff but many people tend to misspell the name as Barinoff or Baronoff, try to obtain not only www.hotelbaranoff.com but also www.hotelbarinoff.com and www.hotelbaronoff.com.

Online Audio and Video Ads

When it comes to online multimedia, there are some similarities to traditional media. Buying ad placement on a podcast, for example, is similar to buying an ad on radio. You have to pay for the spot and may have to invest in creation of the spot, depending on how sophisticated you want your ad to be.

According to Arbitron, a research firm covering the radio industry, 27 million Americans were podcast listeners in the middle of 2006, and more than half of that audience are under thirty-five years of age.

Podcast ads can be placed anywhere within a podcast segment, but they typically fall in the middle rather than the beginning or end. Placement at the beginning doesn't give the listener a chance to hear the podcast first and be engaged. Ads placed at the end of podcasts are less likely to be heard. Ads placed within the segment or between segments are more likely to have a captive audience.

Your URL on Everything

In addition to online and offline advertising, public relations, and other marketing efforts, put your Web site's URL on everything you can. Print collateral from business cards to letterhead and even to envelopes should contain your URL. If you sell products, find ways to include your URL on product packaging. Another way to promote your Web site is to develop branded promotional product such as T-shirts, calendars, and mugs. Some companies, such as CafePress.com and Zazzle.com, offer inexpensive solutions to produce and sell branded product. Getting your URL out there means more traffic for your site.

According to research firm E-marketer, Internet video ad spending represented only 0.6 percent of television ad budgets in 2006, but the firm anticipates a major growth in Internet video advertising in the not-so-distant future. The researcher predicts that by 2010, one in ten dollars devoted to online advertising will go to Internet video. One of the biggest reasons for the growth in popularity of Internet video is the increase in broadband use.

Typically, Internet video ads have been freestanding ads placed like a regular online ad within a Web page. The ad either plays when a person arrives at the Web page, or it has a click button. While not as common, there are also ad placement opportunities within online videos. The latter can still be hampered by slower Internet connections, but even with broadband, not everyone is accustomed to watching longer videos online. Internet video still tends to be displayed within a smaller window, and if it does fill a computer screen, the quality isn't always as good as television. Most extremely popular online videos tend to be very short and are not always optimal for an advertisement.

As with any advertising, you want your Internet video ad to do the following:

- Be brief and concise
- Mention your company name or brand prominently
- Deliver a clear message, especially a call to action, if possible
- Be targeted to your audience, both in design and where it is distributed
- Lead people to your Web site

Don't use the same creative material for your Internet video ads as you are using offline in your television ads. Develop ads appropriately for the medium through which they will be delivered rather than taking the one-size-fits-all approach to your advertising efforts.

TEST DRIVE

Your marketing efforts should be tailored to the audience you are trying to reach, and that includes whether you spend more to market offline versus online. Still, any comprehensive marketing plan should include multiple channels for best results. Some things to think about as you develop a strategic marketing plan include the following:

➲ What online marketing tactics will complement my offline marketing tactics?

➲ Are my online and offline marketing tactics consistent in message?

➲ Are my online marketing tactics appropriate for the medium or just rehashing what I am doing offline?

➲ How am I using my Web site to build relationships with the media?

➲ What features on the Web site encourage visitors to tell other visitors about my site or engage my visitors in spreading the word through viral marketing?

Growing and Maintaining Your Online Presence

PART 5

Online Publishing Basics

Publishing anything online—text, images, audio, video, documents—requires access to the Internet and a place on the Web (a Web server) where the materials can be stored, or hosted. Without a place on the Web to put the content and a way to get it uploaded to that location, the information cannot be made available to the public. A Web site is a common way of publishing content on the Web, as is a blog.

Every year, publishing on the Internet gets easier for non-programmers. In addition to software that can help anyone design a site, there are companies that offer Web-based publishing tools and hosting services to put a Web site online. Having the programming skills or access to the right tools, however, does not guarantee that what is built creates value for a business. Ultimately, it is the content of a Web site that can make or break a Web site as a valuable e-business tool for a company.

Keeping Up with Content

The demand on your company resources can vary depending on what type of online presence you have. If you are building your initial presence online and plan to have an information site that will serve a marketing purpose, your content needs are modest.

Most of the pages on a marketing site remain relatively static, such as these:

Company background: Company background, especially history, philosophy and mission, usually doesn't change although newer information can be added periodically.

List of staff: Key staff members are not likely to change often, so this would be a low-maintenance section.

List of services: Unless you're in a business where the services you offer constantly change, chances are you won't be editing this page much at all.

Client list: This page may be changed occasionally but doesn't have to be modified the moment each new client is brought on. Whom you list and when you list them should be a strategic decision.

List of links: If a resource of links to other sites is a part of your site, the list should be checked regularly to make sure the links work, but adding to it does not have to be a daily activity.

There are areas on your company's marketing site that are more likely to change although the frequency of updating will vary. Knowing the greater demand for new content should be factored into the planning process for these features:

1. **Online press room:** Some things won't change frequently, such as the company fact sheet or team member bios, but the media will expect to see new press releases and news stories on a regular basis, at least several times a month.

2. **What's new:** Any feature that promises new information should never contain year-old information at the top. When people see the word "new," they expect it to be no older than a few weeks.

3, **Blog:** People expect a blog to be updated at least weekly, preferably several times a week.

4. **Products:** If you are starting an online catalog with only a few products, expect to update it within a month's time with more products.

5. **Articles:** If you are publishing articles on your site, some can be archival information, but if an article is dated years ago, you can lose credibility.

Customer service sites need updates when new information is available on products or services that can be helpful to customers or potential customers. An FAQ section should be updated as often as new questions and answers come up to keep growing the resource and increasing its usefulness.

Here are some pros and cons of publishing at different frequencies:

1. **Publishing daily:** This causes a major drain on any company's resources, even publishing companies. If you are not in the business of publishing content and you don't have the right resources in place, this may not be financially feasible or realistic.

2. **Publishing weekly:** While still demanding, this is a much less taxing schedule. Not everything needs to be updated on a weekly basis. Find one or two areas on your site that could be updated each week, such as your blog and What's New.

3. **Publishing monthly:** Monthly may seem a more manageable schedule for companies not in the publishing business, however, it is more challenging to build a loyal audience or following with only monthly updates.

4. **Publishing intermittently:** Sometimes you may have breaking news or new developments that warrant an announcement or information on your company site. If you choose to add new content at another time in addition to your regular schedule, that helps keep your site fresh. To get people to your site the day you publish something off schedule, send a quick notice via an e-newsletter bulletin.

5. **Publishing sporadically:** If you opt not to have an editorial schedule of any kind and just publish whenever something needs to be added or changed, you may not be able to properly build momentum on your site. If you notify your e-mail list about sporadic changes to the site, it could help or it could become an unpredictable annoyance.

Know your audience to help determine the most effective publishing schedule, and know your company to determine the most realistic. Don't overextend company resources to get new content on your site unless you know people are visiting the site and you can have real impact on your business goals with fresh content.

Leveraging Content

Having fresh content on your site can help to bring back visitors. If people know that every week you will post a new tip related to your products or services, they may return to the site more often. Incorporating notices via e-mail to your e-newsletter or e-announcement list can remind people about your site and draw them directly to new content.

Examine the content your company produces every day. Are there things you produce in-house that could add value to your Web site and that would be useful to your potential or current customers or clients?

Not all content must be published directly on a Web page. You can also link to the following:

Word files: Not everyone uses Microsoft Word so you may want to save files as .rtf or .txt.

PDF files: As long as visitors have Adobe Acrobat Reader, they can read PDF files, and these can also be used as fill-in forms that people can mail or fax back. Web-based forms, however, will save everyone time.

Spreadsheets: You can include data as comma delimited so the document is readable in any spreadsheet software program. Alternately, save it as a PDF or use an Excel file with a link to Microsoft's Excel reader.

Graphs, charts, and diagrams: Don't upload diagrams created with special software like a flowchart program that not everyone will have. Save the images as PDF files to be more universally accessible.

PowerPoint presentations: Even though not everyone has PowerPoint, a viewer can be downloaded for free from the Microsoft Web site, so include a link to that resource for convenience.

Another way to leverage content is to aggregate it from other sources. Make sure to properly credit the source and provide a link to the complete article from the excerpt on your Web site. While aggregating content takes up less time than writing content from scratch, it can still be time consuming to sift through other sites or e-mails.

You can also provide a list of links to related content and pull the first sentence or two of each article or piece to accompany each link. Finding the right content takes time, however, and keep in mind that you are leading people away from your site. Make sure any link out of your site opens a new browser window—this is something placed in the HTML code of the link—so that once a visitor reads the article and closes his or her browser window, your company site remains open.

How Much Is Too Much Copying?

While there is no exact number of words you can copy from someone else's copyrighted work before you need to get permission or pay a fee, the general rule is that you should not quote more than a few paragraphs in a row from any text work. Make sure you excerpt a very small portion of any piece. Copying 100 words of a 200-word article is not acceptable although using 100 words of a 10,000 word piece might be fine. When it comes to art, images, illustrations, and other graphics, however, always get permission from the artist. For poetry, the rule is to quote no more than two lines.

Challenges of Online Publishing

Besides the drain on company resources—including time and money—to keep up with online publishing, situations and needs can make online publishing seem nearly impossible. Assessing your resources is the first step in figuring out how frequently you can publish online. Speaking with your Web developer or an Internet consultant can help you find effective ways of addressing the challenges in cost-effective ways. Ultimately, having fresh content on your site should help business, not make you crazy or break the bank.

Coming Up with Ideas

Before you even begin writing or developing other content for your site, you must come up with the ideas. Where do you begin? What will you write about? If you are producing a podcast, what will you talk about? Generating ideas is often half the battle when it comes to publishing online. Sometimes, coming up with the right idea can actually inspire you to produce content quickly while other times, a forced idea languishes and you may get discouraged.

Here are some ways to get ideas for your Web site content:

1. **Current events:** The news, especially online, can be a rich resource to mine for ideas. Subscribe to headline news from your favorite news sources to get bite-sized news items you can peruse quickly for ideas.

2. **Industry news:** Peruse trade publications for articles and information relevant to your company and industry. Think of how your company fits into larger industry trends and write about it.

3. **Blogs:** Because most successful bloggers devote a lot of time to their blogs, they are a rich resource for information and ideas. Never steal an idea, and if you comment on something a blogger has written, credit and link to her or him.

4. **Top topics:** There are sites that keep track of the most popular topics discussed on blogs, such as Technorati and their top tags list (tags are keywords that identify a blog post); Blogpulse and their top blog posts list; and Daypop and their Top 40 blog topics list. Maybe the hot topics of the day will spark an idea.

5. **Articles and op-eds:** Content does not always have to be breaking news. Get ideas from what others are writing or talking about.

As you begin to accumulate ideas, review them and see if you can sort through them, selecting the ones you know you can write quickly and putting them toward the top of your content list and reserving the more complex or less inspiring topics for later.

Dotting I's, Crossing T's

Writing or compiling content for your company site has its own set of demands, but there is more to publishing online than obtaining content. Editing is a major part of the process. The editor for your site should be someone other than the writer. Without some kind of editing and quality-control process in place, your site could be littered with errors including spelling, punctuation, and grammar, not to mention careless typos and errant symbols.

Browser Bookmarks As Tickler File

Whenever you find a Web site that you want to use as a reference or resource, bookmark it. Bookmarks are more than just placeholders to favorite sites. They can act as a tickler file to stimulate content ideas. Keep the sites with the most frequently updated content at the top of your tickler bookmark list to access new information more readily. If you find articles online worth quoting, make sure to bookmark the exact pages and store them in a bookmark folder called "Quoted" or some other name so you can always locate the sources you quote.

You should also have a process in place to check the following:

Link errors: Check the address included in the link code as well as the code itself. If these are all right, the site may be down.

Image errors: Check the image name included in the image code and the code itself. The image may be in the wrong format.

Layout errors: Check the HTML. Most layout issues are problems with the code.

Page errors: Check the link code, the page file name, and make sure the page was uploaded to the right place.

Style errors: Check the code for errors, such as forgetting to close a bold tag or failing to use a consistent font style tag.

Some errors are much harder to identify, such as factual errors. Having a fact-checking process in place during the editing process is important to avoid disseminating erroneous information. Between writing, editing, fact-checking, and basic Web site quality-control processes, you can begin to see why online publishing can be time and resource intensive.

Text Gremlins

Odd, seemingly random symbols, or gremlins, sometimes appear in the text on a Web page and are often caused by copying and pasting content from a word processing document into an HTML text file. Microsoft Word, for example, uses invisible symbols to designate styles. Those symbols can be mistakenly placed in a text file. Web browsers can read invisible symbols then show them on a Web page. Apostrophes, for example, may appear as question marks throughout an entire page. To avoid gremlins, create HTML files in a plain text or Web authoring program or use a content management system (CMS) that can handle text pulled from word processing documents.

Managing Web Publishing

There is a technical side to managing Web publishing and a process side. The process of managing online publishing is similar to traditional print publishing. Your Web developer can make sure you have an easy-to-use, Web-based way of publishing content onto your Web site instead of having to turn to your developer or another programmer to update your site.

Content Management Systems

A content management system (CMS) is a tool for creating, modifying, and archiving content on a Web site. A CMS can be built into a Web site by a developer or can be an integrated feature on a Web publishing tool. Blog publishing tools, for example, are basically built-in content management systems, and blog publishing software used to build Web sites has a CMS automatically included.

Inside Track	Cybergrrl's Content Solutions

When I first started my company, Cybergrrl, Inc., our business was consulting for other companies on building an online presence. In order to showcase my Web design skills, I built a personal Web site that quickly morphed into a general interest Web site for women. At first, I wrote all the content myself but soon realized that my attention needed to be focused on running my company and not developing Web content. Next, I turned to interns to write for the site. Many were students who received credit or built an online portfolio of work by contributing to our site. Eventually, the quality of the content on the site became inconsistent, so we hired a Web editor and writer. She was responsible for reviewing content before publishing it to the site. She also established an editorial calendar, made writing assignments, and did additional writing as needed. We found people willing to write for our Web site for free because at that time, the Web was a new medium, and writers were looking for Web writing experience and to gain exposure. As a small startup company with little budget for content production, we had to look for other ways of getting content onto our site. Our programmer created a database that would feed fresh content to our Web site every day. We used it to publish daily quotes from women throughout history—a "Quote of the Day" feature. Our programmer also created a quick poll feature so visitors could take the poll and see how their choices compared with other visitors to the site. The topics for the quick poll were women's issues-oriented and in keeping with the overall purpose of the site. Getting creative and leveraging technology helped save us time and money.

At a minimum, a CMS should allow you to do the following:

1. **Publish text:** The CMS should either provide templates for page layout or allow some flexibility in programming HTML by hand as needed.
2. **Embed images:** The CMS should allow for images to be uploaded from a computer to the Web server and archived as well as embedded into a page with an option of image alignment, ALT text, and other image specs.
3. **Embed multimedia files such as audio or video:** The CMS should allow for files to be uploaded and archived on the Web server and to easily create links to them on a Web page.

4. Insert links: Even for the non-programmer, creating links in a CMS should be easy, requiring nothing more complicated than highlighting text, pressing a button, and entering the URL.

5. Specify styles: Most CMSs have a toolbar similar to what you might find on Microsoft Word, allowing everything from adding bold and italics to font face, size, and color changes.

CMSs should also have features that facilitate the entire online publishing process. Here are some other features to look for:

⮑ Keeping track of who created a page

⮑ Tracking status of content throughout the editing process

⮑ A draft mode along with an approval for publishing mode

⮑ A way to edit content after it has been published, as needed

⮑ Ability to set limits on publishing permissions for each user

A CMS should be easy to use for non-programmers. Even though adding a CMS to your site could increase development costs, you'll save in the long run rather than having to turn to your Web developer every time you need to update your site. A CMS should also save time because it automates processes that are usually done manually, such as tracking edits and properly placing the HTML onto a page.

Editorial Calendar

If you are not in the business of publishing, chances are you are not very familiar with editorial calendars. These calendars make a plan detailing what content will be developed or aggregated and when it will be published. You can break down the content on your site in a number of ways, including these:

1. Section-specific: A section on marketing tools may include some articles about the basics of marketing.

2. Themes: Overarching themes for your site may rotate over time, such as monthly themes.

3. Current: Some content is timelier, based on current news or upcoming events, for example.

4. Seasonal: Depending on your business and your customer needs, content could be developed based on the seasons and holidays.

5. Evergreen: This is the term for content not tied to a specific timeframe that can be archived on a Web site and remain relevant for a long time.

The frequency of your publishing schedule will dictate how far in advance your editorial calendar should extend. If you publish monthly, you should create at least a six-month calendar. If you publish several times a month, you may be able to get away with creating a quarterly calendar. Try to develop an editorial calendar that covers as many months as possible, even planning out an entire year.

Internal Forums

A good add-on to a CMS is the internal forum, or posting boards where Web staff or editorial staff can post notes, pose questions, respond to questions, and peruse the archive of conversations and information regarding the Web site. Internal forums are password protected so the behind-the-scenes dialogue is not accessible to the public. Archiving messages on a posting board is much better than relying on people to save and properly archive e-mails. Forums can be used to discuss every aspect of a Web site including content creation and editing, images, multimedia, design and layout, programming, testing, and troubleshooting.

Unlike national monthly magazines that have long lead times, on the Web the publishing process is much shorter. You don't need to plan that far ahead other than for convenience, but an editorial calendar spanning the next year is a useful tool to help relieve some of the burdens of coming up with ideas at the last minute and scrambling for content.

Some steps in creating an editorial calendar include these:

1. Determine what content is date specific, and place those topics on their respective dates as publishing dates.

2. Estimate how long the editing process should take; count back that far and mark the calendar to show the date content is due.

3. Decide how long the content development or aggregation process should take, and mark the calendar to show when assignments should be made or development or aggregation should begin.

4. Based on how frequently you want to publish information, make sure you have a content plan at every interval.

5. If you find gaps, fill them in with other content such as fillers or evergreen content, specifying when that content should be developed and edited.

6. Allow for quick changes to the calendar due to current events.

An editorial calendar should also specify who is assigned to write or aggregate the content so assignments are clear. Highlight deadlines so they are not missed. Having a few extra fillers on hand at all times in case of missed deadlines or other unanticipated delays is helpful.

Cost-Effective Content Solutions

If your company is not in the business of producing and publishing content, but content is a necessary component of your Web site, you have options for generating fresh content for your site without having to hire a staff of writers. Some content generation techniques leverage technology, while others leverage site visitors.

Automated Content

You can create the illusion of more frequently updated content by rotating headlines or links on your home page that lead to existing content on your site. If you have an archive of half a dozen articles in a section of your site, your Web developer can build a small database that rotates links to the articles on your home page. Even though you are not publishing a new article each day, a link to a different article appears on the home page each day, drawing a visitor's attention to something new and giving the impression of fresh content. As long as you are not misleading visitors to believe that your content is updated daily, the impression of new content helps alleviate some of the demand for frequent content generation.

The same automated content database can be used to rotate a variety of things onto your home page on a regular basis, even daily. Keep in mind you will need sufficient content in advance to be placed into the database. Try to accumulate at least a month's worth of content in advance to be loaded into the database for rotation on the home page. Some ideas for quick and easy rotating content include the following:

- Daily photographs or illustrations
- Quote of the day
- Daily recipes
- Tip of the day
- Highlighted product of the day
- Daily product special

If you can gather 365 photographs or recipes or tips, you'll have a year's worth of daily fresh content to appear on your home page. Gathering the data may take a few weeks, but you don't have to worry about feeding the content database for another eleven months or so.

Member-Generated Content

An effective but possibly time-intensive way of enhancing the content on your site is to allow site users or members to generate content. Your first step in hosting user-generated content is to include a statement in your terms of service for your site that implies a person who contributes content to your site automatically gives your company permission to publish it. You should specify the ways you may publish the content in addition to on the Web, such as in print or on CD.

User-generated content can take place within forums or on the comments pages of blogs. If you plan to lift the content from a forum or comment page and publish it elsewhere on your site, you should make this clear to the users of your site. Most site visitors are under the impression that the content they produce on your site is theirs. However, you should be clear about ownership. With ownership of comments and discussions comes liability, so check with a lawyer about the best way to sort out ownerships of user-generated content in forums.

If you ask people to submit articles they have written to your site, the writer already owns the copyright. You are asking for the right to host their content on your site or republish it. Post submission guidelines to help minimize the contribution of inappropriate content to your site. Allowing site users or members to publish content to your site without an editorial process is risky. You should request submissions then review, select, edit, and approve the pieces for publication.

Outsourcing Content Development

If you don't have the internal resources to generate content and have determined that content will be an important component of your site, you can outsource development of that content by hiring writers on a freelance basis. To find writers for your Web site, advertise on sites for writers such as Journalism Jobs (www.journalismjobs.com), Mediabistro (www.mediabistro.com), and Absolute Markets (www.absolutemarkets.com), among many others. Because you are looking for a writer familiar with writing on the Web, use online resources rather than print resources to find an appropriate writer.

Specify the skills you are looking for:

➲ Ability to write for the online medium
➲ Familiarity with HTML
➲ Familiarity with content management systems
➲ Ability to insert links into text
➲ Familiarity with Web templates

Because you are looking for an online writer, ask to see not only applicants' resumes but their online portfolios. Look for concise writing styles with a clear voice that matches the voice you want for your Web site. **A good Web writer is able to write in a variety of styles, and an online portfolio should reflect this.**

You can find a freelance editor in the same way you find a freelance writer. Web writers and Web editors tend to frequent similar Web sites and online resources.

Purchasing Content

Depending on the kind of content you'd like to publish on your Web site, you can pay for content generated through wire services or syndication services. Wire services tend to be more news oriented, producing press releases, news briefs, or full-fledged articles. They also can be expensive and are more often used by media companies and publications than general company Web sites. Some wire services include the following:

- Associated Press (*www.ap.com*): News stories
- United Press International (*www.upi.com*): News stories
- PR Newswire (*www.prnewswire.com*): Press releases
- Businesswire (*www.businesswire.com*): Press releases
- Dow Jones Newswire (*www.dowjones.com*): WebReprints of articles from any Dow Jones publication, including the *Wall Street Journal*

Other major newspaper publishers such as the *Los Angeles Times* and *Chicago Tribune* have their own syndication services. You can also get permission to reprint almost any content from Web sites or publications for free or for a fee. To avoid copyright infringement, never publish content on your site from another source without getting express permission.

Syndication services are in the business of aggregating content producers, such as columnists and photographers, then reselling the content to publications and Web sites. Some content syndication services include the following:

- ➲ **FreeSticky.com:** Free content on a variety of topics
- ➲ **Content That Works** (*www.contentthatworks.com*): Includes automotive, real estate, employment, family health, bridal, holiday, home decorating, and lawn and garden
- ➲ **Small Business Resources** (*www.sbresources.com*): Small business, minority-owned business, women-owned business, business technology
- ➲ **Wilson Internet Services** (*www.wilsonweb.com*): Web technology, e-marketing, and e-business
- ➲ **Women's ENews** (*www.womensenews.org*): Feminist news and women's issues
- ➲ **Mochila** (*www.mochila.com*): A "marketplace for syndicated content" where you can purchase content from established publications and publishers
- ➲ Copyright.com (*www.copyright.com*): Another service for licensing copyrighted content

What Is Fair Use?

Fair use refers to the way content that is available to the public is excerpted or used by someone other than the author. Fair use usually applies to copyrighted content that is used by others in the form of comment or criticism, meaning you can excerpt someone else's content if you are illustrating a point, reviewing the material, or criticizing it. Fair use also applies to news reporting such as quoting someone else's copyrighted material in a news report. Other examples of fair use include research and scholarship, nonprofit educational use, and parody. Check with a lawyer before making decisions to publish other people's content on your site.

To obtain photographs or illustrations for your Web site, instead of hiring a photographer or illustrator, you can turn to stock photography sites such as Fotosearch (*www.fotosearch.com*), art sites such as Art Resource (*www.artres.com*), clip art services such as Clipart.com (*www.clipart.com*), and cartoons at Cartoonists & Writers Syndicate (*www.cartoonweb.com*). Major syndicates for famous columnists and cartoonists include United Media and King Features.

If you find content on another Web site that you would like to reprint on your own site, it does not hurt to send an e-mail and ask for permission. Some sites are happy to have their content republished on other sites and will not charge a fee in return for a credit line and link back to their site.

▶▶ TEST DRIVE

Making the decision to publish content on your Web site is a difficult one. On the one hand you know that with fresh content, you could entice visitors to come back to your site. On the other hand, online publishing can be an enormous drain on your company if you are not in the publishing business. Some things to think about before deciding to publish content on your site include the following:

⮑ How will content add value to my Web site, and how will that affect the company's bottom line?

⮑ What internal resources do I have to produce content for my site?

⮑ How can I automate some of my content publishing to alleviate the demands of creating fresh content for my site?

⮑ How will I manage the publishing process, including assignments, deadlines, editing, approving, and publishing?

⮑ Can I outsource content development and editing tasks, and if so, what is my publishing budget?

Growing and Maintaining Your Online Presence

The Nature of Blogs

Contrary to popular belief, blogs are not new to the Internet. They've been around since the late 1990s, although the early versions do not resemble today's blogs. The explosion of blogs and blogging occurred during the 2000 presidential election and the beginning of the Iraq war, when anyone could publish their opinions online easily through a blog.

Just as with Web sites, publishing a blog does not automatically guarantee you an audience. And as with Web sites, you must first determine your business goals before building a blog to make sure it helps you to achieve those goals rather than distracting you and your company resources from them.

Talking About Blogging

A blog consists of posts, which are like articles with headlines. Blog posts can also be referred to as entries, particularly if the blog is written more as a diary. You can create or publish a blog. You can blog. You can post to a blog. Posting to a blog can also be referred to simply as blogging. You cannot post a blog—this an incorrect way of saying that you are posting to a blog or blogging. Someone who blogs is called a blogger, not a poster.

Content Rules

Blogging is about the content first and foremost, although the communities that form around blogs are a close second, making some blogs wildly popular. The format of a blog puts a focus on the timely publishing of content. The basic format of a blog includes the following:

- Time-stamped and dated posts
- Posts listed in reverse chronological order
- Headers or headlines at the top of each post
- List of most recent posts
- Automated archive of past posts, often by category

Because content is the most critical element of a blog, producing content is the most time-intensive aspect of blogging. Before deciding to create a company blog, you need to assess your internal resources and determine the answers to these questions:

1. What will your company blog be about?
2. What will a blog help your company achieve?
3. Who will be allowed to blog on your company's blog?
4. How frequently will someone post to the blog?
5. How will you manage the demand for content for your blog?

Blogs require constant and consistent attention, especially if you allow people to comment on each blog post. People expect blog content to be current and frequent. Although you can opt to blog weekly, it can be challenging to build momentum and a loyal and regular following of readers—or potential customers or clients. Posting every few days can be much more effective. Most business owners are daunted by the content demands of a blog and for good cause. Blogs are not for the occasional writer. To be a valuable resource to customers and to your company, blogs must be fed meaningful and useful content.

Company Internet and Technology Policy

Every company that allows employees to access the Internet should develop a written policy about the company's technology and how employees are allowed to use it. The policy should state that the hardware and software belongs to the company. State that the Internet, Web, and e-mail should be accessed or used for company-related purposes only. Also state that the company has the right to monitor Internet usage at any time. Define what kinds of Internet usage are forbidden. If you allow employees to post to a company blog, provide clear guidelines and rules to follow for posting.

Content Builds Community

Developing content for a blog is incredibly time-consuming, but so is monitoring the comments that people make on each blog post. Blogs usually have a built-in feature that allows visitors to publish a comment on a blog post. You can disable this feature either for all posts or, depending on the blog software or tools you are using, disable comments on certain blog posts. Some blogs allow comments for a limited time. After that time, they remove the comment feature from a post to reduce the need to keep track of comments on multiple posts.

Blog Spam

Most people are familiar with e-mail spam or unsolicited e-mails from unscrupulous marketers known as spammers. Online forums and particularly blogs are susceptible to spammers as well. Some blog publishing tools and software have features to help block or remove blog spam, but this is another thing someone at your company will have to monitor. Most blog spam links directly to pornography sites, so you need to be vigilant about looking at every comment on your company blog. Some blog publishing tools and software allow you to prevent links from showing up in comments.

Some blogs also have a moderating feature whereby all comments on blog posts are submitted first for approval, requiring someone from your company to review each one and determine what to allow on the blog and what to suppress.

Monitoring blog comments is very similar to monitoring online message boards or forums. Some differences between an online message board and a comments page on a blog are these:

1. Message boards usually have threaded messages organized by topic and reply, while blog comments usually appear sequentially down a single Web page.
2. Community members usually initiate conversations on message boards, while blog comments pertain directly to the corresponding blog post created by the blogger.

3. Message board communities tend to focus on a main topic, while a blog can introduce a variety of topics.

Before you decide you will allow comments on your company blog, you should have a terms of use document in place to outline what is expected from visitors who comment and what your company's policy is about removing comments.

Blogging for Business

While anyone can have a blog, blogging is not necessarily useful to everyone, much less every business. Understanding not only the demands of blogging but also the limitations of blogs can help to put into perspective whether or not blogging will be good for your business.

Chief Bloggers

Busy company heads make time to blog about business."I feel it is very important to let customers know that we are real people working really hard to make a difference," says Steve Simonson, CEO of iFLOOR.com, a multi-channel floor provider. "Sometimes a more refined Web site can't deliver on that personal touch." Simonson fits blogging into his schedule whenever he finds a spare moment. His blog serves both customers and a staff that is widespread geographically.

Dave Gray, founder and CEO of XPLANE, a consulting and design firm, receives a couple hundred e-mails daily. Occasionally, he answers one on his blog if the topic is worthy of a wider audience.

For Gray, blogging benefits include attracting new customers and employees. Simonson realizes his competition and supply chain study his blog to learn what his company is doing, so he chooses his blog post topics strategically. Simonson advises, "Only start if you are committed to regular updates that have some level of value to your target audience."

Goals for Business Blogging

Blogging was not started as an e-business or e-marketing tactic. Early blogs were nothing more than Web sites with long lists of links to other Web sites that were updated regularly. These lists were referred to as Web logs, then Weblogs, which was shortened to blogs. Eventually, early bloggers began to add reviews or commentary to their lists of links, and the content often began to resemble diary entries. Soon programmers began creating software or Web-based tools to publish blogs with ease and minimal programming skills.

Today, bloggers run the gamut from moms, hobbyists, and armchair politicians to celebrities, consultants, and business owners.

Blogs tend to be less suited to e-business than a Web site because most people expect blogs to be about content and not about selling products or services. Blogs can be effectively used for the following:

➲ Building a brand
➲ Establishing expertise
➲ Driving traffic to a Web site
➲ Building a following or audience
➲ Leading customers to purchase products

Most people do not expect to be able to shop on a blog. They go for the content and the grassroots, organic community built around the content. That is not to say that your company blog cannot link to product pages within your online catalog. **The blog posts should give context to your products, not be blatant commercials.** Links to product can be embedded in posts about related topics.

For example, if you sell camping gear, you could post regularly to your company blog with camping tips from your staff and even from customers where a mention of one of your products fits naturally into the conversation and is not gratuitous. Keep in mind that when you allow others to comment on your posts, you can open your company to an unprecedented amount of public feedback. Comments on your blog may not always be positive. If your policy is to remove negative comments,

Denali Flavors Digs Into Blogging   Inside Track

Ice cream developers Denali Flavors, Inc., began blogging in early 2005. The company was looking for ways to build their brand because their business model—licensing ice cream flavors such as Moose Tracks to dairies—didn't always put their company's name in consumers' minds.

According to executive vice president John Nardini, Denali Flavors began blogging to build brand awareness and to engage consumers in a grassroots dialogue. The company started with four blogs: TeamMoosetracks.com centered around the company's bike team and fundraising efforts for an orphanage; DenaliFlavors.com took visitors behind the scenes at the company; Moosetopia.com tracked the whereabouts of a stuffed moose around the world; and FreeMoneyFinance.com offered financial tips and advice. The latter two are still active today, accounting for between 10 to 15 percent of the company's main consumer site's traffic (www.MooseTracks.com).

The company places an ad featuring their moose mascot on every blog page, linking visitors to MooseTracks.com. Their blog FreeMoneyFinance.com receives an average of 2,800 visitors per day who view about 2.3 pages per visit. That translates to over 6,000 page impressions for the company's ad on that blog alone. In late 2005, TeamMoosetracks.com and DenaliFlavors.com went into hiatus. However, both blogs still get daily traffic and along with Moosetopia.com account for another 5 percent of MooseTracks.com's traffic.

For a small company like Denali Flavors, the biggest challenge of blogging is finding the time. Blogging on four blogs became too time-consuming, so they pared down to the two blogs receiving the most interest—FreeMoneyFinance.com and Moosetopia.com. Cost has not been a business blogging issue since the company uses Typepad at a cost of about $200 per year. The main goal for their blogs was to build brand awareness, and in 2006, their sponsorship ad on FreeMoneyFinance.com blog received over 1 million ad impressions. The effort to blog is paying off.

you could generate a backlash from customers who may feel you have something to hide. Some companies address negative comments on their blogs by quickly addressing the issue, directly and openly. They may also take measures to take negative feedback to heart and make product modifications based on customer feedback.

Caveats of Blogging for Business

Even if you determine the best way to blog for business, there are many issues to consider before you start blogging.

Some issues you need to think about include the following:

1. The potential liabilities of blogging that are similar to publishing anything online—someone can misunderstand or misuse the information you post and if something goes wrong, try to sue your company for a remedy
2. The potential liabilities of allowing comments on your blog that are similar to liabilities of online message boards
3. The demands for content and constant updates that keep a blog fresh and people coming back to read it
4. The challenges of turning a blog into an effective e-business tool that can generate revenues for your company
5. The possibility that all the efforts you put forth to blogging never build a following or have a positive impact on your business

You may have heard that some people are making a lot of money through their blogs. Most of them are generating revenues from advertising and sponsorship because they have a large and loyal readership. If you are not a publisher selling ad space on your Web site or blog, this revenue model may not be suitable for your company.

Where Blogs Work

Even if blogging doesn't have an immediate and direct impact on a company's bottom line, there are several ways blogging can still be good for business. Consultants, for example, can establish a reputation as experts in their fields. Companies can use their blog to keep customers current on product developments and use a blog in a fashion similar to a customer-service forum. Companies can align themselves with a cause and use their blog to promote this relationship, so a blog can be a cause-related marketing tool. Blogging should add value to a company's online presence and contribute to its overall e-business goals.

Building Credibility

If you or anyone within your company has expertise in a particular subject, you can leverage that on a blog. Consultants have to walk the fine line between demonstrating knowledge and "giving away the store" by providing too much information and less incentive for someone to contact them for consulting services. Companies that are marketing products can showcase experts to blog about issues related to the products. For example, a camping equipment company can have experts within the company blog about camping tips and advice, with or without product mentions within the text.

Independent consultants can benefit from blogging. Blog publishing has a global reach and can be useful for building an audience and loyal following. If you amass a significant amount of traffic, blogging your expertise can lead to inquiries for consulting work.

Blogging Products

A good example of a product-oriented blog is the GM FastLane Blog (fastlane.gmblogs.com) where various people within the GM company blog about their divisions, product research and development, and company news. Each uses a personal approach, includes images and even video in blog posts, and responds directly to blog comments when appropriate.

An effective product blog does the following:

➲ Has a strong and distinctive voice or voices directly from within the company
➲ Balances informational and promotional information
➲ Encourages blog visitors to comment and actively responds to comments when relevant and appropriate
➲ Gives value-added data about products that can help consumers make better purchasing decisions
➲ Leads visitors to areas within the company Web site as appropriate

If you have nothing to say about your products or services other than what appears on your Web site, don't embark on a product blog. You'll quickly run out of things to blog about and potentially alienate customers if you try to fill the blog with irrelevant and useless content.

Issues and Causes

In 2004, the organic yogurt company Stonyfield Farm (www.stonyfieldfarm.com) embraced blogging and set up five separate blogs to serve different purposes and audiences. The Dairy Planet focused on environmental issues; Strong Women Daily News gave updates on their women's issues program; the Bovine Bugle gave a behind-the-scenes look at an organic dairy farm; the Daily Scoop provided a peek inside the Stonyfield factory; and Creating Healthy Kids promoted the company's program bringing healthy food into schools. One single in-house writer did all the blogging for the company. By 2007, the company was down to two blogs, one called Baby Babble (written by Stonyfield Farm employees with young children talking about parenting issues) and the Bovine Bugle. The Stonyfield site still contains archives of the other blogs. Even though they've closed down the blogs that didn't find an audience, the two remaining blogs are updated regularly and are in keeping with the overall mission and philosophy of the company—touting organic eating and supporting families.

An issues- or cause-oriented blog for a company should do the following:

- Promote the company's cause-related efforts
- Clearly support a company's mission and philosophy
- Provide value to customers
- Lead visitors to appropriate areas within the company site
- Provide visitors with a call to action to further promote the cause

Cause-related blogs don't work if the company is not genuinely behind the cause. Partnering with a nonprofit organization associated with the issue or cause can be helpful when it comes to updating the blog. At the very least, the nonprofit can provide related content for the blog to assist with fresh blog post ideas.

Beware of Fake Blogs

In the past, some companies enlisted their advertising agency or public relations firm to create fake blogs (although they probably didn't call them fake). The idea was to invent a blogger without revealing that the blogger was not a real person. In other cases, they created an entire blog around a topic or theme that was fictional but positioned it as factual. Sometimes such fake blogs can be entertaining while positively reinforcing a company's brand. At other times, they come across as deceitful and can damage the trust customers have in a company.

Blogging Tools

If you plan to blog, you'll need to first build a blog. You can opt to use Web-based blog publishing tools, which are provided by blog hosts or companies that will host your blog on their system. You may also want to use blog publishing software that resides on your Web server and can be installed by most skilled Web developers.

Blog Hosts or Providers

While there are dozens of reputable blog hosts or blog providers in business today, there are only a handful of hosts or providers that have been around for many years and continue to provide a reliable product with consistent customer service.

A free blog may save you money initially but in the long run can cost you more in headaches, especially if technical support services are lacking. Free blogs are suitable, however, for testing out blogging. For the best blogging experience with a host, you may be better off choosing one that offers a Web-based blog publishing tool and other services for a reasonable fee rather than a free host.

A blog host such as Blogger.com, owned by Google, can be a good place to start. Setting up a blog on their site takes all of a few minutes, and posting to the blog is easy and straightforward. Another free blog host is LiveJournal.com. Some blog hosts, such as Typepad.com, offer a free trial. After thirty days, the fee kicks in at an average of under $100 per year.

Some features you should look for from a Web publishing tool include the following:

1. **Turning off comments on all posts or individual posts** can help you reduce the need to monitor comments.
2. **Discouraging blog spam** with a feature such as a post verification process can help ensure comments are made by legitimate visitors.
3. **Allowing multiple bloggers to post to a single blog** helps you bring other bloggers into the publishing process.
4. **Deleting comments and banning commenters** as needed helps you manage the comments pages.
5. **Setting future publishing dates on posts** lets you compose many posts in advance and set them to publish over time.
6. **Flexibility in blog template design** helps create a more unified look between your blog and your Web site.

Most popular blog hosts have tools that provide nearly all the above-mentioned features to give you a certain amount of control over the various front-end and back-end aspects of your blog.

Blog Software

The next level of blog publishing tools is software such as Greymatter, Word Press, Movable Type, and ExpressionEngine. While most Web developers are able to install blog software, not all of them are able to configure and customize the software to suit your needs. Check with your Web developer about his or her blog building capabilities if you know that a blog will be part of your overall e-business strategy.

In some cases, Web developers actually prefer using blog publishing software to build a company Web site. **You will want to avoid overuse of templates that make your company site look cookie-cutter and limit the overall design of your site.** Using blog publishing software for Web publishing can provide an integrated content management system that makes publishing content on a Web site as easy as blogging.

The Integrated Blog

You may face a variety of scenarios when considering publishing a blog. You may not yet have a company Web site online and are considering either developing a site with a blog or publishing a blog in lieu of a company Web site. You may already have a company site but are exploring adding a blog to it or even replacing it with a blog. You may also opt to integrate a blog into your site on the home page to emphasize new information on a regular basis while the rest of your site remains fairly static or is updated less frequently.

Contracting Bloggers

Some businesses hire a writer to blog for their company. Here are some things you might want to include in a contract with a writer:

1. A statement that the assignment is "work-for-hire" if the writer is a freelance independent contractor
2. A delineation of deliverables and timelines so the writer knows what is expected
3. A statement specifying ownership of content created so the writer cannot later claim to own what she or he has written
4. Indemnification statements that protect both you and the writer
5. An attachment outlining company policies regarding Web site and blog content

Blog As Home Page

Making the decision to replace a traditional Web site home page with a blog takes some thought and planning. A typical Web site home page serves several purposes, including these:

⊃ Defining who your company is and what it does

⊃ Emphasizing your company's main purposes and goals

⊃ Being a gateway into your site so visitors can access content within the site

⊃ Introducing the main navigation of the site so visitors know how to get around

⊃ Facilitating interactions between you and your customer

⊃ Encouraging visitors to take action such as contacting your company or ordering products

A blog provides fresh content and can also build community. Fresh content in a blog format can do the following:

⊃ Attract readers

⊃ Attract repeat visitors

⊃ Build your company brand

⊃ Demonstrate an expertise

⊃ Build a community

If the best uses of a blog correspond with what your company is trying to achieve with its online presence, replacing a regular home page with a blog or integrating blog posts into a home page can be an effective Web publishing direction for your company.

Blog As Company Site

It's tempting to ditch a traditional Web site for a blog. Publishing to blogs is easy, even for a person lacking technical Web skills. Blog publishing software already includes a content management system, so setting one up doesn't have to be an additional cost.

Using blog publishing software to build a Web site does not mean that the Web site has to look like a typical blog. A good Web developer familiar with blog publishing software can manipulate the templates or integrate other designs into the system so that the site looks like a traditional Web site. The main differences between a Web site created with blog publishing software versus one developed by traditional Web publishing processes are that the blog-built site has a built-in CMS and that a blog can be seamlessly integrated into the site if needed.

Blog publishing software may not be the right tool to use to build a Web site, especially if your Web developer lacks the skills to properly configure and customize blog publishing software to design a traditional site. Also, blog publishing software may not be robust enough to handle a Web site with an enormous amount of content beyond blog posts. A Web developer with the right skills will be able to help you evaluate whether or not to use blog publishing software to develop your company site or use a blog instead of a traditional Web site.

▶▶ TEST DRIVE

As you contemplate publishing a blog as either part of your company site or in lieu of a traditional company Web site, some things to consider include the following:

- ➲ How will a blog help me to meet company goals?
- ➲ How will I integrate a blog into my company site?
- ➲ How will I handle the added demand for content development blogging requires?
- ➲ How will I respond to customer comments to my blog, especially negative ones?
- ➲ How will blogging help to generate revenues for my company or support other forms of revenue generation?

Measuring and Re-Examining Your Site

PART **6**

The Dirty Secrets of Web Tracking

In the early years of the Web, people could say their Web site got 10,000 hits in a month's time and others would believe them and think that number was significant. The reality was, however, that 10,000 hits did not mean 10,000 individuals visited the Web site. "Hits" means the number of files downloaded from a site in any given time period. So if one person visited your Web site's home page and you had eleven images on that page including a logo, buttons, and photographs, that would register as twelve hits—the extra hit was the actual page file. It was inaccurate to say twelve people visited your Web site that day since only one person generated those twelve hits. Also, you knew the visitor went to your home page, but you couldn't track whether she or he went any further into your site.

Today, counting the number of individual visitors to your Web site is more challenging than tracking what visitors do and where they go on your site. **Learning some of the basics of Web tracking can go a long way in making sure you interpret your Web traffic statistics or Web logs accurately and have usable information to constantly improve your Web site.**

What Is a Page Impression?

A page view usually represents a page that a visitor downloads and views through a Web browser. Page impressions are most often used to describe the number of visitors who view an ad, such as a banner on a Web page. Page impressions should match the number of page views, although just because a person has viewed a page does not necessarily mean he also saw the ad. Still, a common way of buying or selling ad space on a Web site is to base the cost on a certain number of impressions—for instance, 1,000 impressions a month.

Counting People

Assessing exactly how many individuals have accessed your Web site is more challenging than it sounds. Most Web traffic software is limited in how it can measure each individual because most people do not access the Internet through their own personal Web server but through an ISP. Each Web server has a unique IP address, like a zip code. If a visitor is using America Online, for example, and so are 200 other people access-ing your company site, your Web tracking software will only register the IP addresses from the servers through which those people accessed the Web. A major service like America Online has a number of servers with different IP addresses; however, your Web tracking software will not tally 201 different IP addresses but more likely a dozen or so.

Most Web-tracking software products measure traffic to your Web site in the following ways:

1. **Page view:** This measures how many pages were viewed during a certain time period. By looking at the page impres-sions for your home page, you can get a sense of how many times people accessed your site, but this does not specify if they continued through to other pages or if it was one or many people accessing the home page. This number, however, is no longer relevant if your Web site is built with technology that doesn't necessarily turn a page, such as if it were entirely pro-grammed in Flash.

2. **Visit:** This measures the number of times someone accesses your Web site but cannot distinguish between new visitors and old visitors. The software therefore inflates the actual number of visitors.

3. **Session:** This measures how long each visit lasts and can be a valuable number to show how much time people spend on your site. Again, it does not break this down by the unique individual.

4. **Individual visitors:** In order to obtain this number, you need to tag visitors' browsers with cookies that let your Web server know whether or not they are new or the same person access-ing your site during a particular timeframe. This requires addi-tional programming on the part of your Web developer and is still not foolproof since often people block cookies or empty their cookie files regularly.

5. **Hits:** Much Web tracking software shows the number of hits. From a business standpoint, this number is not as useful as visits or page views.

As well, keep in mind that there are other ways for people to see your Web content, such as through e-mail using an RSS feed. This may not be measured by Web analytics software. Also, if you are publishing content using audio or video files, make sure all file downloads can be counted separately, to measure the number of times visitors access multimedia content.

Invasions of Privacy

The last thing you want to do once you launch your Web site is to turn off visitors and potential customers or clients by tracking what they do on your Web site without letting them know. Privacy is still a major issue among Web users, and they want to know they can trust your company to not only keep their personal information confidential and safe, but also not to invade their privacy by tracking their every move.

If you are relying heavily on the use of cookies for tracking, remember that some people have an issue with cookies and may even disable them on their Web browser, throwing off your Web tracking. If you decide to use cookies, spell this out for your visitors, explaining what cookies are as well as how and why you are using them. Some people are uncomfortable knowing their shopping habits are being tracked. If you are doing this, you should find ways to add more value for the customer with the data you capture. Explaining that the reason you keep track of their purchases is to make personalized product recommendations may assuage their concerns.

Third-Party Traffic Measurement

In addition to Web site traffic reports generated by your Web analytics software, some larger companies use third-party services for independent analysis of their Web numbers. Both Nielsen//NetRatings, Inc., (NTRT) and comScore measure overall Web traffic and site popularity by enlisting people to keep track of their Web surfing habits. Getting independent Web traffic analysis might be important if you plan to sell advertising on your Web site, but you need the high volume of Web traffic to justify such a marketing expense. Another way to see how your Web site's traffic fits in to the bigger picture is by searching for your site on a site like Alexa.com that shows site rankings.

Most people use a site like Amazon.com without concern because the company has built a reputation of trust and because Amazon.com uses the information it tracks in tangible ways for the customer's benefit. Look for ways that you can build trust with your customers or clients online and be very careful not to break it.

Following the Platform for Privacy Preferences (P3P)

The World Wide Web Consortium (W3, at *www.w3.org*) worked to develop standards for privacy policies. Called P3P standards, for Platform for Privacy Preferences, these rules create a standard format for Web sites to specify their privacy practices. In turn, P3P user agents or software can provide this information to Web users through their browsers. For example, a visitor goes to a site and her browser notifies her if the site tracks her browsing habits or only her purchases and how the site uses cookies. P3P reveals your privacy policy to the public and can affect how consumers use your site.

Elements of a Web Log

When you are measuring Web traffic using Web analytics—either with software or third-party services—look at monthly data first, and then drill down further to weekly or daily. While different Web-tracking software packages or services might use slightly different terms or measuring methods, there are some basic data you should be able to measure. What data to focus on depends on the type of business you are in, the type of customer you are trying to reach, and the goals of your Web site.

Breaking Down a Web Log

Being able to access and analyze more types of data isn't always more useful. Zeroing in on some specific numbers and watching them over time can give you a much clearer picture of how visitors interact with your Web site and how well your Web site is helping achieve business goals.

Some of the measurements to focus on include the following:

1. **Page views:** This represents the total number of pages that are downloaded by visitors.

2. **Top page views:** Pay attention to the top ten pages downloaded on your site each month.

3. **Session lengths:** This measurement tells you how long visits to your site last.

4. **Session depths:** This number tells you the average number of pages viewed per visit.

5. **Entrances:** This measurement tells you the most common ways people access your site. Usually it will start with your home page, but people do access your site through other pages as well.

6. **Paths:** Top paths can show you the most common ways people navigate through your site, such as from home page to online catalog to product page to shopping cart to checkout.

7. **Exits or abandonments:** Measuring where people leave your site can help you determine what pages or sections might not be working well, especially if the exit occurs from the shopping cart before checkout.

8. **Search engines:** Knowing what search engines send you the most traffic can give you insight into the value of advertising with them, such as purchasing keywords.

9. **Search terms or keywords:** Being able to see what the most popular search terms or keywords are being used by visitors to find your site can also help with advertising on search engines and other e-marketing tactics, including improving your meta tags.

10. **Referrers:** These are other Web sites that are referring traffic to your site. You could develop stronger linking relationships with them. This information also gives you insight into your customers' interests.

Make sure the Web traffic software you are using allows you to archive at least a year's worth of data at a time. Comparing traffic over the course of days is not as helpful as comparing month to month.

Other useful data that you may want to pay attention to includes the following:

1. **File downloads:** If you are delivering content, via audio or video in particular, make sure you can measure which files are the most popular.

2. **Errors:** Take note of how many pages on your site are generating errors, and make sure they are fixed.

3. **Geographic locations or geotracking:** For some companies, knowing where customers are located is important. Most Web tracking software can pinpoint this by country and some even by city or region.

4. **Browsers:** Knowing what browsers are most commonly used by your site visitors can help your Web developer make suitable design decisions.

5. **E-commerce stats:** If you are selling online, you may have some built-in tracking with your online store solution. If your Web site tracking solution also can monitor e-commerce, compare the numbers.

Tracking Individual Visitors

Knowing how many individual visitors your Web site receives seems to be the Holy Grail of Web tracking and measurement, but it's also helpful to measure visits. Tracking that 200 individuals visited your Web site this month doesn't mean all 200 will buy your products, hire you, or interact with your company in other ways.

If you only track 100 visits, you may be measuring fewer people, but they may be coming back to your site several times. They may also convert from visitor to buyer. You can then look at session length and see that visits average five to ten minutes, a long time in Web time. Comparing visits to the number of sales in a given month, you begin to get a sense of your average conversion rate.

One way you can better track individuals, however, is to encourage site registration. Once a person is registered with your site and logged in, you not only can count accurately the number of members but also track how they use your site. Tracking site members doesn't include all visitors and also can give a skewed vision of overall visitor habits since registered users are more likely to use your site more often than the casual visitor.

Web Log Visuals

Being able to access graphics along with numbers to view your Web traffic reports is preferable. Sometimes, it is easier to glance at a pie chart or bar graph to get a sense of your Web site traffic and activity.

Web Tracking Solutions

Web tracking or Web analytics solutions can vary in price and features as well as where the software resides. Software is installed on the Web server where a site is being hosted and not on your personal computer. Unless you own a Web server and are hosting your own site, chances are you won't need to purchase Web analytics software yourself. Your Web hosting provider will most likely offer Web logs using a specific software product as part of their hosting package. Charging an additional fee for access to Web analytics is no longer the norm; the cost is probably built in to your monthly hosting fee.

Receiving Web logs via e-mail is not the optimal way of getting the information you need regarding your Web traffic. Most analytics software programs allow access to Web-based statistics, graphs, and charts that should show near-real-time results. That means you should be able to check your Web stats any time of the day or night and see fairly recent data reports generated on the fly.

Other solutions for tracking your Web traffic are Web-based and are offered by companies either for free or for a fee and may involve placing some code on your Web pages to measure activity. The solution you choose should provide some of the key measurements over time that will help you analyze the effectiveness of your site.

Cheap and Easy

For a number of years, one of the favorite Web analytics software among Web developers and marketers alike was a product called Urchin. Google purchased Urchin and incorporated its tracking features into a free Web-based solution called Google Analytics (*www.google.com/analytics*). Other companies offering free or low-cost Web-based tracking solutions include the following:

ActiveMeter (*www.activemeter.com*)
HitsLog (*www.hitslog.com*),
SiteTracker (*www.sitetracker.com*)
StatCounter (*www.statcounter.com*)

If your Web-based traffic tracking solution is only measuring hits, you aren't receiving valuable data. At a minimum, you should be able to measure total number of visits per week or month, top pages, top paths, and if possible, top entrances, top exits, and referrers. This information tells you how many times your site is accessed, the most popular pages, how people navigate through your site, and where they are coming from.

To Show or Not to Show

Some Web sites display a traffic or hit counter on the bottom of their home pages. In fact, many sites offer free hit counters in a variety of designs. You need to consider if you really want people to see how many people have accessed your home page or the rest of your site. You may have a successful site with only 100 visitors because many of them have gone on to do business with you. However, when someone visits a site with a counter that reads 100, the impression may be that your site is not very popular—translation: not any good. From an e-business standpoint, it is best to keep your Web traffic numbers to yourself until you have an interesting story to tell.

For Web Servers Only

Web analytics software that resides on a Web server comes in different shapes and sizes, and if your site is being hosted externally on a shared server you most likely will not have a choice of the software used. If you are co-locating a server at an external host or host your own site internally, an array of solutions is available.

Web analytics solution providers include the following:

ClickTracks (*www.clicktracks.com*)
CoreMetrics (*www.coremetrics.com*)
Omniture's SiteCatalyst (*www.omniture.com*)

VisiStat (*www.visistat.com*)
Visual Sciences (*www.visualsciences.com*)
WebSideStory's HBX Analytics (*www.websidestory.com*)
WebTrends (*www.webtrends.com*)

If you are investing in co-locating a server or hosting in-house, you have most likely based part of that decision on having the financial resources available to invest in these more costly approaches. Therefore, if price is not the issue, you can choose your Web analytics solution based solely on features and capabilities. If price is an issue, this will reduce the number of solutions available to you but should not eliminate quality solutions that will provide you with the valuable data you need to assess the effectiveness of your Web site.

Business Impacts of Web Logs

Tracking your Web traffic can help determine if you are getting an acceptable return on your investment (ROI) for your e-business investments. Seeing an increase in sales through your online store is only one measure of a good return on the cost of building your site. Your ROI may also be determined by an increasing number of leads generated through your site or by the number of customers that click through to your site via your e-mail newsletter. Determine what other goals are important to your company, especially the ones that lead to long-term relationships with customers.

Assessing Web Site Effectiveness

Whether or not your Web site is effective in achieving your e-business goals becomes clear as you look closely at your Web traffic analysis over time. Even before you look at more specific goals, make sure your company Web site is achieving three general goals:

- Acquiring new visitors
- Converting visitors to customers or clients
- Retaining your customers

If you are not acquiring new visitors to your site on a regular basis, the chances of achieving any other goals is slim. Driving more traffic to your site, however, does not always increase conversion from visitors to customers. More traffic doesn't necessarily mean the right traffic. The more targeted you are about who you point to your site, the more likely you are to convert them to customers or clients.

Once you have customers, retaining or holding onto them is a new challenge. Encouraging them to become a registered member of your site and offering them perks and benefits for doing so increases your customer retention rate. Even getting them to sign up for a regular e-mail announcement from your company helps to remind them of your brand, your products or services, and your site. Each time you draw a visitor or customer back to your site, you should take advantage of a new opportunity to build your relationship with him or her.

Comparing All the Data

You should gather data in a variety of ways from your site visitors and existing customers, members, or subscribers. **Make it clear in your privacy policy exactly what kinds of information you are gathering from site users, how you gather it, and how you use it.** Keep track of all the data you are gathering and look at more than just one type of data or one set of statistics to get a detailed picture of the effectiveness of your e-business efforts.

One valuable feature of e-business is that you are able to track customer data more easily, often automatically, and compile the data into databases to generate reports. Here is just a short list of the possible data you should gather, track, and analyze:

1. **Web analytics:** These are your Web traffic reports.
2. **Demographic data:** If you can get visitors to fill out a form, make sure to ask key questions such as age range, education level, household income, location, and anything else that can give you a sense of who they are.
3. **Psychographic data:** Also called "attitudinal data" and gathered through surveys, focus groups, beta testing, and other studies that reveal what your users like, want, and do.

4. **Customer feedback:** Whether you are getting feedback e-mails or customers are filling out feedback forms, keep an eye on customer satisfaction.

5. **Direct customer data:** Using cookies, you can track a customer's habits within your site.

6. **Transaction data:** Purchasing habits, average dollar amount per sale, top items sold, and shopping-cart abandonment is all useful information.

7. **E-mail campaign data:** If you are sending out e-mail announcements, promotions and e-newsletters, track how many e-mails are opened and how many people click on the links to get to your site as well as where they go.

8. **Affiliate data:** If you have an affiliate program, get statistics ranging from what products are bestsellers to which affiliates generate the most sales.

9. **Industry research:** While it may be hard to find data on your exact industry or based on numbers from companies that are the same size as yours, looking for comparables can be helpful when analyzing your own data.

Don't forget to check your competitors' sites and see if they offer any statistics that can give you a better sense of where your own site stands.

Benchmarks and Measuring Progress

Measuring benchmarks for your company is an individual and internal process. A benchmark is a measurement that is established as a comparison for all subsequent measurements of the same thing for a similar time period. Trying to compare your Web site's benchmarks to other companies' benchmarks on a regular basis doesn't work when every company uses a different set of standards for determining their benchmarks. You should establish your own process for measuring and analyzing your Web site's progress in achieving goals.

Establishing Benchmarks

To establish a benchmark for your Web traffic analysis, first determine what unit of measurement will be used for comparison purposes, such as a week of traffic or a month. Benchmarks are different from goals. You may be trying to reach a certain number of site registrations or sales. However, in any given time period, the registrations or sales may meet or surpass your goals. Goals are what you want; benchmarks are what you reach at a given point in time.

If your Web site is online and you have not yet begun tracking your Web traffic but decide to track your statistics month to month, you may need to wait until the following month to gather a full month's worth of data. You don't want to use a partial month as a benchmark for traffic for subsequent months. You want to compare like to like.

Measuring over Time

As time progresses, you will accumulate benchmarks—your first month's benchmark, your quarterly benchmark, your six-month benchmark, and then your one-year benchmark. Now you have more numbers for comparing traffic the next year. You can compare Q1 of last year to Q1 of this year to see if there is significant growth or change.

Don't be alarmed if your Web traffic takes a dip now and then. Blips in traffic can occur for a number of reasons. Here are some things that may decrease the numbers to your site:

1. **Time of day:** In your daily Web traffic reports, notice patterns of preferred times when your site is accessed and also times when you are less likely to get traffic. Often traffic decreases after a traditional workday ends then picks up again later at night. This pattern has shown that many people access the Web from work.

2. **Seasons/weather:** You may notice more traffic during colder months or inclement weather than during hotter months. If your visitors are global, tracking this is more complex but if national, you may begin to see patterns.

3. **Holidays:** Depending on your site, you may see a dip in traffic during the holidays as people tend to spend more time

with family and friends rather than online. If you are selling products and especially gifts, however, you want to see an increase.

4. Outages: Power outages usually should not affect your Web site's accessibility because your Web host should have contingency solutions in place. However, an outage can affect your visitors' ability to use their computers or get online.

5. Stagnation: If you are not building relationships with your visitors or implementing consistent online or offline marketing and promotions for your Web site, you may see a dip in traffic until your next e-newsletter or your next Web site update.

Learning to understand the reasons for the ebb and flow of your Web site traffic will help you identify unusual activity or unexpected lack of activity on your site. Knowing what it takes to keep traffic flowing can dictate a schedule for Web site modifications and updates as well as implementing e-marketing tactics.

▶▶ TEST DRIVE

When you are looking at your Web analytics reports, you want to make sure you are receiving and keeping track of useful data. Some of the things to ask yourself about your Web analytics software include the following:

➲ Can I access my Web traffic reports anytime and receive at least near-real-time data?

➲ Is my Web analytics solution measuring more than just hits so I can best assess the effectiveness of my Web site?

➲ What benchmarks have I established as I track my Web traffic statistics?

➲ How is my Web site meeting or surpassing goals month to month, quarter to quarter, and year to year?

Measuring and Re-Examining Your Site

Business Analysis of Web Traffic Patterns

Monitoring your Web site's traffic goes far beyond determining if your traffic has increased over time. This is only a small portion of what you want to look at in your site's usage logs.

From an e-business standpoint, the way visitors actually use your site is far more telling in determining whether the site is reaching tangible business goals. Comparing the numbers of people who visit your site to how they navigate through the site and what their ultimate action is before they leave the site can speak volumes to whether or not your site is working for you—and for your potential and current customers or clients.

Measuring the Wrong Things

As you look at your Web stats, make sure you are not counting things that will give you false numbers, such as counting pop-up ads (if you are using them) or counting error pages as page views. You also want to make sure that you are not counting the number of times you or your staff members are accessing your company site. Cheaper Web tracking solutions may not allow you to specify what not to track. If you cannot access the Web tracking software on your Web host's server, check with your Web developer to see if there is a way to keep erroneous page views from being counted.

Active Conversions

A conversion rate is a percentage based on the number of visitors to your Web site who act on something instead of just browsing divided by the total number of site visitors. The actions visitors perform through your site will vary depending on what features you've placed on your Web site to help reach your company's goals, such as these:

- ⮌ Requesting information or to be contacted
- ⮌ Signing up for an e-newsletter
- ⮌ Registering as a member of your site
- ⮌ Sending an article to a friend
- ⮌ Filling out a survey
- ⮌ Purchasing a product

Your average conversion rate for each action you are analyzing will give you a sense of how well you are persuading visitors to your site to do the things you want them to do. Tracking these percentages each month can show whether or not the improvements you make to your site layout, design, feature placement, and content increase the conversion rates.

Another aspect of conversion is abandonment, when instead of purchasing or filling out a form, the visitor leaves midway through the process. Compare conversion rates to abandonments (also called exits or bailouts). While it is hard to get accurate conversion rates from industry sources, some conversion rates and abandonment rates that you can refer to as a rough guideline include these:

Industry	Conversion Rate (%)	Abandonment Rate (%)
Catalog	3.1	60.8
Fashion/apparel	2.2	69.7
Specialty	2.0	73.1
Sports/outdoor	1.4	59.4
Electronics	0.6	82.4

Source: Fireclick Index January 2007

Logically, you want to increase your conversion rates for each interactive feature on your site. You also want to decrease the number of exits and bailouts within those interactive features.

You can also segment your conversion rates, and if you are tracking new visitors versus repeat visitors, you can note the difference in conversion rates between them. New visitors will most likely demonstrate a lower conversion rate than those who have been to your site several times or more. The more detailed the analysis of your site's traffic, the more data you can extract to evaluate and increase the effectiveness of your site as a whole or individual features and pages.

Home Page Effectiveness

No matter how great you think the design, layout, and content of your home page is, there is always room for improvement. Looking at your Web traffic statistics, you can figure out how visitors to your site feel about and react to your home page.

Are You Tracking Conversations?

In addition to tracking activity on your company Web site, you should also track what is being said about your company on other Web sites and blogs. The quick and dirty way to do this is to do a search on several of the popular search engines for your company name. Include the name within quotation marks so the results return only hits identical to your company name. eWatch, a product of PR Newswire (ewatch.prnewswire.com), provides a fee-based service for tracking your company mentions in media online and off. A Web-based tool for tracking specific blog posts and blog comments or "blog conversations," is Co.mments (*http://co.mments.com*).

Some of the numbers you can look at to see what happens when visitors arrive at your home page include the following:

Number of visits: This will tell you how many people arrived and downloaded the home page file.

Top entries: Knowing if people are accessing your site first through the home page or via an internal page could tell you if people are getting the benefit of your strategically designed home page or if you need to make sure other pages have easy access to critical parts of your site.

Top paths: Your goal is to get most traffic from your home page to the important business features of your site, such as your online store or your information request form. If the top paths go to other areas, you may need to revisit the way you lead visitors to the most important areas of your site.

Top exits: If visitors are bailing out from your site at the home page, there may be a barrier keeping people from going further into the site.

Home page file downloads: If the statistics for the download of the graphics and other files on your home page are not in line with the number of visitors, it's possible people are bailing because of download issues.

Hiding the Goods

One client I worked with wanted to market a region of a state to tourists. The overall goal of the company's Web site was to show the visual attractiveness of the region and the features that made the area exciting. One of their main measurable goals was to encourage visitors to fill out a form to order a free visitors guide. Their Web traffic logs showed that hundreds of people visited their site each month, but the number of requests for a free brochure was miniscule. Looking more closely at the top paths for the site, it was apparent that visitors were going everywhere on the site but the page with the form to order a free visitors guide.

Analyzing the numbers proved there was a disconnection between the organization's goals and the actual results of Web site usage. The numbers also supported recommendations for a site redesign. One of the first recommendations was a simple fix. On the home page, there was an attractive graphical button that said "Order Your Free Visitors Brochure." But the button was positioned at the bottom right-hand side of the Web page, "below the fold," which meant visitors had to scroll down the home page to even see the button. With the navigation on the left side and right side of the home page—yes, navigation was on both sides—visitors had too many choices and no reason to scroll down the page to see the most important action item. We moved the button to the top right corner of the home page. Other recommendations that were supported by the Web traffic stats included consolidating the navigation and placing it at the top of the home page.

Analyzing Web traffic statistics to get a sense of your visitors' reactions to your home page can immediately tell you if there's something wrong with the design. **A home page that takes too long to load can turn people away.** Home page navigation that is not clear can lead visitors astray. Even clear navigation may be arranged in the wrong order, emphasizing less important sections or features of the site.

Identifying Weak Spots

Your Web analytics software should monitor top exits from your Web site. These numbers show the most common pages where visitors leave your site. Visit the top ten exit pages to get a sense of where visitors are leaving although you may not always be able to figure out why they left a particular page. When you get to a common exit page, check the download time of the page and the navigation. Sometimes, the buttons on a page aren't programmed properly, and clicking on them does not lead a visitor to another part of the site. You may not be able to figure out immediately why visitors are exiting on certain pages rather than others, but over time you may begin to see a pattern. Comparing top exits to top entrances and top paths can show a more detailed picture of visitors' browsing habits and may also give you more insight to whether or not their actions are based on their own preferences or page layout, design, navigation, or other aspects of your site.

If you are selling online, your Web analytics software should also measure cart abandonment or bailout. If an increasing number of customers abandon their shopping carts, for instance, you can test to see if there is something wrong with the process, layout, or technology that is creating a barrier to checking out. A simple bug in a shopping-cart system can tempt visitors into leaving a full shopping cart without completing their purchase. Fixing the bug should result in a decreased abandonment rate the following month. Shopping carts are commonly abandoned on most shopping sites. However, your goal is to do everything you can to decrease loss of sales.

Wrong Paths

By looking at the top paths visitors are taking through your site, you can begin to assess if you are guiding them to the areas and features that will help you achieve your e-business goals. Here are some reasons visitors might not be going where you want them to on your company site:

➲ They are browsing, the online store equivalent of "just looking."
➲ They are following their personal interests.
➲ They are clicking on the most prominent links or buttons.

➲ They are drawn to a link or feature because of site design, layout, or content.

➲ They arrive with a particular goal in mind and act on it.

➲ They are referred to a particular page or feature on the site and bypass your home page entirely, missing cues and calls to action.

By taking a closer look at the top paths, you see your home page in a different light. What may have seemed like prominent placement for key features isn't catching a visitor's attention.

Surgical Web Site Redesigns

If there's a disconnect between the e-business goals of your Web site and the actual actions taken by site visitors, you need to make a change to your site. Evaluate whether the change you should make is simply to a graphic or the placement of a call to action or if you need to make a more extensive modification, such as redesigning the navigation buttons on your site.

Rearranging For Emphasis

If you placed an important call to action on the upper left side of your Web page and it isn't getting any attention, try moving it to the upper right side of the page. Moving a block of text or a graphic to another location on the page should not entail too much work unless your site design is more graphics heavy and the changes you want to make would affect a larger graphical interface element.

A good argument for developing a home page design that is not overly reliant on graphics to produce the look and feel is that you will need to fine-tune your home page over time to improve its effectiveness. Home pages that are almost entirely made up of a single large graphic or several graphics fitted together like a puzzle require a lot more work to modify. Turn to your Web developer to make more complex modifications.

With sites that contain a balance of graphics and text and that have a flexible content management system, making the small tweaks to the pages including the home page should be much easier. Some steps you should take as you make changes to your site based on problems you've identified through your Web traffic analysis include the following:

1. **Save a copy** of the original home page or Web site page that you plan to modify.
2. **Print out a copy** of the original page for your files or take a screen shot to keep in your digital files as an additional record before making the change.
3. **Note the date** you made the change based on your Web traffic analysis along with an explanation of what you are trying to achieve with the change.
4. **Make the change** or have your developer make the change.
5. **Print out a copy** or take a screen shot of the new page for your files.

After you've made the change, keep an eye on your Web traffic reports and the top paths, even tracking weekly to see if there are any significant changes. Unless you have a large and steady stream of traffic to your site and can see results quickly, allow at least a month to note changes in the paths and actions visitors are taking. You should see some change and hopefully an improvement in your Web site's effectiveness. If not, repeat the process, trying a different tactic.

Image Modifications

Changing images on a site can be a more labor-intensive process and may require the help of your Web developer or a graphic designer familiar with the Web. Unless you are able to manipulate images in-house using the array of graphics and imaging software available, you probably don't want to attempt to change your Web site images. The images on your site usually fall into three categories:

- ⮑ Images that make up the overall site design
- ⮑ Images that complement the text
- ⮑ Images that are the focal point of the site (product photos, photographs by a photographer, paintings or illustrations by an artist)

The images that create the overall design of the site may be the most complex to modify although the other images may in themselves take more skills to achieve.

Reasons for modifying images on a site could include the following:

- Images are too large and take too long to download.
- Graphic color combinations are hard to read or not eye-catching.
- Graphic is not attracting enough attention.
- Images are fuzzy, pixelated, or of poor quality.
- Images of products are too dark or hard to make out the items.

Images on a Web site should have a purpose. They should add value to the site, attract the visitor's eye, lead them to calls to action, and help them to better navigate the site. If the images on your site aren't doing this, strategically modifying them could significantly improve your site's effectiveness.

Know Your Visitor Before Redesigning

Some of the statistics tracked by Web analytics software that you may not be monitoring as closely as top paths, top pages, and other action-oriented stats are an analysis of the computers your visitors are using to access your site. Before a redesign, make note of the most popular Web browsers being used in order to optimize your site. Some Web analytics software, including Google Analytics, tracks the number of visitors who have Flash installed in their browser, their screen resolution, platform, and even connection speed. All of these factors could affect what visitors actually see when they come to your Web site.

When to Overhaul Your Entire Site

If you started building your site with a strategic plan, chances are you won't have to rebuild your site from scratch. Most companies do opt to redesign their site on an annual basis, mostly to reflect changes to the company and create new excitement around the site or to take advantage of improvements to Web technology and new Web-based features that could better help the company reach its goals. For others, however, a site redesign needs to take place because the site simply doesn't function well or doesn't play a valuable part in the company's e-business strategy. When a site fails to contribute in any meaningful way to a company's bottom line over a period of time, it may require an entire overhaul to become the effective marketing, customer service, or sales tool that it was intended to be when it was first built.

Changing the Front End

If you put your company site online simply because you knew you had to be online and saw your competitors going online, you are not alone. Many companies put up their first Web site without a plan of any kind in place. Problems tend not to arise in the beginning if the site consists of only a few pages. However, over the course of the next year or so, a six-page Web site is suddenly insufficient, and so additional pages are added. To get to those pages, designers add additional links to the home page and navigation of the site without any rhyme or reason. Suddenly, a basic Web site turns into a labyrinth of pages and links that can lead a visitor in circles but rarely to where they should or want to go. Sound familiar?

If your company site has so many links off the home page that visitors are not funneled to the key areas and actions that are important to your business goals, it may be time to reduce the number of links. There are several ways to change the interface or front end of a site without having to also reorganize the back end, but as you look more closely at the architecture of your site, you may find major flaws in how the files are arranged behind the scenes.

A quick and easy way to figure out if your site architecture has gone awry is to create a flow chart or map for your current site. Draw a box to represent your home page. Then draw boxes below the home page to represent the top-level navigation of your site. If you cannot fit the boxes onto a page no matter how you arrange the page, you have already identified the problem—too many top-level choices. Also, if you cannot draw a short line to the most important pages of your site from your home page or if you are finding lines crisscrossing across the page, you need a site overhaul.

Look for ways to reorganize the content of your site so your top-level categories can encompass more content. Here is an example of top-level categories and how they could be consolidated:

- Company History
- Staff Bios
- Contact Information
- Widgets for Sale
- Gadgets for Sale

- Doohickeys for Sale
- Articles
- In the News
- Resources
- Press Releases

- About Us:
  - ▶ Company History
  - ▶ Staff Bios
  - ▶ In the News
- Our Store:
  - ▶ Widgets
  - ▶ Gadgets
  - ▶ Doohickeys
- Resources:
  - ▶ Articles
- Pressroom:
  - ▶ Press releases
- Contact Us

Consolidated navigation with broader top-level categories gives your site more room to grow. You can do this using drop-down menus or some other visual cue that there is a hierarchy of sections below or beyond each main category.

Modifying the Back End

If you have worked with a Web developer to build your site, chances are you may not have ever seen the ways the files that make up your Web site are organized. A poorly organized back end to a Web site can result in broken links and lost pages. The way files are organized on the back end should reflect a structure or pattern similar to the way the navigation is organized on the front end.

Look at the file structure of your Web site by accessing the site through FTP. Your Web developer, Internet consultant, or ISP can assist you with gaining FTP access to your site. Once there, you'll see your site consists of files and folders, much like the files and folders on your computer. File hierarchy should be reflected in folders within folders or nested folders. If you arrive at the main or root folder of your Web site and see only files—HTML documents, images and other files such as PDF, Word documents, and so on—then you have a back-end problem.

Some basic behind-the-scenes ways to organize the files of a Web site include the following:

1. In your Web site's root directory, create a folder to represent each top-level category.
2. Within the top-level category folder, you can store individual HTML pages related to the category as well as other folders for subcategories.
3. Your home page HTML file (probably named index.htm or index.html) should be stored in your Web site's root directory.
4. Organize photographs and images within folders.
5. Consider creating additional image folders within each category or subcategory folder rather than lumping them together into a single folder.
6. Store your additional files in one separate folder or, if there are many, within individual folders grouped by type such as PDF, Word documents, spreadsheets, PowerPoint presentations, and so on.

The way your Web site is organized from the back end should be in sync with the way the site contents are presented on the front end. If you are doing an entire site overhaul, regroup your Web site files to reflect any changes you make to match the way the content is organized on your site. Trying to change the front end without reorganizing the back end can be a frustrating effort or even an exercise in futility.

Revisiting the Numbers

After you have modified your site in response to what you assessed through your Web analytics software, you will probably need to set new benchmarks. Otherwise you will be comparing apples to oranges when looking at your pre- and post-redesigned site traffic.

Traffic Over Time

Once you set new benchmarks, don't throw out your archival Web traffic reports. Even though you have made some specific site changes that may limit how much of the old reports you can actually compare to the new reports, there will still be some top-line data worth looking at over time.

While your top paths and top pages may change because actual pages have been moved, file names have been changed, and other pages might have been eliminated, you can still compare overall results. Note if the new top pages are the more important pages and if the new top paths are leading visitors to key actions. You can still compare key actions from the old reports and new ones, including the following:

- ⮑ Lead generation
- ⮑ Sales
- ⮑ Registrations
- ⮑ Subscriptions
- ⮑ Feedback

By carefully analyzing your Web traffic reports, you should be able to identify problem areas on your site. By making strategic site modifications based on your Web traffic analysis, you should see positive results in your Web traffic reports and, more importantly, in your overall e-business efforts.

Managing Change

Making site modifications based on your site analysis can become a time-consuming process. Don't let it distract you from the overall business at hand. Determine a manageable schedule for both site analysis and resulting site modifications.

For some, revisiting their site's performance monthly is fine but for others quarterly is more realistic based on available resources and staff. Re-evaluating your site's effectiveness on an annual basis misses many opportunities to improve sales and leads during the year.

Make sure you regularly back up all Web traffic reports and that you document all changes made to your site over time. There is no way to recreate the history of your site's effectiveness, and if you lose the data from previous months or years, you are losing a valuable company asset.

▶▶ TEST DRIVE

Keeping track of your Web site's performance over time is an important way to make sure you are getting a return on the investment you made building your site. As you begin analyzing your Web site's effectiveness, consider the following:

- ➲ What is important to my company as goals for my site?
- ➲ How will I prioritize the goals for my Web site?
- ➲ What is a manageable schedule for my company to analyze our Web site's traffic reports?
- ➲ What is a manageable schedule for my company to modify our Web site?
- ➲ What is a realistic budget we can devote to Web site modifications or redesigns?

Measuring and Re-Examining Your Site

Podcasts and Videocasts for Business

Streaming audio and video can be used for business in a variety of ways, but the jury is still out as to how much impact they have on a company's bottom line. Streaming means that the files begin to play while still downloading rather than older audio and video technologies that needed to download in their entirety before they could be played.

Many obstacles to such files from a few years ago are gone. Barriers to accessing larger file sizes on Web sites are fewer with the continuing increase of broadband connections across the country. Difficulties and expenses in producing audio and video files continue to shrink due to new developments in technology. Still, finding the right business uses of multimedia is an important step to determining whether or not audio or video are essential to your company's site.

There are several things to consider when debating about adding audio or video to your company site. Here are some quick comparisons.

Comparisons of Streaming Audio and Video on Web Sites

Audio	Video
Easy to produce	Requires more editing and production
Smaller file sizes	Much larger file sizes, even for short videos
Easy to access online	Requires more bandwidth
Can be downloaded to various devices	Fewer devices support digital video
Able to listen to anytime	Requires full attention to view

Producing audio or video for your company Web site requires more resources than writing content. From an e-business standpoint, you may not be able to justify the additional resources required to produce quality multimedia, at least not yet.

E-Business Uses for Audio

Audio for business, also known as corporate podcasting, requires more than just the technical means to produce the files. You need the voice talent, not to mention appropriate content to help you achieve your business goals.

Some ways that audio can be integrated into your Web site or used for other e-business or e-marketing efforts include the following:

➲ Ad within existing podcasts
➲ Company news
➲ Press releases
➲ Audio FAQ
➲ Audio blog
➲ Investor relations updates
➲ Audio newsletter

The common audio media format that can be played with relative ease by visitors to your site and that can be downloaded to players and other audio devices is an MP3 file. For radio-quality audio clips, however, stations may request MP2 files.

Tools for Podcasting

There are Web sites where you can produce audio or podcasts, often allowing you to call a phone number or to use Voice over Internet Protocol (VoIP) to record the audio. The site's system automatically produces an MP3 file and posts it to your area on the site. Companies like Gabcast (*www.gabcast.com*), GCast (*www.gcast.com*), MyPodcast (*www.mypodcast.com*) and Blogger's Audioblogger (*www.audioblogger.com*) provide the tools and podcast hosting for either free or a low monthly fee. Some podcasting tools allow you to embed your podcast directly into your Web site so visitors to your site simply click on a button or link to start playing the audio.

E-Business Uses for Video

Finding an e-business use for video can seem more challenging, particularly because video requires much more effort to produce a high-quality recording. While the technology continues to improve, both from the production side as well as the Internet access side, there is more to video than simply recording and publishing.

Before embarking on digital video production, consider whether you have the means to do the following:

- Develop the concept for the video, write the script, and create storyboards or diagrams planning out each shot
- Identify the right onscreen talent
- Find or set up the location for the shoot with the proper lighting and sound equipment
- Have the right equipment to record the video
- Have a means to edit the recording
- Have a place to host the video cast and be able to embed it into your company site

Video Networks, Hosts, and Production Companies

The video equivalent of an audio publishing and hosting site is a video network or video hosting service. Companies that facilitate video uploading and offer hosting for free or a small fee include Veoh (*www.veoh.com*), Photobucket (*www.photobucket.com*), and even Google with its Video Upload Program (*upload.video.google.com*). These sites, however, do not provide the tools for producing videos. Depending on your budget, you can hire video production companies that specialize in video for the Web. Hiring a production company can be costly, so you'll need to first consider how online video can help your company's bottom line.

Even though video sites such as YouTube.com have had explosive success, most online videos have low production values, are just a few minutes long, and tend to be more entertainment oriented. The exceptions are news clips or excerpts from television shows or film, and those are professionally produced, usually for a large amount of money.

For e-business, some uses of online video can include the following:

⊃ Ads within other video segments or on Web sites that allow video advertising
⊃ Viral marketing videos that are available for people to download and distribute
⊃ Customer service featuring product instructions and demonstrations
⊃ Press releases known as video news releases (VNRs)
⊃ B-roll footage to accompany press releases or news stories
⊃ Video newsletters

Whatever you use on your site, make sure it adds value.

Getting Social

Social networking is about expanding one's network. On the Web, online tools can help people not only keep track of their own networks but expand them based on who their contacts know. **Social networking is viral, encouraging people to sign up with a social networking site, tell their friends about it, and invite them to join.** The sites link people together as friends or friends of friends, exponentially expanding one's network. Social networking can be a powerful tool, when used appropriately, to build a loyal following of friends or fans for your company.

Basics of Social Networking

Social networking Web sites have the ultimate goal of linking people together who have shared interests. People can join a social networking site for free and usually can do some or all of the following:

⊃ Create profiles
⊃ Create blogs
⊃ Upload photos and videos

Inside Track   Warming Sales Leads with Web Video

When Koko Fitness (www.kokofitness.com) in Massachusetts first launched its company site in June 2006, the company didn't include online video with the initial public site. It did, however, offer an online video demo to sales prospects via a password-protected link.

"The product is so experiential that video provided the ability to capture the entire experience much more fully than is possible in words," says Lauren Curley, public relations person for the company that manufactures fitness equipment.

When they finally decided to add videos to their public site, they did the production in-house and spent approximately $8,000 for four videos. The video has been updated over time to reflect product enhancements and modifications.

Curley says the video has been instrumental in driving more qualified sales leads for their equipment. The video was initially used to introduce the product but has since become a valuable tool to prepare all parties for initial sales meetings. Their Web site video has also allowed them to demo the product where appropriate without having to transport equipment in their eighteen-wheel trailer.

When the company first looked at video (pre-YouTube.com), they wondered what video file formats to use. Windows Media (.wmv) is the default standard on Windows machines, but they found it would not always play well on Macs. The company also did not have a dedicated server, so both bandwidth and processing requirements made streaming video a challenge.

They uploaded their videos to YouTube.com, now stored on Google Video, and embedded the video directly into a page on their Web site. Using an established video storage and delivery site made their videos easily available.

⮞ Invite others to join their network or join someone else's network
⮞ Communicate with others through instant messages
⮞ Add comments to one another's pages
⮞ Send e-mails through the site's proprietary e-mail system

Every social networking site tries to offer something different or some twist on the traditional concept of networking with others. Some of the more popular social networking sites include the following:

MySpace (*www.myspace.com*): Social, interest-based networking that centers on entertainment interests such as music and film.

LinkedIn (*www.linkedin.com*): Business networking based around people's resumes and making professional contacts.

SoFlow (*www.soflow.com*): Business networking based around forming professional groups and associations.

Gather (*www.gather.com*): Communities built around publishing articles and images and sharing them with people who have similar interests.

Facebook (*www.facebook.com*): Began as a site for students to network but has since expanded to include professional networking.

Friendster (*www.friendster.com*): The social, interest-based networking that was one of the first sites to bring the concept of Web-based social networking into the mainstream.

Some blogging sites are considered social networking sites because of the social interaction between bloggers and visitors who can also become subscribers or in some cases members of the blog. However, blogs blur the definition of social networking because they don't contain tools that help people formally create networks, much less provide ways to organize and expand their networks.

The tools contained within social networking sites allow you to build a network then grow your network by connecting with others through shared interests or by linking through existing contacts. In e-business, establishing a growing network through a social networking site means you have an audience who wants to receive news and information about your company.

Marketing Through Social Networking

Business owners are setting up their own social networks on sites such as MySpace.com and Friendster.com. On MySpace.com, for example, you can find the food company Annie's Homegrown (www.myspace.

com/berniethebunny), with over 1,400 friends, and car company Honda promoting its Element car through a page for Gil the Crab, a character in one of its television commercials (*www.myspace.com/crab*), with over 96,000 friends. Annie's Homegrown also uses a character on its page— Bernie the Bunny from its product packaging. People are compelled to become "friends" with the characters that represent the companies.

Using Tags on the Web

A tag is a keyword or term assigned to information including text, images, or multimedia files such as audio and video. Tags describe or classify an item and are used to relate that item to other items that share the same tag. The producer of an article, image, or file usually assigns the tags to his work based on personal choice. On social networking sites, people are connected through similar interests, and those interests can be designated as tags within their personal profiles. For example, if a person is interested in rafting, swimming, and snorkeling, those interests can be tags in her profile. The tags can link to lists of other people with the same tagged interests.

The company that sells widgets may have a limited lifestyle appeal, but the company that manufactures camping equipment can position itself as a lifestyle brand, as can the company that produces baby gear for new parents. The key is to use social networking to communicate a larger message. Annie's larger message is healthy eating and healthy living. Honda's larger message is fun, leisure time, and friends. The company also has another more straightforward MySpace page for their Element car (*www.myspace.com/hondaelement*) with over 39,000 friends promoting the same lifestyle message as on their Gil the Crab page.

Social networking sites and concepts work best when you can promote a lifestyle aspect of your company. You are creating a way that people who have an affinity toward your company or products can not only connect with you but with one another. As other people connect to your social networking page, they'll draw more visitors and potentially more connections.

Going Mobile

Doing business over mobile devices, also referred to as m-business, is not only the mobile version of e-business but encompasses doing business using multiple devices (multi-device) and across multiple channels (multi-channel). **M-commerce refers to using mobile and wireless devices to transact business over the Web, including buying and selling.** M-marketing is conducting marketing activities via mobile and wireless devices. Conducting m-business can only happen if there are sufficient applications to facilitate publishing to and interacting within the mobile medium.

Delivering on Mobile Devices

The major challenge of m-business is that the devices where the transactions and interactions are taking place have tiny screens compared to a standard computer. Think of the kinds of devices that have become Internet enabled:

- Cell phones
- Smart phones such as Treos
- Personal digital assistants (PDAs) such as Palm and Pocket PCs
- BlackBerries
- Other devices enabled with Wi-Fi or Bluetooth, including gaming devices such as PSPs (PlayStation Portable)

Today, m-business consists of delivering content to portable devices and cellular phones via text messages. However, advertising and marketing have not fully explored this platform. Selling via mobile device has been limited to games and ring tones for cell phones although a move toward purchasing music and audio content is beginning.

Payment methods for m-commerce are mostly conducted using premium rate calling numbers, deducting from the caller's calling credit, or charging through the mobile user's connectivity bill. One company, Text-PayMe (*www.textpayme.com*), is exploring transactions between people using cell phones, a mobile version of making a payment, including buying and selling on CraigsList.

SMS and MMS

Short Message Service (SMS) is a service on mobile phones and devices that allows short messages, also known as text messages, to be sent between devices. While technically text messaging can be used for commercial messaging, consumers' tolerance for text ads in their text-message inboxes has not been fully explored. The most common types of non-personal text messaging are news alerts, sports updates, and financial information. Multimedia messaging service (MMS) allows multimedia messages to be sent through mobile devices that include audio, video, and images. The most common form of MMS is the buying, selling, and trading of ring tones for cell phones.

Getting Ready for M-Business

Most Internet-enabled or wireless mobile devices provide not only text or e-mail messaging but also Web access. Try using a variety of mobile devices to access your company's Web site, and you'll begin to see the challenge of not only using the tiny screen to view the site but also how the mobile device interprets the site's HTML. Take these steps to optimize your site for mobile devices:

1. Check how the site layout appears, especially if you are using tables in the HTML to format your site pages.
2. Check how images appear.
3. Check how multimedia files appear.
4. Check how links appear, particularly how the file names can be used as links, demonstrating how important it is to give your site files logical, clear names.
5. Monitor the download time of each page, especially your home page.
6. Check your site's HTML by entering URLs into a site such as Skweezer.com that strips the pages down to only mobile-safe elements.
7. Check the W3 Web site (*www.w3.org*) for specs and standards for mobile-optimized sites.

While there is not a lot of data on consumer tolerance for marketing messages sent to mobile devices, the current trend leans more toward using the mobile medium for entertainment and financial information than commercials. Business models and standards are still being developed.

Moblogging

One use of mobile devices that has already taken hold is mobile blogging, or moblogging. In general, moblogging refers to blogging remotely using any device other than your computer. Because many cell phones are now capable of taking, storing, downloading, and uploading photographs, a popular form of moblogging is uploading photos to a moblog. Communities of mobloggers have formed including Text America (www.textamerica.com) and Winksite (www.winksite.com). Next came audio moblogging and video moblogging (MoVlogging) using cell phones and other mobile devices. A business benefit of moblogging capabilities is being able to update your blog from anywhere with any Internet-enabled device.

Keeping Up with the Joneses

It is easy to get caught up in the excitement of new technology, but keep in mind that every new e-business tool comes with a cost, and every cost needs to be evaluated for its impact on your company's bottom line. Implementing a new e-business tool just because you can leads to disaster. Step back and look at the big picture.

Make sure that the new technology you want to invest in does some or all of the following:

- ⮑ Saves your company time when performing a task
- ⮑ Saves your company money in the long run
- ⮑ Has a reasonable learning curve that won't bring productivity to a halt
- ⮑ Will seamlessly integrate into your existing systems
- ⮑ Supports revenue generation either indirectly or directly
- ⮑ Can be measured or tracked regularly to evaluate effectiveness

E-business is the electronic version of traditional business, but without a foundation of sound business knowledge and decisions, your company won't find success online.

Twitter and Jaiku

In the category of "what are they thinking," two Web sites emerged around the same time (http://twitter.com and www.jaiku.com) allowing members to post a text message in 140 characters or less about what they are doing at any given moment. Think of these sites as blogs but with faster, more frequent, and much shorter updates. These quick messages can be posted on the member's personal page and made private or public. The posts are generated from the Web, from an instant messaging program online, or from a mobile phone or Internet-enabled PDA. This is a perfect example of a technology that has been developed that requires careful consideration to see if it makes sense for your business. Internet marketing experts, however, have begun examining both sites to see if they should recommend them to their business clients. So far, several companies, nonprofits, and presidential candidates are using Twitter.

Perils of the Bleeding Edge

Think twice before you implement a brand-new technology without a proven track record. Tempting as it is to be first to use a new tech gadget, tool, or feature, the costs associated with being an early adopter can be astronomical. When it comes to new technology, early adopters often help work out the bugs in a new system. They don't usually stake their companies' livelihood on the new technology unless they have a strong technical background or technical support to weather the storm of instability.

Here are some sound business reasons why you don't want to be an early adopter:

Costs of innovation: You don't want to burden your company working out somebody else's technical issues.

Lack of demand: If your customers aren't ready to use a new technology—or are not capable of accessing it because of their own technical issues—you aren't serving your company or your customers.

Inability to integrate: Cutting-edge technology does not always integrate with your existing systems and may require additional purchases and efforts to bridge the gap.

Lack of competition: If a company is first to come out with a new technology, without competitors, prices will be higher until other companies enter the market, often with an improved product.

Buying into the hype: Your judgment may be clouded by flashy demos and slick promotions, and without the proper analysis you'll end up making a rash decision that introduces unforeseen costs to your company.

Technology should be used as a tool, not the driver of your business if technology is not your business.

Making the Right Decisions

If you are not in the technology industry, chances are you are better off adopting a technology once it has gone through a few versions. Watch for the word "beta" next to a technology or the use of "version 1.0." If you are looking for comparables in the market—that is, other companies with similar products—but find none, consider waiting until other companies come out with their versions of the same technology. Prices will be more competitive, and competition forces all companies to keep pace with innovation.

The same caution about early adoption should be applied to upgrading systems. Too many companies have been advised to upgrade to the newest software or a brand-new computer only to find that problems with moving too quickly to new technology renders their systems inoperable.

Know Your Company

Measure your company's basic tolerance for technology. If your company is still crawling along with antiquated computers and dial-up Internet connections, you aren't even close to ready for a brand-new technology without an overhaul of your current technical systems. If you don't have a strong technical team ready to troubleshoot any issue that comes along, you may end up spending more money than you imagined just to get a new technology to work. If your company is not technically savvy, take gradual steps toward integrating new technology tools into your current systems.

If your company is behind the curve, however, you should also evaluate how new technologies can enhance the way you do business, internally and externally. Whereas buying into technology the moment it becomes available can be a foolish business decision, refusing to adopt any proven technology out of fear or lack of knowledge can be equally damaging. **If you don't understand how technology can help your business, hire a consultant to help you evaluate your options.** Remember the person trying to sell you software may push you toward something your company does not need. An impartial consultant can make the difference between a rash decision and a sound one.

Know Your Customer

In addition to examining your company's technology tolerance, look closely at your customers. Through all of the standard methods of identifying, surveying, and communicating with your customers and potential customers, make sure they are ready for the new technologies and systems you plan to adopt. Before the Web became easier to access, companies often hesitated to put up Web sites, and for good reason—their customers weren't online yet. Those who did venture onto the Web early on dealt with early adoption issues but also helped to pave the way for more cautious companies. They also helped to create a market of users who began accessing the Internet and became accustomed to doing business online.

Today, using e-mail, putting up a Web site, and marketing online are less risky; not only are many other companies doing these things successfully, but chances are your customers and potential customers are now online. Knowing your market, customers and vendors, is an essential part of your decision-making process when integrating e-business into your company's business plan. Technology can create many problems. Understanding your company and whom your company is trying to reach can help you map out how e-business will improve your practices.

▶▶ TEST DRIVE

Evaluating if your company is ready to integrate e-business tools and systems into the way you are already doing business requires some honest soul-searching along with sound business planning. Before you move forward with e-business initiatives, consider the following:

- ➲ What is my company's technology tolerance?
- ➲ What is my customer's technology tolerance?
- ➲ What will happen to my company if the technology fails?
- ➲ What will happen to my business if the company fails to adopt to new technology?

Appendix A: Glossary

Aggregated content
Articles and other content gathered from various sources and compiled, often presented on a Web site as excerpts with links to the actual content on other Web sites.

ASCII
Stands for the American Standard Code for Information Interchange; represents the letters, numerals, punctuation marks, and other symbols that are the common format for computer text files.

Back end
Behind-the-scenes technology that enables a Web site or other technical system.

B2B
Business to business. The exchange of products, services, and information between two businesses—one business is the seller, and another business is the buyer.

B2C
Business to consumer. The exchange of products, services, and information between a seller and buyer, often used to describe the retail aspect of e-commerce.

Brochureware
A Web site usually created by taking traditional print marketing materials and putting them online without any strategy for the new medium.

Browser
A software program allowing a person to access and view Web sites. Can also be a person accessing or looking at Web sites.

Catablog
An e-commerce–enabled blog used for selling products. Also refers to a catalog that uses RSS feeds to distribute news about sales and promotions.

CMS
Content management system. A technology system that facilitates content management such as editing and publishing, usually containing Web-based tools.

Cookie
A small text file inserted into a visitor's Web browser cookie file to

tag the user with information such as passwords, preferences, and other personal information gathered by the site.

COPPA
The U.S. Children's Online Privacy Protection Act of 1998, providing guidelines for protecting children under thirteen years old on the Internet.

CPC
Cost per click. An online advertising payment method where the advertiser pays by the number of times visitors click on his or her ad.

CPM
Cost per thousand. A term used by e-marketers to determine the cost of an online ad. A CPM rate of $10 for 10,000 guaranteed impressions of the ad will cost $1,000.

CRM
Customer relationship management. The process by which companies manage their relationships with their customers through the analysis of customer data.

Domain name
The text address of a Web site that can be used in lieu of one or more IP addresses to designate the location of a site on a Web server.

DHTML
Dynamic HTML. An HTML extension enabling small animations and dynamic menus using stylesheets and Javascript.

FAQ
Frequently Asked Questions. A list of questions with relevant answers that is presented as an information resource.

Flame
A personal attack or insult from one community member to another.

Flame war
A disruption within an online community where members of the community personally attack one another, leading to chaos.

Flash
A software product by Adobe used to create animation from vector graphics.

Front end
Also referred to as the interface. Appears in front of the technical system or software to create a more user-friendly presentation.

FTP
File transfer protocol. Used to upload and download files from the Internet, also to upload and download HTML and other files for building a Web site.

GUI
Graphical user interface. The front end of a site or software product that makes it easier to use.

Home page
The opening page of a Web site. Sometimes mistakenly used to refer to a Web site in its entirety.

Host

To provide space on a server for another party's files, often for a fee and usually referring to Web server space for the files that make up a Web site.

HTML

Hypertext markup language. The coding or markup tags used on Web pages that is interpreted by Web browsers to present text and multi-media files that create Web sites.

HTTP

Hypertext Transfer Protocol. Defines how information is formatted and transmitted on the World Wide Web, including how Web servers and Web browsers respond to data.

Information architecture

The way in which information is organized throughout a Web site, particularly using linked documents within different directories (folders) and subdirectories.

Instant message

A software application that allows two people to chat instantly and in real time with one another.

IP address

Information Protocol (IP) address that is like a zip code identifying a particular Web site on a particular server. Usually written as four sets of numbers separated by dots, such as 123.456.78.9.

Knowledge base

The assembly of information and knowledge in a particular area. When assembled electronically, the resulting database is usually searchable.

M-commerce

Mobile commerce. Buying and selling over wireless networks using handheld devices.

Nav bar

Short for navigation bar. The repeated buttons, bar, or links that facilitate navigation through a Web site.

Opt in

The choice to receive an e-mail by submitting his or her e-mail address to subscribe to or to join an e-mail list.

Opt out

The action required to remove a user from a list that he or she may have been automatically subscribed to by someone else.

P2P

Peer-to-peer network. Online information exchange, transactions, or file exchanges occurring between individuals such as what happens on message boards, in auctions on eBay, or on music download sites such as Napster.

Permission marketing

Obtaining permission from someone to communicate with her or him electronically for marketing purposes.

Plug-in
A small piece of software that attaches to a Web browser and enables an additional function, such as a Flash plug-in allowing for the viewing of a Flash animation on a Web site or an Adobe Acrobat Reader plug-in for opening a PDF file.

Privacy policy
A written document stating a company's guidelines for protecting the privacy of its customers or Web site users.

Registrar
A company that sells, manages, and keeps track of domain names.

RSS feed
A file format allowing for easier syndication of content from Web sites and blogs. Said to stand for Really Simple Syndication, Rich Site Summary, or RDF Site Summary.

Search engine
A Web-based database with indexed Web pages where users can submit keywords to search for links to relevant Web sites. Search engines differ from searchable directories in that they use software programs known as spiders, robots, or bots to collect information on the Web.

Second-level domain
Part of a complete domain name. If yahoo.com is the domain name, then yahoo is the second level domain.

Security policy
A written document that defines how a company provides secure measures on its Web site.

Shockwave
A multimedia software and plug-in and predecessor to Adobe's Flash animation authoring software.

Shopping cart
Can refer to the actual software or system that enables online transactions including adding items to an online cart and checking out or paying for the items. Can also refer loosely to the transaction portion of an online retail experience.

SIG file
Signature file. A file attached to the end of an electronic message in e-mail or in online forums that identifies the sender or poster.

SSL
Secure socket layer. Protocol for transmitting confidential data through the Internet, developed by Netscape and used to secure online transactions.

Subdomain
A subset of a domain name; mail.yahoo.com is a subdomain of yahoo.com.

Terms of service
Also called terms of use. Rules dictating how Web site visitors or online community members are expected to behave and their responsibilities

as well as the responsibilities of the Web site or forum owner.

Thread

A conversation on a message board or e-mail list that can be followed and is usually connected by the subject line.

TLD or Top Level Domain

The part of a domain name after the dot such as .com, .net, and .org and country codes such as .ca, .uk, and .jp.

URL

Uniform resource locator. The address for files and documents on the Web including the files that make up a Web site.

Viral marketing

Using electronic word of mouth and online networks to spread the word about something.

VoIP

Voice over Internet Protocol. The technology behind transmitting voice over a data network using IP or Internet protocol.

W3

World Wide Web Consortium. Founded by Web creator Tim Berners-Lee, the W3 is the global group that develops specifications and guidelines that help create standards for the Web.

Web analytics

The study of how visitors use a Web site. Web analytics software measures and details the actions of site visitors.

Web host or host

A company or individual offering space on a Web server, usually for a monthly fee, to house a Web site and make it accessible on the Web.

Web server

The computer that hosts Web sites and that is connected to the Internet at all times.

Weblog

Abbreviated to blog, a Web site with a specific format with diary-like entries in reverse chronological order that are time- and date-stamped.

Wiki

A Web site or online resource that allows group editing, similar to the concept of an online whiteboard.

XML

Extensible markup language for information exchange that can be understood by both computers and humans.

Appendix B: Web Sites

A quick reference guide to useful Web sites in this book.

Chapter 1

Internet World Statistics (*www .internetworldstats.com*): A site with Internet statistics

Chapter 2

Tripod.com or Homestead.com: Examples of free Web publishing sites

Earthlink.net or AOL.com: Examples of ISPs

Register.com or NetworkSolutions.com: Examples of domain name registrars

Blogger.com or Typepad. com: Examples of blog host companies

Chapter 3

SurveyMonkey.com or Zoomerang.com: Examples of sites for setting up surveys

Chapter 4

Great Circle Associations (*www .greatcircle.com/majordomo*): Company that offers majordomo software

L-Soft (*www.lsoft.com/products/ listserv.asp*): Company that offers ListServ software

Seth Godin (*www.sethgodin.com*): Guru of permission marketing

Chapter 5

John T. Unger (*http://johntunger .typepad.com/artbuzz*): Artist selling art through his blog

Chapter 9

Hallmark.com: Company offering e-cards as a viral marketing tool

Hotmail.com: Company offering free e-mail that includes a viral marketing message at the bottom of each e-mail sent

Monk-e-Mail (*www.monk-e-mail .com*): Example of viral marketing using entertaining e-cards, offered by CareerBuilder.com

Web Pages That Suck (*www.web pagesthatsuck.com*): Blog that analyzes bad Web pages

Chapter 10

WebSiteOptimization.com: Site that tests a Web site for errors and programming flaws

SiteReportCard *(www.sitereport card.com)*: Another site for testing Web site HTML

Chapter 11

HTML Color Codes (html-color-codes.com): Hexadecimal color chart

RGB to Hexadecimal Converter (*www.inquisitor.com/hex.html*): Converts RGB numbers into a hexadecimal number

Search Engine Watch (*www.search enginewatch.com*): Compiles information about search engine technology and top search engines

Chapter 14
Examples of companies that offer shopping cart services:
CoolCart.com

Volusion (*www.volusion.com*)

Goecart (*www.goecart.com*)

VirtualCART (*www.virtualcart .com*)

Other online shopping-cart solutions:
Google Checkout (*https://check out.google.com*)

PayPal (*www.paypal.com*)

1ShoppingCart.com

e-Bay (*www.ebay.com*)

GoDaddy.com

Goemerchant (*www.goemerchant .com*)

Miva Merchant *(www.miva.com)*

ShopFactory (*www.shopfactory .com*)

ShopSite (*www.shopsite.com*)

Yahoo! Online Store (*http://store .yahoo.com*)

Zoovy (*www.zoovy.com*)

Shopping-cart software:
X-Cart (*www.x-cart.com*)

Storefront (*www.storefront.net*)

LiteCommerce (*www.litecom merce.com*)

Volusion (*www.volusion.com*)

CoreSense (*www.coresense.com*)

Chapter 15
Companies offering merchant account services:
CardService International (*www .cardserviceunlimited.com*)

Charge.com

Electronic Transfer, Inc. (*www
.electronictransfer.com*)
Merchant Accounts Express (*www
.merchantexpress.com*)
Merchant Warehouse (*www
.merchantwarehouse.com*)

Chapter 16

**Companies providing online
registry services:**
FindGift.com
MyGiftList.com
eWish.com
Marcole Interactive Systems (*www
.marcole.com*)

Chapter 17

**Companies offering online
chat software and services:**
InstantService Chat (*www.instant
service.com*)
Live Person Business Chat (*www
.liveperson.com*)
LiveChatNow (*www.livechatnow
.com*)
LiveHelper (*www.livehelper.com*)
LiveSiteManager (*www.livesite
manager.com*)
Velaro.com

Chapter 18

Top search engines:
Yahoo! (*www.yahoo.com*)
Google (*www.google.com*)
Ask.com
MSN Live (*www.live.com*)

**Sites offering Web site submis-
sion services:**
1 2 3 Submit Pro (*www.website
submit.hypermart.net*)
AddPro.com
Submission-Pro (*www.submission
-pro.com*)
Submit Express (*www.submite
xpress.com*)
Website-submission.com

**Companies that provide affili-
ate program set-up services:**
Commission Junction (*www
.cj.com*)
LinkShare (*www.linkshare.com*)
ClickBank (*www.clickbank.com*)

Chapter 19

**Sites offering free press
release distribution:**
Free-Press-Release.com
24-7pressrelease.com

**Sites offering fee-based press
release distribution services:**
PRWeb (*www.prweb.com*)
PR Newswire (*www.prnewswire
.com*)
Business Wire (*www.business
wire.com*)
Marketwire (*www.marketwire
.com*)
Collegiate Presswire (*www.cpwire
.com*)

Internet News Bureau *(www.inter netnewsbureau.com)*

Sites offering produce-on-demand branded products:
CafePress.com
Zazzle.com

Chapter 20
Sites to locate freelance writers:
Journalism Jobs *(www.journalism jobs.com)*
Mediabistro *(www.mediabistro .com)*
Absolute Markets *(www.absolute markets.com)*

Wire services:
Associated Press *(www.ap.com)*
United Press International *(www .upi.com)*
PR Newswire *(www.prnewsire .com)*
Businesswire *(www.businesswire .com)*
Dow Jones Newswire *(www.dow jones.com)*

Content syndication sites to obtain content:
FreeSticky.com: Free content on a variety of topics
Content That Works *(www.con tentthatworks.com)*: Includes automotive, real estate,

employment, family health, bridal, holiday, home decorating, and lawn and garden
Small Business Resources *(www .sbresources.com)*: Small business, minority-owned business, women-owned business, business technology
Wilson Internet Services *(www .wilsonweb.com)*: Web technology, e-marketing, and e-business
Women's ENews *(www.womens enews.org)*: Feminist news and women's issues
Mochila *(www.mochila.com)*: A "marketplace for syndicated content." A place to purchase content from established publications and publishers
Copyright.com: Another service for licensing copyrighted content

Syndicators of art and images:
Fotosearch *(www.fotosearch.com)*
Art Resource *(www.artres.com)*
Clipart.com *(www.clipart.com)*
Cartoonists & Writers Syndicate *(www.cartoonweb.com)*

Chapter 22
Search engine comparing site statistics:
Alexa.com

Free or low-cost Web analytics solutions:

Google Analytics (*www.google.com/analytics*)

ActiveMeter (*www.activemeter.com*)

HitsLog (*www.hitslog.com*)

SiteTracker (*www.sitetracker.com*)

StatCounter (*www.statcounter.com*)

Fee-based Web analytics solutions:

ClickTracks (*www.clicktracks.com*)

CoreMetrics (*www.coremetrics.com*)

Omniture's SiteCatalyst *(www.omniture.com)*

VisiStat (*www.visistat.com*)

Visual Sciences (*www.visualsciences.com*)

WebSideStory's HBX Analytics (*www.websidestory.com*)

WebTrends (*www.webtrends.com*)

Chapter 23
Companies offering services for tracking news in articles and blogs:

eWatch (*http://ewatch.prnewswire.com*).

Co.mments (*http://co.mments.com*)

Chapter 24
Audio casting services:

Gabcast (*www.gabcast.com*)

GCast (*www.gcast.com*)

MyPodcast (*www.mypodcast.com*)

Blogger's Audioblogger (*www.audioblogger.com*)

Video hosting services:

Veoh (*www.veoh.com*)

Photobucket (*www.photobucket.com*)

Video Upload Program (*upload.video.google.com*)

YouTube.com

Examples of social networking sites:

MySpace (*www.myspace.com*)

LinkedIn (*www.linkedin.com*)

SoFlow (*www.soflow.com*)

Gather (*www.gather.com*)

Facebook (*www.facebook.com*)

Friendster (*www.friendster.com*)

Miscellaneous online services:

TextPayMe (*www.textpayme.com*): Company offering payment services via mobile phone

Skweezer.com: Strips Web site pages down to only mobile-safe elements

Mobile blogging sites:

Text America (*www.textamerica.com*)

Winksite (*www.winksite.com*)

Index

Active server pages (ASP), 159
Advertising, 3, 23–24, 248–51, 264–77
Affiliate programs, 23, 256–58
ALT tags, 167
ARPANET, 5
Articles, publishing, 281, 285–86, 289, 291–94, 298
Audience, 11, 30–34, 170–74, 277
Audio ads, 274–76
Audio content, 69, 342–45
Auto responder, 235

Banner ads, 248–49
Benchmarks, 39–40, 324–25, 339
Beta testing, 185–87
Blogs (Web logs), 27–28, 63–65, 88, 250–51, 298–311, 347
Bookmarks, 286
Brand building, 76
Breach of contract, 119
Bricks-and-mortar businesses, 38, 202
Brochures, 122–23
Business plan, 30
Business practices, 12–13
Business-to-business (B2B), 3
Business-to-consumer (B2C), 3
Business-to-peer (B2P), 3

"Catablogs," 65. See also Blogs (Web logs)
Catalogs, 3, 38, 126, 174, 178, 194–95, 198–203, 259

Cellular phones, 349–50. See also Mobile devices
Clicks-and-mortar businesses, 38
Click-throughs, 248–49
ColdFusion, 159
Comments tags, 167–68
Communications Decency Act (CDA), 81, 82
Consultants, 102–6
Content copyright, 69–71
Content development, 293–96
Content management system (CMS), 287–90
Content solutions, 291–93
Content syndication, 24, 67–71, 295
Contracts, 111–20
"Cookies," 35, 214
Copyright, 69–71
Counters, 321
Credit card payments, 49, 114, 194, 214–19, 233, 242
Customer demographics, 11, 31
Customer psychographics, 31–32
Customer relationship management (CRM), 128
Customer reminders, 220–22
Customer service, 76–77, 126–28, 232–44
Customer support, 127–28, 240
Customers, attracting, 246–59. See also Marketing tips
Customization, 220–22

Databases, 99, 103, 127, 132, 225–26, 238–39, 323

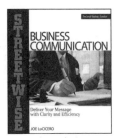

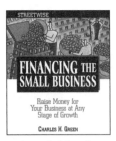

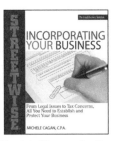

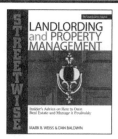

Streetwise® Landlording & Property Management
Weiss & Baldwin
$19.95; ISBN 10: 1-58062-766-8

Streetwise® Low-Cost Marketing
Mark Landsbaum
$19.95; ISBN 10: 1-58062-858-3

Streetwise® Low-Cost Web Site Promotion
Barry Feig
$19.95; ISBN 10: 1-58062-501-0

Streetwise® Managing a Nonprofit
John Riddle
$19.95; ISBN 10: 1-58062-698-X

Streetwise® Marketing Plan
Don Debelak
$19.95; ISBN 10: 1-58062-268-2

Streetwise® Meeting and Event Planning
Joe LoCicero
$19.95; ISBN 10: 1-59869-271-2

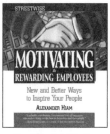

Streetwise® Motivating & Rewarding Employees
Alexander Hiam
$19.95; ISBN 10: 1-58062-130-9

Streetwise® Project Management
Michael Dobson
$19.95; ISBN 10: 1-58062-770-6

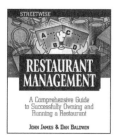

Streetwise® Restaurant Management
John James & Dan Baldwin
$19.95; ISBN 10: 1-58062-781-1

Streetwise® Sales Letters with CD
Reynard & Weiss
$29.95; ISBN 10: 1-58062-440-5

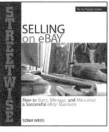

Streetwise® Selling on eBay®
Sonia Weiss
$19.95; ISBN 10: 1-59337-610-3

Streetwise® Small Business Book of Lists
Edited by Gene Marks
$19.95; ISBN 10: 1-59337-684-7

Streetwise® Small Business Start-Up
Bob Adams
$19.95; ISBN 10: 1-55850-581-4

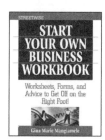

Streetwise® Start Your Own Business Workbook
Gina Marie Mangiamele
$9.95; ISBN 10: 1-58062-506-1

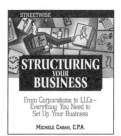

Streetwise® Structuring Your Business
Michele Cagan
$19.95; ISBN 10: 1-59337-177-2

Streetwise® Time Management
Marshall Cook
$19.95; ISBN 10: 1-58062-131-7